The Emerald Diamond

The Emerald Diamond

HOW THE IRISH TRANSFORMED
AMERICA'S GREATEST PASTIME

CHARLEY ROSEN

HARPER

An Imprint of HarperCollins*Publishers*
www.harpercollins.com

HarperCollins books may be purchased for educational, business, or sales promotional use. For information, please write: Special Markets Department, HarperCollins Publishers, 10 East 53rd Street, New York, NY 10022.

FIRST EDITION

Library of Congress Cataloging-in-Publication Data has been applied for.

ISBN: 978-0-06-208988-5

12 13 14 15 16 ov/rrd 10 9 8 7 6 5 4 3 2 1

To the Coyote Man,
for his unwavering friendship

Cast your mind on other days
That we in coming days may be
Still the indomitable Irishry.
　　　　　　　—*William Butler Yeats*

You can take a boy out of Ireland but
you cannot take Ireland out of the boy.
　　　　　　　—*Irish saying*

Contents

Author's Note and Acknowledgments

First off, a pot of gold full of heartfelt gratitude to Marty Appel and David Fleitz, the two baseball historians who have done the most of anyone to record the history of the Irish in baseball, Marty in *Slide, Kelly, Slide* (Scarecrow Press, 1999), and David in *The Irish in Baseball* (McFarland, 2009). I am in debt to them for their research and I have very much enjoyed reading their work as I shaped my own account of the Irish American influence on our national pastime.

Bill Brennan can usually tell the county of origin just from parsing a player's last name. His generous gifts of time, interest, and expertise were invaluable. Bill is both proud and thankful that his great love of the game was passed on to his wife, Mary, and his late son, Neil.

Davey Hannigan's limitless knowledge likewise was a monumental help in identifying who was Irish and who was not.

Bill Francis, of the Hall of Fame library, kindly forwarded a significant amount of material.

Many thanks to *The Baseball Almanac* for the stats of every Irish-American baseball player; likewise, my desktop bible, *Total Baseball*.

Also to books by Robert Creamer, Jerrold Casway, Charles Alexander, and Norman L. Macht; there is a full bibliography in the back of this book.

John Thorn, Major League Baseball's new official historian, gave me the scoop on baseball's true origins. John is a walking baseball encyclopedia, and I am also happy to call him a friend.

To Allison Benoit, an intern for my publisher, who researched the unique photos for this book. We decided not to have the usual player-in-wool-uniform images, but to show you something different.

And a huge thank-you to the folks who established and run the Irish-American Baseball Hall of Fame in New York City. What a great treasure—and pub!

(Courtesy of the Irish-American Baseball Hall of Fame)

I am a former professional athlete and teacher with a master's degree in medieval English, and I was an editor of the *Erasmus Review*, a scholarly journal. I am a student of American history, and I consider it a joy that in researching for this book, I learned about events in our history that were previously unknown to me.

A connection to our past is essential, whether we count ourselves as Irish, Jewish, German, Italian, Hispanic, Asian, or African American. The past is prologue and we have to thank those who came before us, whether a trail was blazed against prejudice, or, on more mundane terms—yet terms essential to our current joy of a game or sport—when we find the first person to have done something so unique that it changed a sport and our enjoyment of it.

Irish Americans were the first to employ many tools of the baseball trade and institute many of the game's major improvements that we take for granted now.

It is my pleasure to recount them—and many big, big personalities—to you in these pages.

The Emerald Diamond

Prologue: The Irish Game

Baseball was mighty and exciting to me, but there is
no blinking at the fact that at the time the game was
thought, by solid sensible people, to be only one degree
above grand larceny, arson, and mayhem.

—Connie Mack (born Cornelius McGillicuddy)

FOR THE MOST part, the unfolding of an exhibition baseball game
played in 1894 between the Pittsburgh Pirates and the Kansas City
Cowboys would seem almost familiar to modern fans, full as the day
was with men in uniform, albeit blousy wool ones, and with green
grass, a blue sky, and scores of enthusiastic fans.

But then some profoundly unfamiliar playing rules would soon
disconcert and confuse the modern onlooker. For example:

The entire game was played under the jurisdiction of only one
umpire.

Balls bunted foul counted as strikes but not as third strikes.

The pitcher threw overhanded—that had been the case for only a
few years—but both feet had to stay on the ground.

A hitter could take full swings and foul off a pitcher's first twenty
offerings and the count would remain 0–0, the only other exception
being a foul tip gloved by the catcher, which would be a strike—but
never strike three.

Pitchers were permitted to use any means to doctor the ball—glomming it with mud, tobacco, licorice, or just plain saliva. These substances served to increase the sinking/curving action of the pitches, as well as to make the ball difficult for the hitters to track. Moreover, even when struck solidly, the heavy ball wouldn't travel very far.

Since the home team was required to provide only a handful of baseballs per game, they frequently opted to bat first in order to hit against relatively unblemished balls.

In the 1800s, the National League was the only universally accepted major league, but there were twenty-five other leagues in North America of varying professional status and stability. Even the NL was financially shaky, so before, after, and even during the season, most clubs sought to increase their revenue by engaging in numerous contests against whichever non-NL teams could offer them acceptable dates.

There were dozens and dozens of such extra games appended to every season.

That's why the NL's Pirates were in Kansas City's Exposition Park to play a midsummer's contest against the Cowboys, one of the premier teams in the Western League. In fact, seventeen of the Cowboys were either once or future major leaguers.

Behind the plate for Pittsburgh was Connie Mack, a second-generation Irishman born to Michael McGillicuddy and Mary McKillop in Massachusetts. Mack was also the player-manager—and would rightfully come to be celebrated as one of the era's most astute tacticians.

The Pirates led 8–6 and the Cowboys were batting in the top of the ninth with two outs and runners on second and third. That's when the batter struck a fly ball that bounced just beyond the reach of Pittsburgh's left fielder.

One runner scored easily, but the accurate relay to the shortstop and then to Mack was a cinch to beat the tying run to the plate by a large margin.

However, a feisty Irishman named Tim Donahue was the K.C.

captain and third-base coach of the moment. As the runner rounded the bag, Donahue took off and ran ahead of him, much like a pulling guard leading a halfback into the line of scrimmage. Taking care to stay on the nether side of the foul line, Donahue plowed into Connie Mack just before the catcher could receive the throw.

Mack bounced one way, the ball bounced another way, and the runner was safe at home. Because Donahue never trod on fair territory, his trick was totally legal!

Since Connie Mack was famous for his own relentless search to discover exploitable loopholes in the existing rules, he was, however bruised, also quite impressed by Donahue's maneuver.

In any event, the run counted and the score was knotted at 8–8 when the Pirates came to bat in the bottom of the ninth. Mack was coaching at third, with a man up and a man on first. The batter smacked a line drive over the third baseman's head that was a sure double. What was uncertain, however, was whether the runner on first could come all the way around to score the winning run.

The odds seemed long when the Cowboys' left fielder made a swift recovery and launched a strong throw toward catcher Fred Lake. Indeed, the ball was already in Lake's glove when Mack waved the runner home—then proceeded to barrel down the line in a duplication of Donahue's successful ploy. Mack crashed into Lake with such force that the ball was, déjà vu, knocked loose.

The umpire on duty signaled that the run counted and the game was over. In a flash, the riotous hometown fans stormed out of the stands and battled the police for control of the field, while Lake turned and punched the ump in the jaw.

Thereby concluding what was deemed to be just another exciting day in the ballpark.

No matter how violent, marginally legal, or downright illegal an action might be, winning a ball game *always* justified the means. And early in baseball's history, there was a name for this ruthless game plan.

Irish baseball.

Part I

HUMBLE BEGINNINGS

Chapter One

Arrival

> Even if the hopes you started out with are dashed, hope
> has to be maintained.
>
> —*Seamus Heaney*

THE PROFOUND INFLUENCE of the Irish people on virtually every aspect of Western culture is well known.

From James Joyce to F. Scott Fitzgerald; Maureen O'Hara to Daniel Day-Lewis. From Eugene O'Neill to John O'Hara; Bruce Springsteen and Van Morrison to John Fogerty and U2. From Ed Sullivan to Stephen Colbert.

The list of American presidents with roots in the Emerald Isle is even more significant: Andrew Jackson, James Polk, James Buchanan, John Fitzgerald Kennedy, Jimmy Carter, Ronald Reagan, Bill Clinton, as well as both Bushes. (And as we've come to learn, Barack Obama is one-eighth Irish.)

But in America, the vital contributions of the Irish to what we call our national pastime remains largely unknown and absolutely unappreciated. Indeed, from the mid-nineteenth to the early twentieth centuries, it was primarily Irish baseball players who popularized and modernized the game.

BACK IN THE 1880s, two out of five players on what were considered to be major league teams were Irish.

♣Throughout baseball's glory years, names like Mickey Cochrane, Joe Cronin, and Joe McCarthy were legendary. Walter O'Malley's was infamous.

That influence has continued into our lifetimes, with the likes of Dennis McLain, Al Kaline, and Mark McGwire. Paul O'Neill is in New York's Irish-American Baseball Hall of Fame, and Kevin Millar told the Red Sox just to believe and they did. Tim McCarver's voice can still be heard on the air.

Even now, there are more than four dozen Irish players in the major leagues, the third largest minority group behind African Americans and Hispanics.

More impressively, Cooperstown includes a total of fifty-four players, managers, umpires, and executives of either full or partial Irish descent.

♣That represents the most numerous ethnic group of inductees.

THE IRISH INFLUENCE on our national pastime all began with an agricultural catastrophe that has been called "the greatest human tragedy of the nineteenth century." At the time, it was believed to be a divine punishment inflicted on either sinful peasants or on greedy landlords and middlemen. Others opined that the disaster most likely had more "rational" causes: perhaps the static electricity and smoke created by the newfangled locomotives, or else deadly vapors leaking from underground volcanoes. In retrospect, it is generally agreed that the Irish Potato Famine was caused by a fungus that originated in Mexico before being transported in the holds of ships.

Whatever the immediate cause, the Great Famine, which translated into Gaelic as An Gorta Mór (The Great Death), killed over a million Irish and compelled two million more to emigrate to either Canada or America.

Throughout its history, Ireland has been invaded, conquered, and subjected to rebellion and civil war. When England first staked its claim in the seventeenth century, James I seized virtually all of the holdings of the prosperous Irish-Catholic landowners and transferred ownership to Scottish, English, and Irish Protestants. Under the rule of Oliver Cromwell, absentee landlords and imported settlers became even more widespread. Subsequently, while the Catholics dwelling in the southern counties were never totally subdued, their lives became increasingly poverty-stricken. And that poverty begat an overreliance on a single crop.

The most widespread and tragic failure of the potato crop was first manifested shortly after the harvest of September 1845. It included most of the rural Catholic sections in the south and west, sparing only Dublin in the west and the Protestant north. Although the diseased plants initially appeared to be edible, within a few days they quickly shriveled and rotted, turning black and emitting a foul odor. All told, virtually all of the nation's potato production was ruined.

The blight was even more evident in the 1846 and 1847 harvests, with the latter blizzard-plagued winter being remembered in Irish history as "Black 47."

In England, governmental efforts to save the starving Irish were inefficient, mainly because the halfhearted and unsanitary work projects, the free soup kitchens (one existed for every ten thousand peasants in need), and the distribution of corn at a penny a pound were pitifully underfunded. (Moreover, funding totally ceased when a banking crisis hit Britain in 1847.) In any case, the prevailing political attitude shared by both the liberal and conservative wings of the British Parliament was laissez-faire. They claimed that giving away too much low-cost corn would make the Irish totally dependent on the British government, and would also short-circuit the machinery of private enterprise.

So the peasants ate everything that grew within their reach, including the bark of trees and, even worse, their own seed potatoes. By 1847 approximately 1.5 million impoverished Irish perished of starvation and related diseases. At the same time, about 500,000 tenant farmers were evicted when they failed to pay their rent. They, along with two million of their countrymen, were ultimately compelled to escape from the dire conditions in the Emerald Isle.

The devastation wrought by the Potato Famine, however, was not the cause of the very first wave of Irish emigration. During the thirty years previous to 1845, nearly a million abandoned their home country and journeyed across the Atlantic. The primary reason for this pre-famine exodus was the inability of young men to secure leased lands, thereby limiting their prospects for advantageous marriages and also preventing any dreams of personal independence. Once in America, many of these early immigrants earned a dollar a day shoveling out the 363-mile length of the Erie Canal.

Empty promises awaited the Irish immigrants who landed in the United States, 45 percent of whom were males aged fourteen to twenty-four. The vast majority of these newcomers to America were farmers ill suited for urban employment, nor could they afford to travel out from their points of entry, mostly Boston or New York. The men wound up working long, arduous hours for meager pay in factories, construction sites, or on the docks, while the women were fortunate to find work as domestic servants. As they flocked to the slums of these cities, the Irish had to endure a new environment rife with poverty, disease, unemployment, and crime.

Even so, the transplanted Irish remained proud of their heritage, and indeed constituted the first significant European "ethnic" group in America.

They gathered by the thousands to march in St. Patrick's Day parades, and when the Civil War commenced, the flower of Irish manhood flocked to what became known as the Irish Brigade to battle the Confederacy.

When Ellis Island opened in 1892, nearly four million Irish men and women were already living in America. Besides working, parading, and fighting to preserve the Union, there were only a limited number of other semi-acceptable public pursuits available to the recently arrived Irish immigrants.

One of these was the new game of baseball.

PRESENT-DAY INTERVIEW

Glenn Patrick Sherlock has been in the baseball business since 1983, starting with six minor league seasons as a catcher in the Astros and Yankees farm systems. He was a savvy receiver, but a gaping hole in his swing reduced his career batting average to a pedestrian .250.

After he retired from playing, Sherlock was variously employed by the Yankees as a roving catching instructor, as the bullpen receiver with the big club (1992, 1994–95), and as a manager in New York's minor leagues. Since 1998, he's been on the coaching staff of the Arizona Diamondbacks, where his current position puts him in charge of the bullpen.

At age fifty-one, and despite his graying hair, Sherlock still looks trim and agile. His well-tanned arms, cheekbones, and neck provide his unmistakable pedigree as a lifetimer in the game. He's got a farmer's tan, but from a different field.

While Sherlock is proud of his own accomplishments in the sport that he loves, he's just as proud of his Irish heritage. His maternal grandparents were O'Connors from Galway, while his father's kinfolk came from County Mayo. Both sets of ancestors arrived in America in the 1880s.

"I've been to Ireland twice and I tried to find the Sherlock homestead in Fauleen, County Mayo. One of my brothers and I were driving a small rented car down a very narrow dirt road when a combine came roaring down from the opposite direction. We expected some kind of hassle, but the driver couldn't have been more friendly.

"'Can I help you?' he said.

"Turned out that he was a farmer who lived on the same street as the Sherlocks used to live. He gave us a tour, then invited us into his home. It was all very inspirational."

SHERLOCK'S FATHER HAD a long career in the U.S. Navy before establishing a car dealership. Along with his five siblings, Sherlock had the chance to attend college—in his case, Rollins College in Winter Park, Florida.

"I appreciate that my parents always emphasized the importance of education," he says, "and also of always working hard no matter what the task. And these are the principles I have always tried to live by."

Sherlock was born in Nahant, Massachusetts, which he characterizes as "a thoroughly Irish community," and he's always embraced the history of his people.

"I'm familiar with the likes of Ed Delahanty, John McGraw, Willie Keeler, and most of the great old-time Irish players.

"But I especially admire how those who came to America because of the famine worked so hard trying to make decent lives for themselves and their families. They were a proud bunch, but not too proud to disdain the grinding manual labor that was just about all that was available to them. Ditch diggers, miners, construction workers—they did what they had to do without shirking."

Chapter Two

Blocked at Home Plate

There are only two tragedies in life: one is not getting
what one wants, and the other is getting it.

—*Oscar Wilde*

AT THE TIME that the famine refugees landed in America, the sport
was still largely unformed. Nevertheless, what was to become baseball as we know it already had a long history.

The claim that Abner Doubleday spontaneously invented the
game in 1839 in his hometown of Cooperstown was more a fanci-
ful act of patriotism than a historical fact. There is no question that
Doubleday was the artillery officer who aimed the first cannonball
fired on Fort Sumter after the rebels had captured what had been an
American stronghold, nor that he was a major general in command of
the Union army early in the Battle of Gettysburg.

However, the Cooperstown Creation Myth is patently false.

Indeed, the first surviving record of a bat-and-ball game dates
back nearly 4,500 years. That's when an Egyptian game called *seker-
bemat* ("batting the ball") was played. The game was so popular that
even over a thousand years later, a wall relief on a temple in Deir

el-Bahri depicted the identifiable figure of Thutmose III holding a ball in one hand and a stick in the other. A nearby inscription reads: "Catching it for him by the servants of the gods."

Sounds like the very first case of good field, no hit.

Several millennia later, a game called rounders became a part of the sporting scene in England. Originating sometime in the late sixteenth century, rounders featured a small, hard, leather-covered ball, a round wooden bat, and four bases that had to be rounded to record a score. This was probably the most immediate ancestor of baseball, but was blithely ignored so that what became our national pastime could be considered quintessentially American.

Even more evidence exists that Doubleday was inappropriately canonized. As long ago as Christmas Day 1621, verifiable records state that Governor William Bradford of Plymouth Plantation castigated a group of men for "frolicking in ye street, at play openly; some pitching ye barr [ball]" instead of attending church.

There were several other "baseball" games played in the New World, for instance "barn ball," "town ball," and the "cat" games (one o'cat, two o'cat, three o'cat, etc., depending on the number of players). During the 1780s, Dartmouth, Penn, and Princeton prohibited the playing of what most of the players called wicket, but which at least one participant referred to as "baste ball," near on-campus windows. In the same vein, a 1791 town meeting in Pittsfield, Massachusetts, made playing "baseball" too close to a newly built meetinghouse a violation of the law.

Into the 1800s, playing the game was a leisure-time activity primarily engaged in by genteel young middle-to-upper-class businessmen and students. Almost exclusively native-born Protestants of English ancestry, they strictly adhered to amateur guidelines and competed with impeccable sportsmanship. Other ethnic groups usually had neither the free time nor the social standing to participate.

♣The first traceable Irish involvement in baseball was logged in 1837, when the Gotham Baseball Club was formed in New York City.

One of its founding members was a well-known Irish hotel-keeper, John Murphy. This was a sign of things to come. Six years later, the New York Magnolia Ball Club was established, with Irish-born John McKibbin Jr. elected president.

The Gotham's charter is credited with codifying several rule changes.

Most important, the previously popular triangular infield now became diamond-shaped.

Instead of a runner's being put out by being hit by a thrown ball (or "plugged"), a "baseman" had to tag him with the ball while the runner was unattached to any of the four bases.

The bases themselves were sandbags instead of tree stumps, bushes, or stones.

A single umpire would be on hand to adjudicate any disputes that the players themselves couldn't settle.

With the formation of the Knickerbocker Baseball Club in 1845, more radical rule changes were established, including authorizing the lone umpire to immediately fine players for cursing, arguing with him, or flagrantly breaking the rules. That summer, Ebenezer R. Dupignac was fined six cents by umpire Eugene Plunkett "for saying s—t."

Other restrictions limited pitchers to underhand—yes, underhand—deliveries similar to the modern softball pitch, except that the pitcher's arm had to be perpendicular to the ground, and no wrist snaps were permitted. At that stage in the development of the game, the pitcher was deemed to be more of a facilitator than an adversary, and was obliged to make high, middle, or low offerings at the batter's request. It was the fielders who were the batter's true opponents.

It wasn't until 1858 that the still-solitary umpire was empowered to call properly positioned pitches "strikes." Called balls weren't admitted into the rules until 1863. Two years later, the modern fly-out rule was instituted, and batters were no longer declared out when fly balls were caught on one bounce.

The rules governing the game may still have been in flux, but there was no question that baseball had a special allure for the recently arrived Irish immigrants.

♣BACK IN IRELAND, sports and games always had an important place in Irish popular culture.

Hurling (*iomain* in Gaelic) was an ancient stick-and-ball game that resembled lacrosse and had been played on the Auld Sod for more than two thousand years. Gaelic football, an ultraphysical cross between rugby and soccer, was another traditional sport. Also popular were foot races (called "pedestrianism"), throwing light and heavy stones, swimming, hurdling, cricket, rowing, both high- and long-jumping, and especially boxing. All of these contests proceeded on both amateur and professional levels.

In addition, considerable evidence suggests that all-Ireland "Tailteann Games" predated the athletic festivals of ancient Greece.

In the modern era, the international Olympic Games provided a showcase for the outstanding athleticism of Irishmen. For example, in the 1900 Paris Olympics, Irish-born Mike F. Sweeney won the high jump and long jump events as well as the hundred-meter race, John F. Cregan won the triple jump, and John F. Flanagan won gold in the hammer throw. A Mr. (first name unknown) McCracken captured second place in the shot put. Indeed, such native Irish as Matt McGrath, Pat McDonald, Martin Sheridan, and Pat Ryan dominated the international hammer- and discus-throwing competition for so many years that they were collectively known as the "Irish Whales."

THE PARTICULAR PASSION of the Irish for the developing game of baseball was understandable for several compelling reasons.

Aside from low-paid physical labor, only four paths of advancement were readily available to young Irish males: politics, police work, the priesthood, and sports. Of these endeavors, politics and police work were the most easily accessed because of the multiple opportunities existing in urban areas—precisely where most of the Irish resided. The priesthood required many years of study and utter devotion.

Even the sporting life offered limited opportunities.

Once in America, the absence of leisure time and the unavailability of appropriate urban venues made participation in their homegrown sports virtually impossible for the newly arrived Irish. Moreover, popular American sports such as tennis and golf were strictly country-club activities, football and track-and-field teams were almost exclusively sponsored by universities, and swimming pools were for the upper crust.

The primary exception to these various exclusions was boxing, where fans would eagerly pay to see a pair of Irishmen beat each other bloody. The likes of Sam O'Rourke, Cornelius Horrigan, John C. Heenan, James Sullivan, John Morrissey (recognized in the 1850s as the first American heavyweight champ), James Ambrose, Paddy Ryan, and Jake Kilrain made their mark as exceptional bare-knuckled pugilists immediately before and after the Civil War.

For many years, the heavyweight champion of the world was the most famous athlete of the time—and both John L. Sullivan (who reigned from 1882 to 1892) and "Gentleman Jim" Corbett (1892–94) were proud Irishmen who celebrated their heritage by wearing green trunks and robes in the ring. Other Irish prizefighters who would eventually dominate the sport included Gene Tunney, Jack Dempsey, Tom Sharkey, and James Braddock.

Baseball was especially appealing because the basics of the sport involved manipulating a bat (which strongly resembled the ancient Irish war club known as the shillelagh), running fast, and throwing a ball hard and accurately—all skills familiar from the traditional sporting pastimes in Ireland.

Also appealing was the fact that the rules of the game were essentially unformed, which encouraged spontaneity and cleverness.

By participating in baseball, Irish immigrants found a comfortable niche in their new environment that enabled them to assimilate into American life. Moreover, the formation of all-Irish town and neighborhood teams presented multiple opportunities to engage in "peaceful" warfare with other ethnic groups—most particularly teams whose players were descended from hated England.

Other immigrant groups discouraged participation in sports as a waste of time and energy. For Germans and Jews, education was deemed to be much more important than any trivial game. But many Irish families encouraged their sons' interest in baseball, particularly when the building of an enclosed stadium (1862 in Brooklyn) led to admission fees and paydays for players.

IN 1869, THE first ever all-pro team was organized: the Cincinnati Red Stockings, so named because, instead of playing the game in long trousers like everybody else, these guys hiked up their pants to display their manly calves in carmine hose.

Suddenly, baseball became an even more lucrative career option. Indeed, the player-manager and star of the Redlegs earned $1,200 for six months' work, whereas the salary for skilled laborers averaged $780 for an entire year. (It should be noted, however, that although the Reds were virtually unbeatable on the field, the team showed a year-end profit of only $1.40.)

Because of the financial straits suffered by most Irish immigrants, children were forced to seek full-time employment by the time they were ten years old. Many found jobs in textile mills, where the continual need to move large rolls of fabric across factory floors developed strong arms and wrists—among the most vital physical attributes needed to excel at baseball.

However, despite all the requisite qualifications—considerable physical skills, generations of culturally conditioned gamesmanship, and spontaneous pragmatic enthusiasm—young Irish males were routinely disdained by the insular baseball establishment.

Chapter Three

NINA

I am troubled, I'm dissatisfied, I'm Irish.
                                    —*Marianne Moore*

WHEN THE TIDAL wave of Irish Catholics first broke across America during the late 1840s, the newcomers encountered a huge majority of already entrenched citizenry whose ancestral roots were in Protestant England. And since these two ethno-religious groups had slaughtered one another in periodic blood feuds for centuries, a renewal of the mutual enmity was inevitable.

Still, this was new turf for both, and the Irish immigrants found in their adopted country a sudden freedom from generations of oppression. They recognized that America was indeed a land of opportunity where they might now have the power to achieve success by their own efforts. Authority was meant to be challenged, and, regardless of any preexisting rules or prevailing system, the overriding imperative of the not-yet-assimilated Irish was to succeed by any means.

Therefore, it was easy for the staid Protestants to remain staunch in their long-held view of the Irish Catholics as ignorant, rowdy, and addicted to gambling and thievery. On the other side of the class divide, the Catholics deemed the "Brahmins" to be aristocratic, flabby, heartless, and eager to fleece poor folks of their last pennies.

The friction between these two classes was palpable in an 1860 series of three baseball games played in New York between the Excelsiors and the Atlantics. The outcome would ostensibly determine the baseball championship of the city, but what was really at stake was honor and class supremacy. After all, the Excelsiors were clerks and small-time merchants of elevated social standing in the Protestant community who prided themselves on being gentlemen. By contrast, their opponents were Irish Catholic workingmen who, God forbid, had dirt under their fingernails.

Ten thousand fans turned out for each of the first two games, which were split between the teams with no untoward incidents. However, the deciding game was witnessed by an estimated fifteen to twenty thousand fans, most of them rooting for the Catholic team, the Atlantics. Not only did the Atlantic partisans offend fans of the opposite persuasion with foul language and boisterous behavior, but they loudly voiced their crude objections to several of the lone umpire's calls that went against their heroes. The hooting and jeering eventually became so menacing that not even the pleas of Atlantic players nor the poised billy clubs of the hundred policemen stationed at the game could control the rowdy fans.

The Excelsiors' captain eventually had no choice but to pull his team off the field. As the fearful Protestants hastily retreated in their horse-drawn omnibus, the riotous Atlantics fans (called "cranks" in the current lingo) pelted them with stones.

The local press unanimously castigated the "spirit of faction" with which the "foreign element" and their offspring had polluted the peace and quiet of the entire metropolitan area.

UNTIL THE 1930s, when Branch Rickey developed a minor league farm system for the St. Louis Cardinals, the recruiting and signing of players was strictly a cash transaction.

In rural areas, a young hopeful with sufficient talent might begin his baseball career by playing for his town team. In urban settings, a point of entry might be a club team like the Atlantics. (By the late 1860s, there were more than a thousand similar amateur teams in the United States.) The only means of advancing to a higher level of competition would be for the player to give an outstanding performance in front of an interested spectator with the proper connections. Since not even upper-echelon teams employed scouts, the influential observer might be an ex-player, the friend of a manager, the owner of a low-level pro team, or even a sportswriter. A positive verbal scouting report would then be passed along, followed by either another look-see or a contract offered sight unseen. Should a player manage to attract the interest of a more advanced ball club, his contract would have to be purchased at a mutually agreeable price. The player, of course, would receive nothing in this transaction.

As the player advanced up the ladder, the process would be repeated, with both the individual's salary and the sale price increasing. The primary exception to this practice would be a relatively high-level team signing a player straight out of college.

Occasionally, though, when a team had immediate need of a player to fill a specific role, it would place an advertisement in a local or regional newspaper. But a promising Irish player still had to face the prevailing anti-Irish and anti-Catholic discrimination.

Here's a typical ad that appeared in the *Brooklyn Eagle* in the spring of 1868:

NOTICE TO FIRST BASEMEN—The National Club of
Washington are looking for a first baseman about here. They have
been to Brooklyn, but they were not successful in obtaining one.
Terms—First-rate position in the Treasury Department; must

work in the Department until three o'clock, and then practice base
ball until dark. "No Irish need apply."

The restriction was so commonplace that it was often reduced to a universally understood acronym: NINA.

It should be noted, however, that this bias existed even before the Irish came to America en masse. For example, James Harper successfully campaigned for mayor of New York in 1844 on a platform whose central feature was a virulent anti-Catholic prejudice.

One contemporary reporter for the *Chicago Post* claimed that putting the Irish "on a boat and sending them home would end crime in this country."

Not even Henry David Thoreau was immune to ethnic intolerance. In reacting to the influx of Irish immigrants who worked on canal-digging projects in New York and Chicago, Thoreau wrote: "If the Irishman did not shovel all day, he would get drunk and quarrel."

Perpetually smarting from the pain inflicted by these and other exclusionary practices, the Irish turned the other cheek and often welcomed ethnic diversity within their own organizations. That's why the Greater New York Irish Athletic Association, unlike the prestigious New York Athletic Club, granted membership to several outstanding Jewish athletes at the turn of the century.

Despite these many cultural handicaps, the sons of Ireland could not be denied. Irish baseball players were so talented and so persistent that they simply could not be kept off the green diamonds of America's popular new game.

Chapter Four

The First Irish Stars

I would rather die than give up any part of my father's name.

—*"Orator" Jim O'Rourke*

ON MARCH 17, 1871 (St. Patrick's Day, as it turns out), representatives of ten professional teams met to plan the first all-pro league in America: the National Association of Base Ball Players (NA). Already in existence were several touring pro teams, some salaried clubs funded by commercial establishments, and a number of cooperative nines that shared gate receipts. The increasing popularity of the game was also demonstrated by scores of amateur leagues that organized competition among various trades (including a Wholesale Grocers League in Chicago), colleges, schools, cities, towns, villages, and social clubs—with many of these paying ringers on a per-game basis.

These diverse leagues and teams especially proliferated in urban areas such as Boston, Cleveland, Philadelphia, Providence, Hartford, New York, and Chicago, cities that had significant Irish populations. If NINA was the byword in most outlying locales, the teams in these metropolitan areas pointedly recruited a number of Irish players, even if in limited numbers, to lure their fellow countrymen through the turnstiles.

♣Historians consider the NA to have been a bona fide major league, making Andy Leonard the first Irish-born major leaguer. Leonard (of County Cavan) made his debut with the Washington (D.C.) Olympics in 1871 and went on to play the infield and outfield for more than five hundred games with the Olympics and Boston Red Stockings of the NA, as well as the Boston Red Caps and Cincinnati Reds of the National League (which was founded five years later, in 1876), finishing with a lifetime batting average of .299.

♣Perhaps the most influential of the Irish players in the NA was William Arthur "Candy" Cummings, who is often credited with being the first pitcher to throw a curveball.

According to Cummings, he was inspired as a boy in Massachusetts by his habit of tossing seashells into the ocean. Recalling the swooping movement of the shells later encouraged him to find a way to make a baseball move the same way. His experiments to discover the appropriate wrist twist came to fruition during an 1867 game in Worcester, near his hometown of Ware.

"I became fully convinced that I had finally succeeded," Cummings said, "because the batters were missing a lot of balls. I began to watch the flight of the ball through the air, and distinctly saw it curve."

Yet Cummings rarely threw his curveball, relying instead on pinpoint location, changes of speed, and an effortless delivery.

There were, however, other claimants to the creation of this back-, bat-, and ground-breaking pitch.

Fred Goldsmith (English, not Irish) offered the first publicly recorded demonstration of the curveball on August 16, 1870, at the Capitoline Grounds in Brooklyn. Bearing certifiable witness was Henry Chadwick, a sports reporter for the *Brooklyn Eagle*.

The Cummings-Goldsmith debate raged on for a few years in

the press and in later historical documents, but only Cummings got the Hall of Fame nod, voted in by the Veterans Committee seventy years later.

♣Another notable Irish player in the NA years was "Orator" Jim O'Rourke, a young outfielder for Connecticut's Middletown Mansfields. In 1872, O'Rourke was offered a lucrative contract to move from the Mansfields to the Protestant-owned Boston Red Stockings. But there was a catch: He would have to conceal the obvious Irishness of his name by dropping the "O" and playing as Rourke.

Emphatically declining the offer, O'Rourke said that "a million dollars would not tempt me."

O'Rourke eventually graduated from Yale and became a longtime manager of several National League clubs. Orator Jim proved the appropriateness of his nickname when he refused a player's request for a raise by saying this: "I'm sorry, but the exigencies of the occasion and the condition of our exchequer will not permit anything of the sort at this period of our existence. Subsequent developments in the field of finance may remove the present gloom and we may emerge into a condition where we may see fit to reply in the affirmative to your exceedingly modest request."

Orator Jim was voted in by the Hall of Fame Veterans Committee in 1945.

♣The Philadelphia Athletics were the champions of the NA's maiden season, led by the exploits of their left-handed catcher Fergy Malone (born in County Tyrone), who sported a scintillating .343 batting average.

However, the Boston Red Stockings dominated after that, winning titles in the league's next four seasons. The ease with which Boston prevailed from 1872 to 1875 proved disastrous for the league's survival, as several of the weaker teams went broke and folded in midseason. Moreover, the vague players' contracts couldn't prevent players from bouncing from team to team, causing several other franchises to cease operations out of sheer frustration. The integrity of NA competition was also compromised by persistent (but never proved) rumors of players fixing games.

NEVERTHELESS, IN AN indirect way, the NA made a significant contribution to the long-term "greening" of the game. Midway through the 1874 season, a team made up of players from the Boston and Philly franchises undertook a three-week tour of England, with a two-day side trip to Dublin. The squad was stocked with Irish players, including the aforementioned O'Rourke and Leonard, plus Mike McGeary (with his roots in County Tyrone), John McMullin (Antrim), Tim Murnane (County Cork), and pitcher-manager Dick McBride (Donegal).

The Americans split two games in Dublin, but defeated an Irish all-star team in cricket by the lopsided score of 165 to 79. Despite the presumed attraction of the visiting Irish American team, the two baseball games only attracted a total of 1,500 paying customers.

Even so, this first exposure to American baseball created a small coterie of passionate fans that would gradually increase over the decades.

In 1876, fearing that the National Association's egregious flaws threatened the very existence of the pro game, the Chicago White Stockings owner convinced several of his peers to abandon the shaky league and form a new one. The result was the National League of Professional Baseball Clubs (NL), which featured ironclad player-team contracts and severe financial penalties for franchises that didn't complete any given season's quota of ball games, as well as a team of detectives whose task was to make sure the competition was above board.

The NL also tweaked many of the abiding rules of the game. Yet the whys and wherefores of the on-field action would still have completely mystified modern fans.

Truly bizarre rules, in retrospect.

For example:

- Instead of throwing off a mound and pushing off a rubber, there was a six-foot-square pitching box with the nearest point located only forty-five feet from home plate, which was totally situated in foul territory.
- Although pitchers still had to deliver the ball with an underhand motion, they were now permitted to snap their wrists to enable the throwing of curveballs—thereby legalizing what Candy Cummings had already been doing.
- A "pitcher's balk" would be called should the ball be released above the waist. Three such balks would result in the game being forfeited.
- Before facing the initial pitch of any at-bat, the hitter could still demand that pitches be thrown "high" or "low." Once the declaration was made, these preferences remained unaltered during the entire at-bat.
- Any three consecutive pitches that were not within the constraints of the batter's demands would be called a "ball." Three balls (totaling nine pitches) would entitle the batter to advance to first base.
- With two strikes already recorded, the umpire delivered a warning if a hitter failed to swing at a "good" pitch. Subsequent to the warning, the umpire would declare a second taking of a "good" pitch to be a third strike, but instead of automatically being declared out, the runner would dash toward first base as though he had struck a fair ball.
- Except for what we now call a pinch runner, no substitutions were permitted after the completion of three innings.
- The umpire allowed precisely five minutes to elapse while the players and the fans searched for a lost ball. Only after that time had elapsed was he permitted to put a new ball in play.

- Should the umpire not have a clear view of wheth█████████ ball was fair or foul, or caught on the fly or t████████ was instructed to question the fans nearest the pla██████en abide by the "fairest testimony."

IN 1876, THE National League's maiden season, approximately 31 of the 133 players on the eight charter teams had Irish roots, whether of Irish parents or actually born in Ireland.

Several of these Irishmen recorded historical firsts in the new league.

♣Boston's Jim O'Rourke clouted the NL's first-ever base hit—a single on April 22 against the Philadelphia Athletics.

♣Candy Cummings, he of first curveball fame, won both games of the NL's first doubleheader, ostensibly with the aid of at least a few curveballs.

Two other Irish-born players excelled in the early years of the NL:

♣Patrick Joseph "Patsy" Donovan (from Queenstown in County Cork), who eventually retired with 2,253 base hits and a lifetime batting average of .301, and went on to be considered one of the most successful Irish-born managers in history. (In his very late years, he coached a young George H. W. Bush, who was in his last year at Andover.)

♣Tony Mullane (also of County Cork) won 284 games and, after his retirement in 1894, became one of the most influential sportswriters in the early twentieth century. He is tied with Ferguson Jenkins for wins, but didn't make the Hall; he is behind only Bobby Matthews (297 wins) and Tommy John (288) for eligible pitchers *not* in the Hall of Fame. He was also known for being ambidextrous on the mound. (More on the player known as "Count" to come.)

According to the *Baseball Almanac*, six other players born in major league debuts in the 1870s, but alas, except for ha▓▓▓▓▓▓l Irish names, they didn't accomplish much—with a few exc▓▓▓

♣First ▓▓▓ n John James McGuinness played three modest seasons.

♣ John Henry Curran played just three games, and even that statistical footnote was almost lost, until SABR researchers found him listed at Peter Curran.

♣ James "Jimmy" Hallinan played shortstop here and there over five seasons.

♣ William Sullivan played one season for the Chicago White Stockings.

♣Patrick A. McManus pitched one season for the Troy Trojans.

♣ And Charles "Curry" Foley, hailing from Milltown, Ireland, played only two seasons but was officially the first player to hit for the cycle.

During the NL's formative seasons, the first generation of American-born Irish males were coming of age and would exhibit sufficient skills and aptitude to be well represented on every team in the league.

Even so, the game had yet to be "Irish-ized."

Chapter Five

More Irish Firsts

If you're enough lucky to be Irish, you're lucky enough!
—Irish saying

♣ON JULY 4, 1876, James Francis "Pud" Galvin (a first-generation Irish American born in St. Louis) pitched a perfect game for a touring professional team out of St. Louis against another outfit of on-the-road pros from Philadelphia. This was probably the first such accomplishment in baseball history, professional or otherwise.

As the nickname Pud supposedly came from his proclivity for turning bats into pudding, within three years Galvin would become the mainstay of the Buffalo Bisons, using only a blazing sidearm fastball that was augmented by his uncanny control.

However, it was subsequently discovered in 1889 that Galvin recorded still another milestone, being the first major league player to be injected with a performance-enhancing substance. This was "Brown-Sequard," an extract made of the brains and/or sexual organs of various animals, an elixir that many doctors believed could prolong human life. Except for an article in the *Washington Post* claiming that the latest pitching gem by the thirty-three-year-old Galvin demonstrated the value of the drug, the news caused no reaction whatsoever.

By the time he retired in 1892, Galvin had become the sport's first 300-game winner (365–308). He was inducted into the Hall of Fame by the Veterans Committee in 1965.

♣Greatly aided by the potent bats of a pair of second-generation Irishmen—first-basemen Cal McVey (.347) and outfielder John Glenn (.304)—the Chicago White Stockings cruised to the NL's initial championship in 1876.

There was one significant and one minor rule change for the subsequent 1877 season: the installation of a six-foot by three-foot batter's box that permitted the hitter to take his stance anywhere from three feet in front of or behind home plate. Also, should rain persist for ten minutes after the umpire suspended action, he was required to terminate the game.

The 1877 season also saw the birth of not one but two additional pro leagues that vied with the NL to sign quality players: the League Alliance featured thirteen teams, while the International Association comprised sixteen clubs. All three of the self-proclaimed major leagues prohibited Sunday games, but the NL was still unique in several ways: most of its franchises were situated in thriving metropolitan areas, admission to games was fifty cents (twice the normal fee), and the sale of alcohol at games was forbidden.

Still, with three leagues bidding for the services of the elite players, salaries jumped to such a degree that the NL could only field six teams in 1877, down from eight. (Surprisingly, the New York and Philly franchises were disbanded.)

THE IRISH NUMBERED 23 of the 98 active NL players, almost the same percentage as in the previous season, when Irishmen numbered 31 of 133.

A trio of Irish pitchers totally dominated the competition in the NL's second season:

♣Tommy Bond (hailing from Granard in County Longford) led his fellow hurlers in wins (40), winning percentage (.702), strike-outs (170), shutouts (6), and ERA (2.11), while finishing second in games (58), complete games (58!), and innings pitched (521). No wonder Bond's team, the Boston Red Caps (nicknames were frequently changed), won the NL's second season's championship.

Bond would finish with a career record of 193–115. (The Tommy Bond Award is given to the best pitcher in the modern-day baseball league in Ireland.)

♣As good as Bond was, Charles "Kid" Nichols (born in Wisconsin to parents who had fled the famine) got the more important Cooperstown enshrinement in 1949 by dint of being, at age thirty-two, the youngest pitcher to win three hundred games, compiling a lifetime mark of 361–208.

♣Another Irish pitcher, Jim Devlin (from the Irish enclave of Troy, New York), with the Louisville Grays, was nearly as accomplished—leading the NL in innings pitched (559, every inning of every game the Grays played; yes, *every* inning), games and complete games (61), while finishing second to Bond in wins (35), winning percentage (.583), and strikeouts (141).

His devastating out pitch was a "drop" (perhaps the first known sinker), and he also led his team in hitting with a .315 average. Despite his extraordinary accomplishments, Devlin's name is remembered primarily because of his participation in the NL's one and only betting scandal.

It seems that the Grays led the second-place Boston Red Caps by a considerable margin as the 1887 season neared its climax. But then Louisville went winless during a seven-game road trip, games that were marked by uncharacteristic boneheaded plays and bush-league pitching. Eventually Boston won the pennant with the Grays lagging three games behind. Immediately after the season, Devlin and several of his teammates were seen dining in Louisville's most expensive restaurants while wearing gold watches and diamond rings that were all well beyond the purchasing power of their baseball salaries.

A postseason investigation was launched by Charles Chase, Louisville's vice president, causing Devlin and teammate George Hall to quickly confess. Chase then demanded that he be allowed to read any telegrams that passed among them and any other Louisville players.

A wire to Devlin from Louisville's right fielder, George Bechtel, was incriminating:

Bingham House, Philadelphia, June 10, 1876. We can make $500 if you lose the game tomorrow. Tell John [Chapman, the team's manager] and let me know at once. BECHTEL.

Devlin's response was righteous:

I want you to understand I am not that kind of man. I play ball for the interest of those who hire me.
DEVLIN

But other telegrams confirmed that a utility infielder named Al Nichols was coordinating payoffs from New York gamblers to himself, Devlin, and Hall. Even though nothing could be proved against Bechtel, league president William Hubert issued a lifetime ban, prohibiting Devlin, Hall, and Nichols from ever playing in the NL again.

PERHAPS THE MOST significant landmark of the 1877 season was the debut of Michael Joseph Kelly—a player destined to become not just an Irish superstar but also the first national baseball celebrity.

When Kelly joined the Columbus Buckeyes of the International Association, he was only nineteen years old, and his paltry .156 batting average in twenty-three games bore no hint that he would someday be hailed as "the King of Ballplayers."

Born on December 31, 1859, to immigrant parents in Lansingburgh, New York (an Irish neighborhood near Albany), Kelly inherited a thick Irish brogue. He was still a child when his father joined the Union Army after the outbreak of the Civil War and moved the family to Washington, D.C. It was there that young Kelly came into regular contact with a man who would have a dramatic impact on his life—General George McClellan, notorious for his stylish dress, the carefree spending of his considerable wealth, and his ebullient personality. Kelly was so dazzled that he swore that when he grew up he'd find a way to duplicate McClellan's flamboyant lifestyle.

After the war, the Kellys moved to Paterson, New Jersey, where the numerous textile mills offered ready employment. By then Kelly had grown into a sturdy 5'10", 170-pound teenager, whose strength and large frame enabled him to earn three dollars per week hauling baskets of coal from the basement to the top floor of the Murray Silk Mill.

But baseball was his passion.

At age fifteen, he was good enough to be the starting catcher with the Paterson Stars, a semipro outfit that successfully competed against some of the best teams in the New York metropolitan area. Having delivered his daily quota of coal, Kelly would sneak away from the mill to play with the Stars. On one occasion, his boss caught Kelly jumping out of a second-story window, a transgression that nearly cost him his job.

♣Two of Kelly's teammates with the Stars were Irish pitchers Ed Nolan and Jim McCormick, who (like Kelly) were destined to have outstanding careers. In 1877, both Kelly and McCormick joined the Buckeyes, and shortly after the Columbus franchise folded, Kelly was signed by the NL's Cincinnati Reds.

Kelly proceeded to hit a steady, if not spectacular, .283, and proved to be a versatile athlete, variously playing all of the outfield positions, plus third base and catcher. Fielding, however, was never his strong point.

In an era when most fielders played either barehanded or with thin, fingerless gloves, cleanly fielded balls were rare. Still, in sixty games, Kelly committed a whopping 43 errors. Years later, Kelly would respond to his manager's anger at his muffing an easy fly ball by smiling and saying, "By Gad, I made it hit me gloves, anyhow."

Kelly's natural talents as a batsman were evidenced when he hit .348 in 1879. Even so, his fumbling efforts afield (58 miscues in 77 games) were so egregious that the Reds released him after the season.

Within two months, Kelly was signed by the Chicago White Stockings, and his brilliant, nomadic—and hard-drinking—Hall of Fame–bound career began in earnest.

Boston repeated as champs in 1878, but was usurped by Providence a year later when the NL expanded back to eight teams.

♣Several of the Irish veteran players continued to thrive, especially Tommy Bond, who won 43 games and led the NL in strikeouts, along with Jim O'Rourke, who matched Kelly's handsome .348 batting average. (O'Rourke, however, was an even worse fielder than Kelly.)

♣Meanwhile, the league's rosters featured an increasing number of up-and-coming stellar Irish players. Foremost among those making their major league debut in 1879 was a square-shouldered, square-jawed Irishman named Dan Brouthers.

The son of Irish immigrants who settled less than two hours north of New York City in Wappingers Falls, Brouthers was commonly called Big Dan even before he fully matured into a 6'2", 205-pound, lefty-swinging, power-hitting first baseman. He was still a teenager when he was recognized as one of the best players in the Hudson River valley—home to several highly competitive amateur and semipro ball clubs. But Brouthers temporarily quit baseball as a nineteen-year-old when he slammed into a catcher in an attempt to score on a close play. Unfortunately, the catcher suffered a head injury and was dead within twenty-four hours.

Most likely, this was the first instance of an on-field death in the recorded history of the game, and Brouthers was so grief-stricken that he sat out the rest of the season and contemplated giving up the game for good.

But he resumed his career with a team in Lansingburgh the next spring, and was signed by the NL Troy Trojans for the 1879 campaign. He was a mere twenty years old when the season began, yet batted a respectable .274 and clouted the only four homers the Trojans managed for the entire season. However, after he went 2 for 12 at the start of the 1880 season, Troy cut Brouthers loose and he spent the rest of that season playing for several independent teams in the area. It wasn't until he joined the Buffalo Bisons in 1881 that Brouthers became a major league stalwart, and he would later find his way to fame in New York City.

Shortly after the conclusion of the 1879 season, the franchise owners adopted a ruling that was designed to reduce their expenditures— and would serve to create bitter controversy throughout the next hundred years.

Each team could designate five players presently under contract to be on their "reserve list." This action bound these players to their teams of the moment for the duration of their playing career in the NL.

The underlying anthem of each of the National League's early seasons was provided by the disharmony of musical franchises. If the NL's initial four seasons established it as the most competitive of the three extant major leagues, there was still considerable doubt about the financial health of many of its franchises.

By 1880, the only surviving charter members of the NL were Boston, Chicago, and Cincinnati. Long gone were teams in Hartford, Worcester, Troy, Buffalo, Syracuse, Providence, Louisville, Indianapolis, and Milwaukee.

Yet the next decade would feature several developments that would increase the game's popularity while further testing the stability of the league:

- The massive influx of many more outstanding Irish players into the NL, including the arrival of Ned Hanlon, arguably the most influential Irish player-cum-manager the game has ever seen.
- The coming of age of young stars like Kelly and Brouthers.
- Serious labor problems instigated mostly by Irish players.

The end result, though, would be the emergence of baseball as America's undisputed national pastime.

PRESENT-DAY INTERVIEW

A lefty reliever with the Atlanta Braves, Eric O'Flaherty was born in Walla Walla, Washington, where nobody was aware of, or paid much attention to, his being Irish.

"Except my dad," Eric says. "He's into all that family tree stuff. But the only way the rest of the family knew about being Irish was when my dad made Irish stew on St. Paddy's Day. It was very low-key. When I was over twenty-one, though, I really started to celebrate in my own way."

Nowadays, O'Flaherty notes that there's one major league curse in the mix: "The whole team wears green hats every St. Paddy's Day. And every time I've pitched with my green hat on I've gotten lit up. I've never had a good outing on March seventeenth."

The un-luck of the Irish?

"Nah. What happens in spring training doesn't really matter."

As the Braves travel through the season, O'Flaherty is fascinated by how much of a fuss fans in Boston and New York make over his heritage.

"Everybody takes very good care of me whenever I walk into an Irish pub."

Part II

THE EMERALD AGE

Chapter Six

They Would Be Giants

There is no language like the Irish for soothing and quieting.
—*John Millington Synge*

THE LATE 1800s ushered in the Emerald Age of major league baseball.

According to the research of the late Hall of Fame historian Lee Allen, that's when a full 41 percent of the rookies in the NL, the American Association (AA), and the Union Association shared a common Irish heritage.

Because of the still-prevailing NINA bias, Irish players still had to be demonstrably better than their respective competitors in order to secure spots on pro teams. And the statistics bear this out: in 1880, Irish players exceeded non-Irish players by 11 points in batting average, 14 points in slugging percentage, and 12 points in on-base percentage. (The latter two categories have been compiled retroactively.)

♣Prominent among these Irishmen was Tony Mullane, who won 30 games in five consecutive seasons. During the 1880s, Mullane's excellence was rewarded with an average salary of $6,000 (equal to $85,000 in today's economy), which rightly placed him among the top earners of the time.

Because of his stylish clothes, his magnificent handlebar mustache, and his way with the ladies, Mullane had several nicknames, most notably "Count" and the "Apollo of the Box." His incredible athleticism was proved both during and after he injured his right arm in throwing a baseball the prodigious distance of 416 feet, 7¾ inches, to demonstrate his strength. This feat was all the more remarkable since the leansome 5'10" Mullane weighed only 165 pounds.

Mullane responded by pitching left-handed, with only minimal loss of effectiveness, until his right arm was fully healed.

Other Irish pitchers who dominated NL action in the early 1880s included two league leaders—and two more who set all-time records that stand to this day:

♣ Jim McCormick of the Cleveland Spiders led the NL in wins in 1880 (45) and 1882 (36).

♣ Larry Corcoran of the Chicago White Stockings was the NL's strikeout king in 1880 and the win leader in 1881. Corcoran didn't make the Hall of Fame, despite being the first pitcher to throw three no-hitters in a career, not surpassed until Sandy Koufax tossed his fourth in 1965.

♣ "Sir" Timothy Keefe played with Troy, the New York Giants, and Philadelphia, twice leading the league in wins, strikeouts, games, and complete games. In 1880, Keefe was only 6–6, yet recorded an ERA of 0.86, a still-standing single-season record for pitchers with at least ten decisions. He was voted into the Hall in 1964.

♣ Hall of Famer Mickey Welch holds the record for most strikeouts to start a game (9) and was the third pitcher ever to reach 300 wins, finishing with 304.

What makes these achievements even more notable is a brace of rule changes that were instituted, starting in the 1881 season:

- The number of called balls that entitled a hitter to a free pass was reduced from eight to seven. And, more significantly, the closest edge of the pitcher's box was moved five feet farther from home plate, from 45 out to 50 feet.
- In 1882, a runner was declared out if he failed to *run* back to his base after a foul ball.
- For the following season, pitchers were charged with errors for walks, balks, hit batters, and wild pitches.
- In 1884, the number of balls required for a walk was reduced to six.
- A major change occurred in 1885: pitchers were allowed to throw overhand, but to reduce the velocity of their offerings they were required to keep both feet on the ground throughout their deliveries—and were still compelled to throw their pitches at the heights demanded by the hitters.
- In 1886, the pitcher's box was reduced to four-by-seven feet.

EVEN SO, THE most influential Irish players of the time were position players.

. ♣ First up was Roger Connor, a handsome man with a wide jaw and a requisite mustache overhanging a grim mouth. He also measured 6'3" and 220 pounds, about seven inches taller and sixty pounds heavier than the average contemporary American male.

A slugging lefty-hitting first-baseman, Connor began his major league career with the Troy Trojans in 1880, and went on to total 138 home runs during his eighteen-year career—a mark that stood until Babe Ruth surpassed him in 1931.

Given that the baseball Connor faced was discolored by the use of so many foreign substances, that only three or four balls were used per game, and that the balls quickly became lopsided and spongy, home runs were rare occurrences during his tenure in the pros.

Yet one of Connor's round-trippers not only was dramatic but also historic. On September 10, 1881, Troy was hosting a team that was a strong candidate for having the most unimaginative nickname ever—the Worcester Worcesters—and trailing 7–4 with two outs and the bases loaded in the bottom of the ninth inning.

That's when Connor blasted the first grand slam in the history of the NL.

However, Connor was more than just a strong-armed hitter. His lifetime totals of 441 doubles, 233 three-baggers, and 244 steals (which weren't recorded as an official statistic until 1886) are convincing evidence of his all-around skills.

In 1883, the Troy franchise was expelled from the NL and had its players transferred to the New York Gothams. Two years later, New York's Irish manager, Jim Mutrie, was speaking of Connor when he said: "My boys are not only giants in stature but in baseball ability."

That is how, why, and when the Gothams officially became the Giants.

♣Batting second for the Giants was Dan Brouthers, the big man newly arrived from the Buffalo team. Brouthers twice led the NL in homers, with eight in 1881 and eleven in 1887. He was also credited with 256 stolen bases and a lifetime batting average of .342.

Brouthers was also infamous for being a cheapskate. One evening, a Giants teammate was so shocked when Brouthers bought a round of drinks that he exchanged the dollar bill with the bartender and had it framed.

After his loyal service in a Giants uniform, the team provided Brouthers with a lifetime job as a gatekeeper at the Polo Grounds.

♣In the third slot for the Giants was Edward Hugh "Ned" Hanlon, standing just 5'9" and weighing 170, but most noticeable for his high forehead, long nose, thick soup strainer of a mustache, and slightly crooked dimple on his abbreviated chin.

While Hanlon was not an accomplished hitter (.260 over his thirteen-year career, spent mostly with the NL's Detroit Wolverines), he made his mark as a smart, speedy, highly motivated, and sure-handed centerfielder. Above all, Hanlon was a winner—he led off, hit .274, and pilfered 69 bases when Detroit copped the NL pennant in 1887. Hanlon was forced into premature retirement in 1892 after straining a tendon in a previously broken leg.

It was Hanlon's post-active career, however, that made him a major factor in the theory and practice of baseball for the next three decades.

DURING THIS TIME, Irish players continued to stand out.

♣In 1880, the White Stockings had an all-Irish battery: Larry Corcoran on the mound and the tobacco-chewing Frank "Silver" Flint behind the plate, the latter so named because of his prematurely white hair. He was also one of the last backstops to catch barehanded.

The two of them worked out a pitcher-catcher signal system, the first ever in the game. For a fastball, Flint put his chaw on the left side of his mouth, moving it to his right cheek for a curve.

♣The summer of 1882 marked the pitching debut of Irish-born Hugh "One Arm" Daily for the Buffalo Bisons. Actually, a gun accident had cost Daily his left hand, not his entire arm. For the season, Daily was 15-14, all complete games, and even hurled a no-hitter against Philadelphia on September 3. However, when overhand pitching was adopted, Daily's NL career was over. He did go on to have much success in the Union Association, a pro league that lasted for only the 1884 season; there he won 28 games and led the league with 483 strikeouts in 500 innings.

♣John Alexander "Bid" McPhee was a sure-handed second baseman for Cincinnati from 1882 to 1899. All told, he hit .271 for his career, led the NL in homers with nine in 1886, and stole 95 bases in 1887. According to the surviving percentages he was the league's best fielder at his position for eight seasons.

♣McPhee's prowess afield is even more remarkable since he was the last second baseman to play his position without using a glove, and was only just elected into the Hall by the 2000 Veterans Committee.

MANY PEOPLE DON'T know that before Billy Sunday was an internationally known evangelist, the Irishman was a speedy reserve outfielder for the White Stockings. He played in his first NL game on May 22, 1883, striking out in all four at-bats. As a sidekick of Mike Kelly, fast becoming famous for playing hungover, Sunday would often get drunk, smoke, play cards, and attend vaudeville performances.

But one day in 1886, Sunday, Kelly, and several teammates were lounging on the corner of State and Madison in Chicago when the sound of a gospel choir singing across the street reached their ears. Sunday believed it was a message from God to change his ways. He began to cry and told his teammates, "Good-bye, boys, I'm through. I'm going to Jesus Christ. We've come to a parting of the ways."

Then he left his flabbergasted teammates and joined the choir as it entered the Pacific Garden Mission.

When Sunday returned to the ballpark the next morning after a sleepless night, he was afraid that his teammates would ridicule him. But Kelly encouraged Sunday, saying, "Bill, I'm proud of you. Religion is not my long suit, but I'll help you all I can." Kelly's words made it easy for the other players to likewise encourage Sunday.

Even so, Sunday played for another four seasons, but he forswore smoking, drinking, and gambling. In his spare time, he began delivering the Good News to local YMCAs. Ultimately, Sunday quit the game in 1890 after compiling a career batting average of .248 and stealing 249 bases.

OTHER SIGNIFICANT ACHIEVEMENTS by Irish players in the early to mid-1880s included:

♣Mike Tiernan's record-setting impotence in making five outfield errors in one game. (Tiernan later went on to lead the NL in homers in 1890 and 1891.)

♣Billy O'Brien smacking 17 home runs to lead the NL in 1887.

♣The 1885 edition of the New York Giants featured an all-Irish outfield consisting of Mike Dorgan, Pete Gillespie, and Jim O'Rourke. Ireland-born Pat Deasley served the Giants as a backup outfielder and backup catcher.

♣Over the course of the entire 1885 Giants season, all but two innings were pitched by Irishmen, with Mickey Welch the staff's ace (44-11), Tim Keefe winning 32 games, sore-armed Larry Corcoran appearing in three games, and Danny Richardson (7–1) doing emergency mound duty. (The non-Irishman who took the mound for the Giants for those two innings was Buck Ewing, who was otherwise employed as the starting catcher.)

♣And the most conspicuous Irishman on the team was slugger Roger Connor, who had taken to wearing a bright green shamrock patch sewn to the sleeve of his jersey.

In addition, several Irishmen made their mark in the NL's rival leagues.

In the Union Association:

♣Joe Quinn became the first Australian-born Irish player in the majors, hitting .270 with the St. Louis Maroons. (Quinn went on to have a successful nineteen-year career in the National and American leagues.)

♣Charlie Sweeney won 40 games and set a single-game record by striking out 18 Boston Red Stockings.

In the American Association:

♣Matt Kilroy set an all-time strikeout record by fanning 513 in 1886.

♣Joe McGinnis won 25 games in 1882.

♣Catcher Jack Corcoran became infamous for spitting birdshot at batters' hands and faces just as a pitch was being delivered.

♣With walks counting as hits, James "Tip" O'Neill batted .492 for the Maroons; discounting his bases on balls, O'Neill's average was still an awesome .435.

What was undoubtedly the American Association's most curious incident involved a pair of non-Irish players, but it still had an Irish twist.

During a game played on August 22, 1886, William Van Winkle "Chicken" Wolf hit a line drive that landed just out of Abner Powell's reach in deep center field. Because of Powell's speed and strong arm, the hit seemed ticketed for a stand-up double. But a stray dog chanced to dash out onto the field to bite and hold on to Powell's pants, thereby enabling Wolf to circle the bases for a game-winning homer.

Rumor had it that the dog was an Irish setter.

IRISH PLAYERS WERE valued for more than their obvious skills.

The *Sporting News* claimed that the baseball-playing descendants of the Emerald Isle were distinguished by their ability to think "quickly and devise plans and schemes."

Sportswriter Henry Chadwick celebrated the Irish players' "pluck, courage, endurance and physical activity."

According to the American Press Association, the superiority of Irish players was due to their "love of a scrap and . . . proficiency in the use of a club."

However, after the conclusion of the 1887 season, it was an off-field trait of the Irish that would challenge the entire structure of professional baseball.

Chapter Seven

Molly Maguires

It's not that the Irish are cynical. It's simply that they have a wonderful lack of respect for everything and everybody.

—*Brendan Behan*

THE ANTHRACITE COAL mines in and around Scranton, Pennsylvania, were death traps. No provisions were made for ventilation, and there were no second exits that could be used in case of fires, explosions, or cave-ins. During a typical seven-year period in the 1850s, 566 miners were killed and 1,665 maimed in Schuylkill County alone; most of them were Irish.

In addition, virtually all of the flimsy housing provided for the workers and their families lacked adequate heat, windows, and even wood floors. Also, the underground workday could last up to fourteen grueling hours, and the miners' already meager pay was further reduced by deductions made for overpriced goods from the company store. Premature deaths from accidents as well as black lung disease were common.

In 1869, after a particularly devastating fire in the Avalon mine killed 179 miners, a bill was passed in the state legislature that ostensibly mandated various safety measures, but the bill was largely ignored by the all-powerful coal mine operators.

In an attempt to protect their lives and their livelihood, the miners formed a union—the Workingmen's Benevolent Association (WBA).

The vast majority of union members also belonged to the Ancient Order of Hibernians (AOH), a semisecret fraternal society founded in 1565 by an Irish chieftain, Rory O'Moore, to protect Roman Catholics from religious persecution. In Ireland, the AOH was essentially a militant movement that guarded churches and church members.

The owners reacted to the formation of the WBA by siccing goons and local policemen on the union members to violently break up meetings, smash picket lines, and bust heads. However, far from being intimidated, large numbers of WBA members took up arms in self-defense. Ferocious battles between the miners and the lackeys of the bosses became common. The miners' resistance became even fiercer when they discovered that British investors were in control of many of the area's mines. Before long, numerous groups of the WBA with AOH roots formed assassination squads that targeted the most vicious foremen and policemen, as well as several of the local mine superintendents.

These murderous squads were dubbed the "Molly Maguires" after a group of bloodthirsty Irish peasants who used to dress up as women in order to get close enough to their landlords and their landlords' properties to inflict severe damage. This appellation was used by the mine operators and parroted by the press to their advantage. Anyone who was pro-union was a "Molly," implying that they were deeply involved in murderous activities and that all miners were criminal by nature.

The WBA officially denounced the "Mollies" and revoked their union membership. But large numbers of desperate miners took it upon themselves to continue the Mollies' deadly reign of terror, especially since control of the WBA was being taken over by conservative elements.

The Mollies were eventually infiltrated by an Irish-born detective, James McParlan (né Seamus Mac Parthalain), who was hired by the mine owners under the aegis of the Pinkerton Agency. In June 1877, twenty Mollies were arrested, tried, then hanged, and the underground movement was rendered extinct.

Even so, the Molly Maguires were heroes to virtually every Irish worker throughout America.

Including numerous professional baseball players.

At the same time, Irish laborers were engaged in various other pro-labor movements, most notably the Noble and Holy Order of the Knights of Labor (KOL). First established in 1809 as a secret and obscure labor society by a group of tailors in Philadelphia, the KOL was chartered as a national organization in 1869. Under the presidency of Terence Powderly, the son of Irish immigrants, the KOL's wish list included the eight-hour workday and the inclusion in their ranks of unskilled female and black workers, along with the general uplifting of the social and cultural lives of the working class. The KOL reached its peak in 1886, when it boasted nearly 700,000 members nationwide.

But by the early 1890s, poor organization caused the Knights to dissolve.

AT THE END of the 1885 baseball season, nine members of the New York Giants caucused and formed the Brotherhood of Professional Base Ball Players.

♣Six of the founding members were Irish—Roger Connor, Mike Dorgan, Mickey Welch, Danny Richardson, Jim O'Rourke, and Tim Keefe (who transcribed the constitution in longhand).

The Brotherhood's immediate objections were to the expansion of the existing reserve clause to cover most (instead of just six) of a team's players, arbitrary fines, low salaries mandated by a salary cap, nonguaranteed contracts, pay cuts even for players who had enjoyed superb seasons, and the practice by some NL teams of forcing their players to rent their uniforms.

In return for the satisfaction of their demands, the Brotherhood pledged to support the establishment and enforcement of a code of conduct that would reduce the rampant rowdyism that plagued the sport.

The Brotherhood's gospel was spread throughout the NL during the 1886 season. A major boost to recruitment efforts was the Haymarket Square Riot, which erupted in Chicago on May 4, 1886—and for which the KOL was wrongly blamed.

By the end of the 1886 season, there were Brotherhood chapters on each of the NL's eight teams, with more than a hundred major leaguers agreeing to join the union. Although several radical players lobbied for immediate action—a strike or outright but ill-defined rebellion—the Brotherhood's officers counseled patience. Even more members were needed to make such an overwhelming show of strength. Plus there were vague plans afoot to eventually form still another rival league.

On November 11, 1887, the Brotherhood, now led by John Ward, Ned Hanlon, and Dan Brouthers, was officially recognized by the NL owners. But this recognition was merely an empty device designed to perpetually shelve the Brotherhood's demands. The only results were a series of fruitless meetings.

THE GAME OF baseball carried on, fueled by the desire to play.

The most significant new rule in effect for the 1888 season made walks no longer count as hits. As a result, batting averages were greatly reduced. After regular .400s by league leaders in earlier seasons, Cap

Anson set the pace with .344 and was followed by a trio of Irishmen:

♣Jimmy "Pony" Ryan (.332)

♣Mike Kelly (.318)

♣Dan Brouthers (.307)

Ryan was the home run king (16); Connor was second with 12.

An Irish theme that would run throughout baseball history—Irish brothers in baseball—got kicked off in style in 1888.

♣Pitcher Mickey Hughes had one outstanding season in the big leagues, winning 25 games for the Brooklyn Bridegrooms in 1888. Younger brother James would pitch a no-hitter a decade later.

♣On May 22, Ed Delahanty made his inauspicious debut (0 for 4 with two errors at second base) with the Giants. The son of Irish immigrants, Delahanty would be the first of five brothers to play in the bigs and would turn out to be one of the most potent batsmen the game has ever seen.

Behind Tim Keefe's league-leading 35 wins, 335 strikeouts, and 1.74 ERA, the Giants cruised to the 1888 pennant, finishing nine games ahead of the White Stockings.

The game took a huge step toward modernization with the institution of four balls and three strikes for the 1889 season.

♣Brouthers was the best hitter (.373) and Connor set the pace in RBIs (130).

♣John Clarkson led a quartet of dominant Irish pitchers with 49 wins—his fellow countrymen being Keefe (28 wins), Welch (27), and Galvin (23).

Another Irishman made history on September 10, 1889, when Mickey Welch became the first pinch hitter in major league history. A career .224 hitter, Welch's eventual whiff was true to form.

Off the field, the Brotherhood was finally poised to make a daring move as the 1890 season approached.

Chapter Eight

Superstar

I'm Irish. We think sideways.
—*Spike Milligan*

WAY, WAY, WAY before Elvis Presley or Babe Ruth, an Irishman became a bona fide American pop icon. Mike "King" Kelly, from a small town in upstate New York, was a baseball celebrity whose fame transcended the game and his rural roots.

Kelly's virile good looks were enhanced by his abundant mustache, his arched eyebrows, and the self-assured look in his stone-colored eyes. Kelly was often posed in full uniform while casually leaning on the remains of some ancient stone pillar, his left hand holding his bat at rest as though it were a sword or a scepter. Sometimes, a sprig of laurel was close by to further underline his regal presence.

KELLY DIDN'T NEED any tutoring from his manager Ned Hanlon to find ways to win at all costs. He made his own history of sorts with the Chicago White Stockings on May 20, 1881, when he was perched as a runner on second as a teammate punched a routine ground ball to the second baseman. While the lonely umpire tracked the batted ball and throw to first, King took a shortcut to home plate, avoiding third by about twenty feet as he scored the go-ahead run.

Indeed, Kelly was always an imaginative base runner. Early in his nine-year tenure in Chicago, the White Stockings were up in the bottom of the ninth with two out, runners on first and second, and the score knotted at two all. Immediately after executing a double steal that resulted in Kelly safe at third and teammate Ned Williamson at second, Kelly howled in pain and called time. Williamson rushed over to help and was loudly instructed by Kelly to pull on his right shoulder in hopes of snapping it back in place. But there was nothing amiss with Kelly's shoulder. His act was just a ruse for him to clue Williamson in on a trick that Kelly had devised.

As soon as the pitcher raised his arms and initiated his set position, Kelly took off for home. Both the opposing pitcher and catcher were stunned by Kelly's miraculous recovery, but the ball was in the backstop Charlie Bennett's hands with Kelly still ten feet from scoring the winning run. As Bennett prepared to tag Kelly, the King came to a stop and spread his legs as far apart as they could go without his falling down. Bennett was simply frozen with confusion. Then just as suddenly, Williamson, who had cut third base by some fifteen feet, dived through Kelly's legs and tallied the winning run.

If his antics on the bases were eventually outlawed and the infractions enforced by adding more umpires, Kelly also invented a particular maneuver that has become standard: the hook slide. He was so proficient in the execution of this evasive tactic that Chicago rooters took to shouting "Slide, Kelly, slide!" every time he approached a base.

Kelly also had a few trick plays when he was stationed in the outfield, the primary one being hiding an extra ball in his uniform shirt. One day, as darkness was rapidly approaching, Kelly gave a high-speed chase after a long line drive that concluded with his making a headfirst dive, then jumping to his feet and happily raising the ball in the air to indicate the spectacular catch had been accomplished. The Chicago fans cheered lustily, but when the White Stockings' manager, Cap Anson, complimented Kelly on his catch, Kelly laughed and said, "Not at all. Twent a mile above my head."

A versatile athlete, Kelly variously played the outfield, all the infield positions, and even pitched in 12 games (sporting a record of 2-2) during his sixteen years as a pro. When first basemen were taught to always keep a foot on the bag, either Kelly or Charles Comiskey came up with the idea of increasing their defensive range by disconnecting from the base and playing several feet back and off the bag.

Yet Kelly's primary position was behind the plate. And that's where he really opened his bag of tricks. One was to casually drop his mask on the plate just as an opposing runner was about to slide. This last-second obstruction often caused the runner to stumble and/or miss touching the plate.

Moreover, at a time when a caught foul tip was recorded as an out, another of Kelly's ploys was to fill his mouth with birdshot. Kelly picked his spots carefully as he snapped several of the shots between his teeth, producing a sound designed to fool the umpire into believing that contact had been made between the bat and the ball.

But this particular jig was up late in his career when Kelly accidentally began choking and coughed up his cache at an umpire's feet.

Other of Kelly's more legitimate innovations included determining what pitches would be thrown by giving finger signals to the pitcher, backing up first on routine groundballs, and making a science of stealing opponents' signs.

At the plate, Kelly was dynamic, leading the NL in doubles and runs three times each, then capping his tenure in Chicago by outhitting his peers with a gaudy .388 batting average.

EVEN SO, IT was Kelly's off-field antics that were the most troublesome.

His inveterate drinking and nighttime barhopping were bad enough, but what was even worse was his convivial nature, which made him an irresistible leader. As a result, there were frequent games in which both Kelly and several other players were still drunk, or else so hungover that their play was listless and disinterested. But Kelly remained carefree. He once blamed a poor performance on "too much temperance."

Fully embracing his youthful admiration of General McClellan, Kelly kept his late hours in resplendent silk suits, patent leather shoes, top hats, and gold-knobbed canes. When the owner of the White Stockings, Albert Spalding, complained about his behavior and the bad influence he had on the younger members of the team, Kelly said: "What are you running here? A Sunday school or a baseball club?"

At one point Spalding hired a detective to tail Kelly and his cohorts. Spalding then read the report in front of the team, emphasizing the most reprehensible incidents of carousing, revelry, and debauchery. When Spalding was finished, Kelly said, "I have to offer only one amendment. In that place where the detective reports me as taking lemonade at three a.m., he's off. It was straight whiskey. I never drank lemonade at that hour in my life."

Kelly and the six other teammates who were implicated agreed to pay a total of twenty-five dollars to reimburse Spalding for the cost of the detective. Still, their promises to reform soon proved meaningless.

Through it all, the White Stockings were the NL's most successful franchise, winning pennants every year from 1880 to 1886 except '83, with Kelly hailed as the league's premier player and biggest gate attraction. But both owner Spalding and manager Anson had had their fill of Kelly's escapades.

On February 14, 1887, Kelly was sold to the Boston Beaneaters for the unheard-of price of $10,000—twice the previous sum ever paid for any other ballplayer.

Upon being notified of the deal, Kelly denied any and all charges that he was routinely intoxicated. The accusations and the resulting fines, Kelly claimed, were "simply drummed up in order to lessen the salary list of the club."

MEANWHILE, KING KELLY'S arrival in Boston was greeted with unabashed and unprecedented adulation by the city's huge Irish population in some unusual ways:

- Whereas a lithograph of Custer's Last Stand used to occupy a prominent spot in Boston's Irish saloons, it was quickly replaced by a replica of Kelly sliding into second base.
- A Kelly-endorsed shoe polish was introduced.
- A sled manufacturer produced a "Slide, Kelly, Slide" model.
- Seemingly on a daily basis, Kelly's fans showered him with trophies, floral arrangements, and gold jewelry.
- Several of his most ardent admirers pooled their resources to provide Kelly and his wife, Agnes, not only with a fully furnished house, but also with a carriage and a matching pair of white horses to transport him from his new home to the ballpark. On several occasions, his fans became so enthusiastic that they unhitched the horses and propelled the carriage to the ballpark with their own manpower.

In addition to all that, some more significant occurrences took place.

- Kelly was asked for and readily agreed to sign his name on the numerous scraps of paper proffered by crowds of adoring young fans. Kelly's signature soon became treasured as undeniable proof that a personal encounter had been made, and it initiated the cultural phenomenon of collecting celebrity autographs.

- John W. Kelly (no relation) composed a ditty titled "Slide, Kelly, Kelly" that became a hit record.
- Before the 1888 season, Kelly became the first baseball player to become a vaudeville star. He sang snippets of popular songs, acted in brief skits, and performed some elementary dance steps.
- Also prior to the 1888 season, Kelly set another precedent when his autobiography, *Play Ball: Stories of the Ball Field*, was published. The ghostwriter of this "tell no evil" book was Jacob Charles "Mike" Morse, a sportswriter for the *Boston Herald*, and it was the first presumably self-authored life story presented by a baseball player.

At the same time, the Beaneaters' management had to make several concessions to keep Kelly happy. According to the official limitations recently imposed by the NL owners, Kelly was only entitled to a $2,000 salary. However, the Boston brass shelled out an additional $3,000 for the right to use a photo of Kelly for publicity purposes. More significantly, Kelly demanded that he be named the team's captain.

The current practice was for a manager to make out the lineup cards, oversee trades and roster moves, institute fines for his players' miscreant behavior, and generally supervise any other necessary off-field activities. The captain's responsibilities covered all game-time decisions—when to steal, hit-and-run, issue intentional walks, and make strategic substitutions.

There were no restrictions on when or how these substitutions might be made, and this loophole led to one of Kelly's most famous antics.

For a game in Indianapolis, Kelly happened to be out of the lineup because he was simply too drunk to play. Edward "Dimples" Tate was behind the plate for the Beaneaters, who were leading by a run with two out in the bottom of the ninth and the bases loaded. The batter lifted a high pop foul close to the Boston bench and, although

Tate made a desperate run to make the game-ending, game-winning catch, the ball was clearly beyond his reach. That's when Kelly made a loud announcement—"Kelly now catching"—and snagged the ball in his bare hands.

Another occasion in which Kelly was too inebriated to leave the bench didn't end so fortuitously. On October 2, 1887, Boston was playing a critical game against the Spiders in Cleveland with Kelly shivering under his overcoat, in the throes of a severe hangover. But Kelly roused himself into action to dispute a close call rendered by a rookie umpire named John McQuaid.

"You're stealing the championship from us!" Kelly screamed. His protestations became so virulent that McQuaid believed the Cleveland fans were on the verge of storming the field, so he summoned the ballpark police to remove Kelly from the grounds. The cops were glad to do so, one of the officers going so far as to threaten to bash Kelly's noggin with an upraised billy club. Kelly was then bum-rushed out of the park.

"We've heard of this chap," the outraged policeman said later, "and think he's a disgrace to the business."

Boston's manager, Jim Hart, hurried to buy a ticket for his banished captain, but the police refused to readmit Kelly.

Kelly was reduced to helplessly screaming at a locked gate as Cleveland won, 7–1, to oust Boston from first place and enable the Giants to win the NL pennant.

Through it all, Kelly was one of Boston's most accomplished hitters. With his left hand secured at the bottom of the bat and his right hand usually positioned twelve inches higher, Kelly sacrificed power for average. In 1887 he hit .322, and encored in '88 by batting .318.

And win or lose, Kelly strode through his kingdom with a swagger, oftentimes with a pet monkey perched on his shoulders or secured at the end of a golden chain as it skipped at Kelly's side.

THE LATE 1800s saw another milestone of baseball—and literary—history: the publication of "Casey at the Bat," by an Irish poet named Ernest L. Thayer. No surprise, then, that the main character—mighty Casey—was an Irishman. Nor that two of the other four players named in the poem, Cooney (who "died at first") and Flynn (who "let drive a single"), were likewise sons of Erin. And "Jimmy Blake" (who "tore the cover off the ball") could very well be Irish, too. The main character, of course, was Casey, who brought a sense of high drama to the game.

Then from 5,000 throats and more there rose a lusty yell;
It rumbled through the valley, it rattled through the dell;
It knocked upon the mountain and recoiled upon the flat,
For Casey, mighty Casey, was advancing to the bat.

There was ease in Casey's manner as he stepped into his place;
There was pride in Casey's bearing and a smile on Casey's face.
And when, responding to the cheers, he lightly doffed his hat,
No stranger in the crowd could doubt 'twas Casey at the bat.

But there was "no joy in Mudsville" because "mighty Casey has struck out."

Note King Kelly's exuberantly adoring fans, his own flamboyance both on and off the field, his penchant for clutch base hits, and the rarity of his striking out (once every 14.1 at bats).

Is there any doubt that King Kelly 'twas the model for Casey?

Chapter Nine

Brotherhood

When I was young I thought that money was the most
important thing in life; now that I am old I know that it is.
                                            —*Oscar Wilde*

AFTER THE BROTHERHOOD of Professional Base Ball Players successfully solicited financial backers and recruited players, a Players' League was officially chartered on December 10, 1889—a move that had the blessings of Samuel Gompers, president of the American Federation of Labor. Franchises were established in Boston, Brooklyn, Buffalo, Chicago, Cleveland, New York, Philadelphia, and Pittsburgh, with every team except Buffalo competing with an already existing NL outfit.

What set the upstart Players' League apart from its rivals were its rules of governance:

- The players and owners were to have equal voices in the league's administration.
- At season's end, $20,000 in prize money would be dispersed to

the first seven teams in the standings. From top to bottom the rewards would range from $6,250 per team to $400.

- No player could be traded or sold without his permission.
- None of the player contracts included an option clause.

EIGHTY PERCENT OF the 168 players were refugees from the National League. Another twenty-eight were from the American Association, the best of these being Tip O'Neill, Tommy McCarthy, and Denny Lyons.

More important, 40 percent of the Players' League's players, five of the eight managers, and six of the franchise owners were Irish.

♣The list of future Hall of Famers who jumped from the NL includes King Kelly, Roger Connor, Tim Keefe, Hugh Duffy, Jim O'Rourke, Dan Brouthers, Connie Mack, Charlie Comiskey, Ed Delahanty, and Pud Galvin.

Quite a lineup.

Nobody was surprised when King Kelly's change of uniforms came with some complications. The owner of the Boston Beaneaters offered King a $10,000 salary to stay, besides lending the always-broke Kelly $500 on the spot. But Kelly wound up in the new league's Boston entry and never paid back the loan.

♣Ed Delahanty was a twenty-one-year-old, 6'1", 170-pound strongman who swung a 50-ounce bat as though it were a toothpick and once hit a ball so hard that the cover of the horsehide split. He favored slicking back his black hair and parting it just to the right of center, which gave his roundish, thin-lipped face a somewhat lop-sided aspect. Delahanty's journey from the NL Philadelphia Phillies to the Players' League's Cleveland Infants was filled with dead ends and detours.

After two seasons as a part-time outfielder/infielder for the

Phillies, Delahanty was still refining his skills; he hit only .228 in 74 games as a rookie in 1888, but followed that with .293 in 56 contests in '89. He desperately wanted a chance to play every day, and to boost his salary above the $1,750 that the NL mandated, so he signed a contract with the PL's Philadelphia Quakers. Shortly thereafter, he changed his tune and re-upped with the Phillies for an upfront $500 bonus. However, it seemed that Delahanty's enduring dream was to play in Cleveland, so he inked still another contract, this one with the Infants—for a salary of $2,800 with a $600 cash advance.

The lawsuits flew as thickly as snowflakes in a Lake Erie winter storm, with the ultimate outcome being that Delahanty could play for Cleveland on three conditions:

- He had to return the $500 bonus to the Phillies.
- Under the threat of arrest, he was prohibited from setting foot in Philadelphia even when the Infants were scheduled to play the Quakers there.
- If or when he ever returned to the NL, Delahanty was obliged to play only for the Phillies.

With the Infants (second to the Worcesters as the worst name for a team, ever?), Delahanty divided his playing time between short, second, and the corner outfield positions, but he did appear in 115 games and sported a .296 batting average in 1890, his first PL season. The highlight came on June 2, when he collected six hits in as many at-bats during a 20–7 rout of Chicago.

Thirteen years later, Delahanty would create another round of legal havoc by simultaneously signing contracts with two teams in competing leagues—and arguably die as a result.

Yet wherever he played, Delahanty always took enormous pride in being Irish. He frequently wore a small Irish harp pinned to the lapel of his uniform. No matter how ritzy the restaurants that Delahanty frequented, he usually ordered "Irish turkey"—corned beef and cabbage.

And the biggest compliment he could think of was given to English-born Harry Wright, who managed Delahanty in 1891 upon his unavoidable return to the Phillies fold: "God breathed pure Hibernian oxygen into the heart of Harry Wright."

The PL Giants built a ballpark that was adjacent to the NL Giants' home field, the Polo Grounds, in such a way that the new team's fans could easily view the game action in both venues. And with Connor (who led the PL with 14 home runs), O'Rourke (who hit .360), and Keefe (17-11 before breaking a finger) on their roster, the upstart Giants were deemed to be a lock to win the league's first pennant. Too bad they finished third, eight games behind the freshly minted Bostonians, who were paced by the heavy-hitting Irish quartet of Hardy "Old True Blue" Richardson, Kelly, Harry Stovey, and Brouthers.

♣Other stellar Irish PL performers who had excelled in NL play were Charlie Ryan, Harry Stovey, Richardson, Tom Brown, and Ed "Cannonball" Crane.

♣But it was John Tener, a mediocre pitcher born in County Tyrone, who turned out to be an influential figure, for a different reason.

After two respectable seasons with the NL Chicago Cubs (pitching to a combined mark of 22-20), Tener posted a dismal 3-11 record with PL's Pittsburgh franchise. He was so distressed by his lack of success and the real prospect that he could never make a living in the game that Tener quit the game to work as a bank cashier in his wife's hometown of Charleroi, Pennsylvania. By 1897 he was president of the bank. In his new position, Tener became involved in Republican politics.

From there, Tener was elected to Congress and, in 1910, he became the governor of Pennsylvania. He only served four years as the state's chief executive, because of term limits.

From 1913 to 1918, Tener was president of the National League.

Also noteworthy were the Irish NL stars who refused to join the new circuit. Three erstwhile Irishmen/Brotherhood promoters re-signed with NL teams after initially agreeing to terms with Players' League ball clubs—Mike Tiernan, Jack Glasscock, and Jerry Denny.

♣Foremost among these, however, was Mickey Welch, a stalwart pitcher for the New York Giants and one of the founders of the Brotherhood. Even though the PL Giants offered him a guaranteed one-year contract that was $2,000 less than that offered by the NL Giants, Welch originally agreed to transfer his allegiance.

"I offered to play with the new club," Welch said, because the move "suited the leaders of the movement." However, he eventually agreed to re-sign with the NL Giants for a counteroffer that featured a three-year guarantee. Welch then said, "I am in the business for dollars and cents."

Left unsaid was that the thirty-year-old Welch had already had 450 complete games and nearly 300 wins to his credit, and wondered how many more bullets he had left in his right arm. Turned out that Welch went 17-14 for the NL Giants in 1890, then 5-9, before appearing in one game in the last year of his guaranteed deal. In retrospect, it was an excellent dollars-and-cents decision for Welch.

Tim Keefe, the secretary-treasurer of the Brotherhood and longtime teammate of Welch, was brimming with forgiveness. "Mickey," he said, "you are your own boss."

As ever, Jim O'Rourke reacted with a suitable oration: "The poor, miserable wretches who have permitted bribers to label upon their flesh the price of dishonor excited my pity rather than my anger, and I shall allow them to rest in peace if it is possible for them to find it on this green earth."

THE PL'S MAIDEN—AND sadly, only—season was highlighted by two extraordinary feats accomplished by Irish players.

♣The youngest player in the history of major league baseball was a sixteen-year-old Irish lad named Willie McGill, who pitched Cleveland to a complete-game 14–5 victory over Buffalo on May 5.

♣On July 5, Harry Stovey cracked a home run that made him the first major leaguer to amass a lifetime total of 100 round-trippers.

♣But certainly the most significant PL happenstance occurred on September 9, 1890, when Buffalo's manager, Jay Faatz, was banished from the game for too vociferously protesting an umpire's call, and was replaced in the command seat by Connie Mack.

Although Mack would continue playing on a sometimes basis for another six seasons, in 1896 he became a full-time manager—a position he would retain for more than fifty years.

During his active career, Mack measured a gangly 6'1", 150 pounds, and was considered to be too tall and too lean to be an effective backstop. Not to mention his being a decidedly inferior batsman. In 733 career games, he produced only a .245 average.

Ah, but he could catch, throw—and think.

His long face and grim aristocratic bearing gave the impression that Mack would never deign to smile. But his ultra-serious mien revealed his obsession with studying and analyzing every detail of the game.

When Mack was a rookie with the NL's Washington Nationals in 1886, the accepted procedure was for the thin-gloved catchers to stand as far back from the plate as possible so as to snare the pitches on one bounce. If a catcher crouched directly behind the plate, all-out fastballs would be too hot to handle, and the pitcher would be forced to throttle back all of his offerings. Only with a man on base or if the hitter was one strike away from whiffing would the catcher cozy up to the target.

But Mack was one of the first catchers to set up behind the plate for every pitch. Since the rules then in effect recorded an out if a foul tip was caught no matter what the count, Mack's repositioning enabled him to perform one of his favorite tricks whenever a hitter hacked and missed a pitch: mimicking the sound of a tip by clicking his tongue, slapping his glove, or snapping a small strip of elastic that was sewn to his mitt.

Indeed, because of Mack the rule was changed in 1891 so that a caught foul tip meant an out only when the count registered two strikes.

Mack was likewise one of the first catchers to counter a double steal by trying to throw out the trail runner at second base. Credit Mack, too, with instigating the practice of physically blocking the plate to tag a runner attempting to score.

In addition, Mack was an inveterate bat tipper, lightly touching his glove to the bat as a hitter launched his swing. This "accident" totally destroyed a hitter's timing and invariably resulted in swinging strikes. However, a Louisville catcher-outfielder named Farmer Weaver once got so fed up with Mack's recurring accidents that he altered one swing so that his bat cracked across Mack's wrists.

"I didn't tip his bat again," said Mack. "No, sir, not until the last game of the season and Weaver was at bat for the last time. After he had two strikes, I tipped his bat again and got away with it."

One day Cap Anson was at bat with two outs and the bases loaded. After Anson took two quick strikes, Mack returned the ball to the pitcher, tossed his glove to the ground, removed his mask, and began to unhook his chest protector. Anson turned to Mack, saying, "What's the matter, Connie?" Even as Anson was talking, Mack flashed a secret signal to the pitcher, jumped back behind the plate, and barehanded a fastball down the middle that the surprised Anson took for strike three.

What other tricks did Mack have up his sleeves?

With Washington leading late in a game but the home ball club involved in an extended rally that put them ahead, Mack feigned an extremely painful injury. The prolonged delay was designed to force the umpire to call the game because of darkness. The score would then revert to the last complete inning when the Nationals still had the lead and, presto-chango, a sure loss was transformed into a victory.

Mack would go on to become one of the most durable, successful, and respected managers in the history of the game.

Although the PL Giants outdrew the NL Giants, both teams lost a great deal of money. Thanks to King Kelly's popularity, the PL's Boston entry was the only team in any of the three pro leagues to show a meaningful profit.

After the PL season ended, the owners of the PL Giants rushed to make a secret agreement with the NL Giants to merge their teams and play in the National League. Before long, the owners of the PL Chicago franchise made similar overtures to the NL's Chicago White Stockings. Although Ward, Keefe, and several other stubborn hard-liners were eager to keep the Players' League alive, all of the new league's moneymen had already hoisted the white flag.

The PL's official death certificate was signed on October 10, 1890, whereupon the Cleveland Infants and the Brooklyn Bridegrooms sought entry into the National League but were rebuffed.

The *Sporting News* wrote the obituary: "Goodbye Players' League. Your life has been a stormy one. Because of your existence many a man has lost by thousands of dollars. And before long all that will be left of you is a memory—a sad, discouraging memory."

PRESENT-DAY INTERVIEW

Ryan Roberts of the Arizona Diamondbacks
(Caitlin Cunningham)

Ryan Roberts has remarkable tattoos.

Thin, wiry, and intense, Roberts has black hair and dark eyes, marking him as one of the so-called black Irish.

"Although my mom was born in Paris," he says, "her mom was born in County Kilkenny."

While Roberts's Irish heritage is not "dominant," he does have an affinity for all things Irish. "When I played in Toronto, I had a flag of Ireland mounted on a wall of my bedroom."

His first-ever major league base hit was a solo home run struck against the Yankees on August 3, 2006. However, in a total of 26 at-bats over the course of the 2006 and 2007 seasons, Roberts only managed two hits for a minuscule batting average of .077.

"After the Blue Jays released me," he reports, "I gave the flag to my favorite bar in Toronto."

Subsequently, Roberts signed a minor league deal with the Texas Rangers, but was hitless in his only plate appearance in a Ranger uniform. He's been with the Diamondbacks for three seasons, finally establishing himself as a big-time major league hitter in 2011 and becoming a fixture both at second base and in the leadoff slot.

"Normally Irish players are very aware of each other," he says, "but being black Irish like me, my ancestry is not widely known."

All the same, Roberts does advertise his heritage in an offbeat fashion.

"I'm really into Celtic symbols," he says.

That accounts for the two Celtic images among his thirty body tattoos.

"One of my favorite tats is a Celtic cross on the left side of my back," says Roberts.

He also proudly displays a series of Celtic leaves on the left side of his neck, representing faith, hope, love, and luck.

"I guess you could say that my heart is Irish."

Chapter Ten

Spikes Up

It's my rule never to lose me temper till it would be
detrimental to keep it.

—Sean O'Casey

THE GAY NINETIES spilled over into the baseball community, and
the reigning spirit of pleasure before business was personified in the
1891 season by (who else?) King Kelly.

After the Players' League went kaput, the American Association
was now the National League's only rival, and a team in Pendleton,
Ohio (adjacent to Cincinnati), made Kelly an offer he couldn't, and
wouldn't, refuse. Not only did the franchise provide Kelly with the
chance to return to the area where he had made his major league
debut thirteen seasons past, but they also dangled the manager's job.
This position was more important than ever since a team's captain
had mostly been reduced to motivational duties.

Instead of having an official nickname, his latest team was simply
known as "Kelly's Killers." Under his misguidance, Kelly's Players'
League team had won the pennant in 1890 without his implement-

ing the merest shred of discipline. Perhaps Kelly's promoting the pleasures of booze and women, betting on horses, and keeping late hours had kept his charges loose enough to finish 6½ games ahead of second-place Brooklyn. If this was so, Kelly saw no reason to change his managerial game plan in Cincinnati.

His Killers were one of the wildest, most carefree baseball teams in history, spending more time at racetracks, bars, and brothels than on the ball field. One of Kelly's staunchest disciples of debauchery was 5'5" "Wee" Willie McGill, who at seventeen was still the youngest player in the big leagues at the time.

In the opening game of the 1891 season, Kelly had a beef with umpire Bill Gleason after Cincinnati's pitcher walked six consecutive St. Louis hitters. Gleason quickly thumbed Kelly-as-player from the field, but allowed him to sit on the bench and resume his managerial duties. Darkness was gathering in the top of the ninth with the score knotted at 7 all. Kelly then ordered his pitchers to walk every opposing batter, and his fielders to flub any ball that might be hit in their vicinity—his idea being to force a suspended game that would eventually be replayed with Kelly back in the lineup. But Gleason foiled Kelly's plan and forfeited the game to St. Louis.

As the season painfully neared an end, the only thing the Cincinnati fans could count on from game to game was at least half of the team being drunk. The hometown fans responded by seeking other sources of amusement. After eight losses in a nine-game span before ever-shrinking crowds in Cincinnati, the moneymen pulled the trigger and Kelly's Killers were exterminated.

Kelly was sufficiently sober to have appeared in 82 of the team's 102 games (43-57 with two ties) and batted .297. It was expected that he would next re-sign with the NL's Boston Beaneaters, but Kelly chose to join another American Association outfit, the Boston Reds. However, his tenure with the Reds lasted only four games before he indeed did rejoin the Beaneaters for the final sixteen games of their pennant-winning season after happily accepting a grandiose contract that would pay him $25,000 through the next season. Kelly's paltry .231 batting average with his third Boston team in two seasons did little to help the Beaneaters' stretch drive.

In fact, his dismal performance signaled that the thirty-four-year-old Kelly had already dissipated his considerable skills.

♣Although young Willie McGill was only 2-5 during Cincinnati's brief existence, he was signed by the AA's St. Louis Browns when the Killers were declared dead meat. The Irish manchild went 19-10 for the Browns, becoming the youngest pitcher in major league history to hurl a shutout—a record that still stands.

Unfortunately, McGill was frequently too inebriated to play and he only managed a lifetime record of 40-51 until a sore arm ended his career.

Other milestones achieved by Irishmen in that 1891 season included:

♣Billy Hamilton leading the NL with a .340 batting average, as well as with 111 stolen bases.

♣Bill McGunnigle, the manager of the Pittsburgh Pirates, tooting a tin whistle coupled with gesticulations from the bench to properly move and position his fielders for each hitter.

♣Dan Brouthers emerging as the AA's premier hitter with a .350 average.

♣Duke Farrell leading the AA in both home runs (12) and RBIs (110).

♣John "Sadie" McMahon's 35 wins leading the AA's moundsmen.

YET THE MOST significant event of the 1891 season—one that would have an immense impact on the future of the game—was the first appearance in a major league uniform of a pugnacious Irish player named John McGraw.

At 121 pounds and 5'6½", the seventeen-year-old McGraw was thrilled to be paid $200 a month to play for the AA's Baltimore Orioles. But his older teammates gleefully exercised their veterans' prerogatives by mercilessly abusing him during the team's opening game.

Wherever the scrawny rookie tried to find a seat on the bench, he was bumped and jostled while his teammates laughed at his obvious distress. McGraw managed to maintain his composure until he was pushed off the end of the bench and had to scramble to his feet. That's when he jumped up and loosed several wild roundhouse punches aimed at everyone and no one. Since McGraw was the son of an abusive father and the product of brutal upstate New York winters, his quick trigger and ready fists came naturally to him. Embarrassed by the public spectacle, manager Billy Barnie chastened his vets, soothed his feisty rookie, and cleared a safe space for him on the bench.

McGraw appeared in only thirty-three games, primarily at shortstop, batting a respectable .270 while displaying a spectacularly unreliable arm on the field. As all part-time players were required to do prior to games, McGraw frequently manned the ticket booths in full uniform.

Realizing that his diminutive size precluded him from hitting with any semblance of power, McGraw quickly understood that his job was to get on base by whatever means possible. Accordingly, he held his bottom hand six inches from the knob end of the bat, sprayed the ball to all fields, became an expert bunter, drew an inordinate number of walks due to his ability to foul off pitches when fouls were still not counted as strikes, and crowded the plate to deliberately get hit by pitches. His bat control was so magnificent that, throughout his career, McGraw struck out only once every 46 at-bats.

In 1892, the Orioles joined the National League, and late in the season Ned Hanlon was installed as manager. Hanlon was intrigued by McGraw's cleverness—especially when the youngster urged Baltimore's Irish groundskeeper, Tom Murphy, to pack hard clay directly in front of the plate. This rock-hard surface enabled

McGraw to deliberately use a downswing that resulted in the ball heading sharply down, then bouncing either over the infielders' heads or high enough to enable McGraw to reach first before the ball could be fielded. The maneuver came to be called the Baltimore chop.

Hanlon also took note of McGraw's relentlessly enthusiastic activities when asked to coach at either third or first base. Baseballs cost $1.25 each and because they were understood to be the property of the home team, spectators were expected to return any balls hit into the stands. During one game at Union Park in Baltimore, McGraw was coaching at third when a foul ball skipped over a low fence and was clutched by a fan, who was clearly intent on keeping his souvenir. Whipped into a froth of anger, McGraw hurdled the fence, approached the fan, and snatched the man's hat. A brief confrontation ensued until the fan agreed to exchange the ball for his hat. Hanlon rewarded McGraw's zeal beyond the call of duty by inserting him in the lineup the next day.

By 1893, McGraw was the Orioles' starting third baseman and would be a fixture there for the next six seasons.

Whether in meaningless exhibition games or regular-season contests, McGraw proved to be ruthless, ferocious, and unprincipled. In a single preseason game in Chattanooga, Tennessee, McGraw held a runner by the belt to prevent him from advancing on a fly-out, slid into second base while slashing the opposing shortstop with his spikes, and bloodied a sliding runner by deliberately tagging him in the face with the ball. It was all the local police could do to stop the irate crowd from spilling onto the field and assaulting McGraw.

Through it all, several sportswriters reported that his face most resembled a map of Ireland and dubbed him "Mickey Face." But the nickname that stuck was "Mugsy," after both a cartoon character and a crooked Baltimore politician. Even so, McGraw didn't care what he was called so long as his roughneck tactics helped the Orioles to win.

And win the Orioles did. Eventually.

McGraw was certainly instrumental in Baltimore's relentless

climb up the NL's standings. But the team's primary catalyst was Ned Hanlon, who assumed control of the team in 1892.

Both before and contemporaneous with Hanlon, clever Irish managers were already a grand tradition:

♣Tommy Bond, who managed Worcester (1883) after he hung up his spikes.

♣Mike Scanlon (County Cork), manager of the Washington Senators in 1884–85.

♣From County Clare came Ted Sullivan, who directed the respective fortunes of St. Louis, Washington, and Kansas City.

♣Patsy Donovan, who managed five different teams from 1897 to 1911.

♣Bill McGunnigle managed in various pro leagues for fifteen years.

BUT NED HANLON was a cut above.

As manager of the Baltimore Orioles (1893–98), the Brooklyn Bridegrooms (1899–1905), and the Cincinnati Red Stockings (1906–7), Hanlon generously seeded his rosters with Irish players, deeming their aggressiveness, resourcefulness, and ability to make quick, clever decisions to be unparalleled.

From 1894 to 1900, Hanlon's teams in Baltimore and Brooklyn won a total of five NL pennants. Along the way, Hanlon also tutored some of the most successful managers of the early twentieth century, the most significant of these being John McGraw.

Hanlon's most notable legacy was his role in developing what became known as "inside" or "scientific" baseball. In so doing, his innovations covered virtually every aspect of the game.

- Whereas the standard practice was to use the double steal only when runners were on first and second, Hanlon made a habit of employing this maneuver with runners on first and third.

- When opponents attempted this tactic, his counter was to have the second baseman abandon his base, move forward to meet the expected throw, then quickly return the ball to the catcher in ample time to catch the runner trying to score from third. Another alternative was the catcher faking a throw to second and then turning to deal with the oncoming runner.

- Another of Hanlon's innovations was to have his pitchers cover first on grounders hit to the right side of the infield.

- Hanlon was responsible for the routine deployment and perfection of the hit-and-run.

- He encouraged base runners to smash into infielders (and umpires) whenever possible, and also to slide with file-sharpened spikes held high enough to menace a fielder's legs. Such a tactic was extremely dangerous because, before the development of antibiotics, the threat of a cut developing into a serious infection or even gangrene, lockjaw, or blood poisoning was something that ballplayers dreaded.

- Hanlon's minions were also prompted to initiate ferocious disagreements with umpires (an activity known in the current parlance as "kicking"), not necessarily to get a specific call reversed, but to rouse the hometown fans into riotous behavior and thereby intimidate the solitary ump to make subsequent calls in his team's favor.

- Under Hanlon's imprimatur every possible rule was bent to the breaking point in the name of winning a game. Hanlon called his ruthless game plan "disorganizing baseball."

In 1893, his first year at the helm of the Orioles, the team moved from tenth to eighth in the NL standings. In '94, he'd take first with the aid of an Irish-stocked lineup.

Through it all, Hanlon wore civilian clothes that prohibited him by rule from stepping on the field, and was even more resplendent in a top hat. Yet he was a surprisingly nervous presence on the bench. And if Hanlon was an accomplished teacher, his students were frequently unappreciative.

"He'd wring his hands when a game was close," said Sam Crawford, a future Hall of Famer who played against several of Hanlon's Oriole teams, "and start telling some of the old-timers what to do. They'd look at him and say, 'For Christ's sake, just keep quiet and leave us alone. We'll win the ball game if you only shut up.'"

Ty Cobb taking a picture of Sam Crawford

The fans loved the show—the bloody warfare, the fierce arguments that often degenerated into fisticuffs, the players dramatically preening in the batter's box and executing theatrical bows to the stands after making good plays.

Meanwhile, the owners publicly deplored this rowdy behavior, even as they relished the increasing gate receipts.

Chapter Eleven

Last Slide

I can't go on, I'll go on.
—*Samuel Beckett*

WHILE NED HANLON retooled the Orioles, several other important developments took place. By far the most important of these
were several rule changes.

The pitcher's box was gone in 1893, replaced by a rubber slab
twelve inches long and four inches wide with which the pitcher's back
foot must now be in constant contact. In addition, the rubber was
situated ten feet farther from home plate than the nearest edge of the
pitcher's box had been.

This new distance of 60 feet, 6 inches, represented the last tweak-
ing of the separation between pitcher and hitter and still remains in
effect today.

Also, whereas bats were previously permitted to be flattened on
one side, they now had to be round, which radically diminished the
effectiveness and dominance of the bunting game.

These alterations were effected on the assumption that paying
customers were more attracted to lusty hitting than they were to

stingy pitching. One predictable result was a dramatic increase in overall batting averages.

♣Whereas Dan Brouthers's .335 led the NL in 1892, the top five batters in 1893 (fellow Irishmen Hugh Duffy, Billy Hamilton, and Ed Delahanty, along with Sam Thompson and George Davis) all hit .355 or higher.

Overall, the National League's collective batting average jumped from .245 to .280. By 1895, hitters would be successful in nearly 31 percent of their at-bats.

At the same time, a quartet of young pitchers of Irish extraction—Amos Rusie, Kid Nichols, Frank Killen, and Bill "Brickyard" Kennedy—were among the few hurlers able to make successful adjustments.

With hitters feeling much more comfortable, on August 7, 1893, Roger Connor decided to attack a particularly tough lefty pitcher by moving into the right-handed batter's box for the first and only time in his career. The result: two homers and a single.

♣On the last day of the 1893 season—September 30—another Irishman had a memorable performance. Before a doubleheader, the *Sporting News* presented Australian-born Irishman Joe Quinn with a gold watch to commemorate his being selected as the most popular baseball player in America. Quinn was so inspired that over the course of the two games he blasted a total of eight hits.

UNFORTUNATELY, ANTI-IRISH BIAS came to the fore again. With home attendance down, the Phillies' owner, Colonel John I. Rogers, attempted to curry favor with the city's Irish population by lavishly praising their intelligence and loyalty at every conceivable opportunity. But then he offended the nationalistic sentiments of both the fans and his players when his correspondence with Prime Minister William Gladstone, passionately defending England's iron-fisted rule over Ireland, became public.

More often, however, this bias was still out in the open.

White Stockings owner A. J. Spalding took every occasion to disparage the inferior quality of Irish players' mental and physical abilities. He also promised he'd totally purge the roster of Irish players and never even consider signing another one—a vow that eventually yielded to the necessity of fielding a competitive team. Spalding was also idiotic enough to limit home attendance by briefly having a NO IRISH NEED APPLY sign tacked over the front entrance of his ballpark.

Hugh Duffy played in Chicago for two seasons (1888–89) before moving elsewhere.

"Captain Anson, of the Chicago Club," said Duffy, "has no use for players with Irish blood in their veins and he never loses an opportunity to insult those men who have played with him in the past."

Anson's jaundiced attitude was fueled by his lingering resentments over the aberrant behavior of King Kelly and his cohorts when they were all teammates in the early 1880s. Anson would later lash out again when he was fired, and looked for Irish scapegoats.

Moreover, while gambling, drinking, and general carousing were traits common to a substantial population of major league players, the press concentrated on the undesirable off-field proclivities of Irish players. Knowing full well that revelations of these colorful misdeeds sold more newspapers than game-time exploits, the foibles of such free-living players as King Kelly, Mickey Welch, Mike Dorgan, Jim Keenan, John McGraw, Ned Hanlon, Charley Sweeney, John O'Connor, Hugh Duffy, Tony Mullane, and Denny Lyons were frequently emblazoned in back-page headlines.

Conversely, Ned Hanlon loaded his Orioles lineup with fellow Irishmen for the 1894 season. Included were a host of Irishmen, some future Hall of Famers.

♣Hughie Jennings, all of 5'8½" and 165 pounds, manned the shortstop position. He had previously played with a total lack of distinction for three seasons with Louisville teams in the AA and NL. However, he suddenly blossomed into a potent hitter (.355 in 1894, followed by successive seasons of .386 and .401), a hot-footed base stealer, and the best-fielding shortstop in the league.

A local scribe described Jennings as "a red-headed Irishman who would fight at the drop of a hat."

Opponents concurred, complaining that Jennings would always slide into a base "spikes first and with malicious intent."

In other words, he was a perfect fit for Hanlon's new combative crew.

♣At first base, the thirty-seven-year-old Dan Brouthers was in the last season of his prime. Still, hitting .347 with 128 RBIs, he remained an uncanny contact hitter (only nine whiffs in 525 at-bats) and, as such, was an accomplished hit-and-run man.

♣Willie Keeler was a two-year NL vet going into his initial season in Baltimore. His birth name was actually O'Kelleher until his parents went with the more Germanic Keeler at some unknown point and for some unknown reason—perhaps to increase employment opportunities in the face of NINA prohibitions.

Measuring only 5'4½" and barely tipping the scale at 140 pounds, the lefty-swinging outfielder was inevitably nicknamed "Wee Willie." With his fierce, perpetually squinting eyes and his slicked hair parted precisely in the middle of his dome, Keeler had a grim appearance and, accordingly, always played with all his diminutive might no matter what the score. He choked up almost a full foot on the bat and took short, downward swings. The Baltimore chop lived on.

"Hit 'em where they ain't" was his famous Yogi-esque mantra, and he eventually twice led the NL in hitting—highlighted by a .424 average in 1897—on his way to a sterling .341 lifetime average.

♣John McGraw was Baltimore's keystone performer at third base. Still as rambunctious as ever, McGraw's ultra-aggressive base running precipitated a brawl in Boston on May 15 that had cataclysmic results.

While sliding into first to avoid being picked off, McGraw kicked first-sacker Tommy Tucker squarely in the head. Immediately the two Irishmen started exchanging punches, a melee that soon involved every player on both teams. While the fans were understandably absorbed in watching the fight, a discarded cigar or cigarette was inadvertently dropped into a trash can and a ferocious blaze quickly ensued. Because the stands were fashioned of wood, and because there were huge storage bins filled with hay to feed horses and barrels of oil used for lamps, the fire spread so quickly that the several thousand spectators were fortunate to escape with their lives.

When the smoke had cleared, Boston's South End Grounds and $70,000 worth of baseball-related equipment were destroyed, along with 170 other buildings in the neighborhood.

♣Another Irish addition to the Orioles was pitcher William "Kid" Gleason, previously a four-time 20-game winner with Philadelphia and St. Louis who had peaked with 38 wins in 1891. Gleason went 15-5 for Hanlon's transformed ball club, while also serving as a valuable part-time infielder and pinch hitter, batting .349 in 86 at-bats. After the season, Gleason forswore pitching and lasted fifteen subsequent seasons as a slick-fielding, light-hitting second baseman for several other teams.

♣Hall of Fame–bound Wilbert Robinson was Hanlon's catcher, already a distinguished veteran of five seasons with the Orioles. Robinson's affable presence was announced by his thick mustache as well as his slight paunch. Known for his smarts, a howitzer-like throwing arm, and an ability to nurse pitchers through difficult situations, "Uncle Robby" had a career year in 1894, batting .353, which was eighty points above his lifetime average. (He would return later as the first pitching coach ever in baseball.)

♣Another holdover, Sadie McMahon, had earned 35 victories for the 1891 Orioles and was in his last successful season (25-8) before a sore arm turned him into a pedestrian performer.

♣At the ripe old age of fifty, holdover Tony Mullane started the season with the Orioles by compiling a record of 6-9 before being cut and temporarily salvaged by Cleveland (1-2). Age, and the increased distance from rubber to plate, meant the end of Mullane's Hall of Fame career.

♣ Perhaps the most overlooked future immortal on the squad was Joe Kelley, a fleet-footed (53 stolen bases) slap hitter (.393), half of whose at-bats resulted in his reaching base safely. His pale face and thin red hair gave the lie to his bloodthirsty intensity. Kelley was inducted into the Hall of Fame in 1971.

With their own ends-justify-all-conceivable-means game plan, the Orioles fought off a determined, season-long challenge from the Giants to cop the 1894 pennant by three games.

MEANWHILE, A QUIET event in 1894 signaled the beginning of one of baseball's most famous Irish ownerships.

During his thirteen years on the field, Charles Comiskey compensated for his weak bat (.264) with his fielding wizardry. He made his pro debut in 1882 with the St. Louis Brown Stockings, playing first, pitching in emergencies, and also directing the ball club whenever player-manager Ned Cuthbert was in the lineup. Comiskey assumed more managerial responsibilities over the course of the next two seasons.

With his round face and a smile that always bordered on a smirk, Comiskey perpetuated the Irish traditions of physically intimidating umpires and opposing players, inciting hometown fans to violence, and discovering new ways to win ball games. Before the coaching lines became law, Comiskey would often station himself just a few feet away from an enemy's catcher and curse both him and the umpire up, down, and sideways. He was also the first manager who tried to deny a runner scoring from third base on a routine groundball with less than two outs by moving his infielders closer to home plate.

And then, in 1894, Comiskey bought a Western League franchise located in Sioux City, Iowa, then quickly moved the team to St. Paul,

Minnesota. In 1901, he relocated the St. Paul Saints to Chicago, where, as the White Stockings, they became a charter member of the American League.

Sadly, tragedy and infamy lay in Comiskey's future.

Three baseball records were set by Irishmen in the summer of 1894.

The most significant of these occurred on May 30 in Boston's new home field, the Congress Street Grounds.

♣Robert Lincoln "Link" Lowe (whose father was German, but his mother was a refugee from the famine) was considered to be a good-fielding second baseman with some pop in his bat. At 5'10" and 150 pounds he was somewhat scrawny, but his bushy black eyebrows and matching facial hair gave substance to his appearance. Unlike many of his fellow countrymen, Lowe was praised by the press for being a "gentleman."

In his previous four seasons with the Beaneaters, Lowe's batting average topped at .298, yet his 1894 campaign was downright historic. Although he finished the season hitting .346, well above his eventual thirteen-season average, his performance on that Memorial Day was one for the ages.

With a large holiday crowd on hand, and facing the slants of Cincinnati's Elton "Ice Box" Chamberlain, Lowe belted four consecutive homers, including two in the third inning. Although the left-field wall in Congress Street Grounds was a mere 250 feet from the plate, the *Boston Globe* reported that all of Lowe's four-base knocks "would all be home runs on an open prairie." Other observers, however, swore that three of his clouts were really routine fly balls that were lofted into the grandstand.

After his fourth homer, the happy hometown fans showed their appreciation by tossing coins in the general direction of home plate.

Lowe was equally as delighted to collect a scattered silver bonus that amounted to $160.

Several sluggers would eventually equal Lowe's feat, but none has ever surpassed it.

♣In 1894, a pair of Lowe's teammates were nearing the end of a more continuous run of excellence. Tommy McCarthy in left and Hugh Duffy in center were universally known as "the Heavenly Twins."

One reason was that Duffy hit 18 homers, drove in 145 runs, and batted a remarkable .440, leading the NL.

That made Duffy pro baseball's first-ever Triple Crown winner.

If McCarthy's 1894 statistics were not quite as gaudy—13 homers, 126 RBIs, .349—he was respected by his peers as being the smartest player in the game.

Among McCarthy's brainstorms were the delayed steal, the fake bunt-and-swing, and the deliberate trapping of a fly ball to confuse runners and hitters and create unexpected double plays.

In addition, McCarthy's speed and uncanny instincts enabled him to play a shallow left, so much so that he was often involved in rundowns in the infield. Indeed, every clever ploy on the part of any player was commonly referred to as "a Tommy McCarthy."

♣Moreover, New York's Amos Rusie led NL pitchers in wins (36), shutouts (3), ERA (2.78), and strikeouts (195).

An unofficial Quadruple Crown.

MEANWHILE, THE KING of Baseball's skills had eroded to such an extent that Mike Kelly had begun the 1894 season with Allentown in the Pennsylvania State League, where he hit .305 in 75 games against inferior pitchers. When the Allentown franchise folded on August 6, Kelly's contract was transferred to Yonkers of the Eastern League. This was an even lower class of competition, as evidenced by Kelly's hitting .377 in fifteen games despite continuing to drink himself into oblivion and haunting various faro tables.

Even so, the King remained a popular presence on the vaudeville circuit. He couldn't sing or dance, but he charmed the audience by reciting "Casey at the Bat," and exchanging suggestive repartee with the chorus girls. After completing a week's engagement at the Bijou Theater in Paterson, New Jersey, Kelly dallied in New York before boarding a boat heading up Long Island Sound to Boston, where he would next perform at the prestigious Palace Theater. No doubt he was looking forward to making a triumphant return to Boston.

A severe snowstorm blew up in the late afternoon of November 8, just before the boat left the pier, but Kelly's attention was arrested by a poorly dressed man who was slumped over a bench near the ticket window and copiously weeping.

Kelly approached the stranger and heard his sad tale: After many years of dissolute living, the poor soul was anxious to return to the bosom of his family in Boston. But he was penniless and unable to purchase passage on the steamship. Kelly had always been a soft touch, freely giving anything of value in his possession in response to a sob story. This time, he presented his own topcoat to the ticket master as security for the stranger's fare.

As a result, Kelly caught a cold on the boat ride, which quickly evolved into pneumonia. By the time the steamer docked in Boston, Kelly was unable to walk. A stretcher was fetched from a nearby hospital. But while he was being carried there, one of the stretcher bearers slipped and Kelly fell to the ground.

It was then that the thirty-six-year-old King Kelly gasped his last pronouncement: "Well, boyos, that's probably my last slide."

He died at 9:55 that same evening.

Chapter Twelve

Nice Guys Finish First

People who say it cannot be done should not interrupt those who are doing it.

—*George Bernard Shaw*

SEVERAL FRANCHISE OWNERS were disgusted with Baltimore's savage brand of baseball. At the same time, they understood that hand-to-hand combat and freely flowing blood were potent gate attractions.

So they instituted a rule to take effect in the 1895 season that would levy fines on "boisterous coaching." Cursing and otherwise intimidating opponents and umpires, either by managers or players manning the coaches' boxes, would no longer be tolerated. Despite this toothless attempt to bring a degree of civility to the games, the 1895 and 1896 seasons continued to be raucous and unruly.

But whereas several teams—most notably Chicago and Cleveland—adopted Baltimore's crude strategies, Frank Selee, the manager of the Boston Beaneaters, believed that teams playing clean baseball could also be winners. To try to prove his point, Selee pointed to Boston's superstar Hugh Duffy and sought to fill his roster with similarly intelligent and disciplined gentlemen. However, Tommy Tucker, Boston's veteran first baseman, went public with his disdain for both the new legislation and Selee's plans, complaining that "this lawn tennis business is killing baseball."

Selee endured Tucker's over-the-top aggressive play for two seasons, during which the feisty Irishman fielded his position brilliantly while hitting .249 and .304. Then Selee traded him away.

Selee was also motivated to clean house when his 1895 team was racked with ethnic conflict—the Irish Catholics versus the non-Irish Protestants. The religious and political differences largely remained unspoken while other issues became focal points of the mutual hostility.

Chief among these was the physical condition of Tommy McCarthy, who reported to training camp so overweight that his teammates called him "Pudge." Then his extra poundage resulted in McCarthy's suffering a leg injury that kept him on the bench for much of the early games. His Protestant teammates blamed McCarthy for the team's slow start.

The simmering tension erupted in late May when a game-time disagreement between McCarthy and Jack Stivetts led to a bloody fight in a Louisville, Kentucky, hotel room. When the fight was headlined in the next morning's newspapers, any semblance of team harmony was gone.

Even worse, the fading McCarthy and his younger "Heavenly Twin," Hugh Duffy, had become partners in a Boston bar. The strain of running the business, coupled with their careers moving in opposite directions, led them to frequently indulge in loud arguments on the field. Heavenly Twins gone to the devil.

Also, Duffy longed to be named team captain, a position that belonged to Billy Nash. Throughout the season, Duffy continued to snipe at Nash in a most ungentlemanly fashion, trying to goad him into a fight that would force Selee to replace him. And Nash and Herman Long, together the left side of Boston's infield, either didn't speak to each other at all or else loudly bickered during games.

After a sixth-place finish, Selee banished the troublesome Irish trio of McCarthy, Nash, and Jack Ryan.

Still, Irishmen captained many of the NL's teams.

Captains of the twelve clubs in the National League, 1895
(Library of Congress)

MEANWHILE, THE ORIOLES were not at all deterred by the league's behavioral modification legislation and beat down a thrust by the Cleveland Spiders to win their second consecutive pennant in 1895. But sometimes the continuing roughhouse tactics of the defending NL champs had unexpected results.

During an exhibition game in Virginia, prior to the 1896 season, Hugh Jennings was successful in stealing second base, primarily because his sharp spikes bloodied the shins of the local player who attempted to tag him. While this maneuver was barely tolerated in the pros, slicing up a hometown hero was a call to both individual and community action.

In a flash, a rigorous brawl ensued between Jennings and his latest victim. Just as quickly, the enraged fans stormed the field and succeeded in roughing up whichever Orioles they could get to before the hugely outnumbered visitors could make a mad dash to the presumed safety of their nearby hotel. But their sanctuary failed to protect them after the still irate crowd stormed the hotel, clobbered several more of the players, and then proceeded to ransack the entire building. Ultimately, the champion Orioles required a considerable police presence to safely escort them to the railroad station and onto a train.

Simultaneous with the Orioles' narrow escape, another Irish-centric ball club chose more peaceful ways to manifest their ethnic heritage. By a fortuitous coincidence, Ed Delahanty's Philadelphia Phillies opened spring training in Hampton Roads, Virginia, on St. Patrick's Day. Prompted by "Big Ed's" relentless insistence, the waiters were compelled to cover the team's training tables in green.

The celebration of Delahanty's proud Irishness continued unabated when the Phillies played their home opener. In what soon became a proud tradition, two groups of loyal Delahanty "cranks" paraded into the park before the game while shouting rehearsed cheers.

"Kelly's Rooters" were led and organized by Ed J. Kelly, while the "Grey House Rooters" were captained by Harry Donaghy. Over the course of the 1896 season, there were plenty of smiling Irish eyes among the Philadelphia faithful as Delahanty hit .397, banged out 13 homers, and drove in 126 runs.

♣Another son of Erin provided a chest-swelling moment for Irish fans of every persuasion on June 3, 1895. That's when Roger Connor, playing for St. Louis, smacked his 122nd career home run, tying fellow Irishman Harry Stovey for the all-time leadership.

A MORE UNUSUAL event took place in an Eastern League game on August 12, 1895, when boxer Jim Corbett, the reigning heavyweight champion of the world, played first base for Scranton. Gentleman Jim had previously played in games with the Hartford, Meriden, Derby, and Bridgeport teams in the Connecticut League—and usually acquitted himself with a surprising level of competence. With Scranton that day, the jovial Corbett slugged two singles and drove in two runs.

♣ A sidebar to that game was the presence of Corbett's younger brother Joe at shortstop for Scranton. Strong-armed and square-shouldered, Joe stood a shade under 6'0". He had already had a taste of the big leagues as a scatter-armed fastball pitcher with the Washington Senators, going 0-2 in three games early in the 1895 season. The surprise was that Corbett the younger was destined to win 24 games and become the ace of Hanlon's pitching staff in 1897.

Neither Jim Corbett's appearance nor his effectiveness surprised any of the spectators on hand, because notable prizefighters routinely cashed in on their fame by making well-paid guest appearances for minor league teams. As a top-shelf draw, Corbett bragged that his share of the gate receipts for his baseball exhibitions netted him about $17,000 per annum. If less famous boxers were also in great demand, they were not so handsomely rewarded and their on-field antics were much less predictable.

A decade earlier, a pair of Irish boxers living in New Haven, Connecticut, were involved in a famous incident. Playing on opposing teams, Tommy Donahue and Tommy Sweeney were both repeatedly dissatisfied with an umpire's calls, and eventually refocused their hostility on each other. The game halted as the two men squared off and exchanged prodigious blows. In the end, Sweeney was a double loser, absorbing a beating from Donahue, then suffering a twenty-dollar deduction from his fee for throwing the first punch.

IN ADDITION TO his season-long brilliance, two specific performances by Ed Delahanty in 1896 thrilled his fans despite the Phillies languishing in eighth place. For starters, Delahanty knocked out ten consecutive base hits in a July 7 twin bill at Louisville. But the main course occurred six days later, when the Phillies visited Chicago and faced William "Adonis" Terry, a handsome curveball specialist who already had accumulated 180 wins during his illustrious career.

Chicago's West Side Park had spacious dimensions—340 feet down each foul line and nearly 500 feet to an on-field clubhouse in dead center. In addition, a scoreboard and a canvas screen (to block the view of the local treetop spectators) raised the overall height of the right-field wall to forty feet.

In the top of the first inning, Delahanty dug himself a toehold in the batter's box with two out and a runner on base. Then he lined an outside pitch into a narrow alley that separated the right-field wall from the center-field wall. By the time Jimmy Ryan, Louisville's fleet-footed Irish outfielder, retrieved the ball, Delahanty had easily circled the bases with Home Run No. 1 on the day.

In the third inning, Delahanty smashed a low liner that literally tore the glove off the shortstop's hand for a single, but two innings later, Delahanty unloaded a sky-high drive that sailed far over the right-field wall and landed across a road, where it scattered a flock of chickens. Veteran observers believed Delahanty's Home Run No. 2 to be the longest ever hit at West End Park.

Despite Delahanty's heroics, his team was behind 9–6 when he came to the plate in the seventh inning with the bases empty. Home Run No. 3 was another skyscraping drive that soared over the center fielder's head and rolled untouched to the center-field wall.

The drama increased with Delahanty due to bat third in the ninth inning and the White Stockings still clinging to the 9–7 lead. Chicago's manager, Cap Anson, threatened to fine each of his players "the price of three meals at World Fair rates" (the World's Columbian Exposition, held in Chicago in 1893, had already become a cultural byword) if a runner got on base ahead of Delahanty, thereby making the Phillies slugger the potential tying run. Fortunately for Anson's players, the bases were unoccupied when Delahanty assumed his stance.

To prevent a duplication of Home Run No. 3, Chicago's center fielder positioned himself at the base of the clubhouse steps as Adonis Terry went into his windup. Even the Chicago fans were on their feet, yelling "Line it out, Del!" Then Delahanty fooled everybody in the house by bunting the first pitch, but the ball quickly rolled foul. Terry's next offering was a slow curve that bent around the outside corner. This time Delahanty was swinging for a place in the record book, and onlookers reported that his bat hit the ball with a sound like that of "a rifle shot."

Indeed, the ball traveled as fast and as far as if it had been fired out of a gun, not landing until it bounced off the top of the distant clubhouse roof. Home Run No. 4.

A ten-minute standing ovation greeted Delahanty as he crossed the plate.

Also there was Adonis Terry to shake his hand.

Delahanty's only postgame reward for his prodigious feat was provided by a Chicago businessman, William Wrigley Jr., who presented him with four boxes of his newfangled product, chewing gum.

EVEN SO, DESPITE the stupendous accomplishments of Delahanty, and notwithstanding the contentious Orioles winning their third consecutive pennant, the most momentous development of 1896 was a passive protest by an outstanding half-Irish pitcher.

It was so critical to the entire future of the game as to spill over into the off-season.

♣While pitching for the New York Giants earlier in the decade, Amos Rusie used his blazing fastball and snapping curve to average more than 31 victories and twice lead the league in strikeouts. It was generally believed that Rusie's virtually unhittable express was the main reason why the pitching distance was moved back ten feet in 1893. Not that the increase hindered Rusie any, since he recorded 33 wins in '93 and 36 in '94. His continued prowess made Rusie's $3,000 salary one of the highest in the game.

Then a notorious jackass and cheapskate purchased the Giants.

Andrew Freedman resented having to pay Rusie top dollar, especially after the muscular 6'1", 200-pound pitcher had a mediocre 23-23 record for the sad-sack ninth-place Giants in '95. To remedy what Freedman believed to be an unfair situation, the owner fined Rusie a total of $200 for repeatedly breaking curfew on the road as well as playing with a noticeable absence of enthusiasm during the last game of the season. In his own defense, Rusie pointed out that he had never left his hotel room on the dates in question, and always played hard.

Freedman then added injury to insult by offering his star pitcher a reduced $2,600 contract for the 1896 season. Rusie countered by demanding that his new contract should be for $3,000 plus a restoration of his fine money. When Freedman refused, Rusie simply spent the entire season at home in Indiana.

The citizens of New York were united in their outrage. The *Sporting News* was moved to declare: "Every independent fair-thinking man is with Rusie."

Even the archconservative brokers of Wall Street were up in arms, arranging for a sign to appear in a popular department-store window calling for a boycott of the Giants. The sign caused such a ruckus that the police had to be summoned to disperse the roiling crowd.

Then, in January 1897, Rusie sued Freedman for $5,000 in lost salary and assorted damages. Even more threatening to Freedman and the entire baseball establishment was the risk that Rusie's lawsuit would evolve into a legal challenge to the reserve clause.

The stubborn Freedman refused to budge, but his fellow owners were aghast at the mere possibility of losing their ironclad control of contracted players. The dilemma was resolved when NL officials anted up the $3,000 that Rusie demanded as an out-of-court settlement. The other owners then pressured the fuming Freedman to offer Rusie a $3,000 deal for the upcoming season.

However, when Rusie finally returned to the Giants, Freedman prohibited the manager from playing him. A long losing streak and increasingly vociferous complaints from the fans eventually forced Freedman to yield.

Rusie completed the 1897 season with a 28-10 record as well as a league-leading ERA of 2.54. It was largely due to Rusie's efforts that the Giants climbed five rungs in the final standings to finish two games behind Baltimore and 9½ behind the pennant-winning Beaneaters.

Amos Rusie had another sterling season in 1898, winning 20 of his 31 decisions. But late in the season, he tore muscles in his shoulder while making a whirling throw to pick a runner off first. Rusie rested for five weeks, but never recovered the zip on his fastball.

However, to complete a complicated deal, the Giants sent Rusie to Cincinnati to secure the rights to Christy Mathewson. After a brief comeback attempt in 1901—getting cracked for 43 hits and 37 earned runs in 22 innings—Rusie finally retired.

When John McGraw became New York's manager, he came to the aid of his half-Irish compatriot by arranging for Rusie to be the superintendent of the Polo Grounds, just as McGraw had done for Brouthers before him.

Selee's domesticating of the Beaneaters' roster led to a bitter pennant race between Boston and Baltimore that wasn't decided until the closing days of the 1897 season.

♣It should be noted, however, that the Beaneaters' team featured such gentlemanly and high-quality players of Irish extraction as Duffy, Bobby Lowe, Billy Hamilton, Kid Nichols, Jimmy Collins,

Fred Tenney, Dan McGann, Mike Sullivan, and Patrick "Cozy" Dolan.

The Orioles had reacted to Boston's challenge by instigating more fights, battling more umpires, and filing their spikes to sharper edges. The ultimate victory of the competitively correct Beaneaters over the lethal game plan of the Orioles was hailed by the majority of the sportswriters covering the game, including even several scribes in Baltimore.

The O's subsequently made a solemn collective vow to regain the pennant in 1898 by establishing new definitions of on-field ferocity.

All for naught.

Down to only six Irish players, the good-guy Beaneaters nevertheless beat Baltimore to win the pennant in 1897 and 1898.

Chapter Thirteen

Kill the Ump

Umpiring does something to you.
—*Frank "Silk" O'Loughlin*

As baseball continued to evolve in a more organized fashion through rule changes, the lone umpire continued to suffer the slings and arrows of players, managers, and fans.

According to the ubiquitous president of the White Stockings, Mr. Spalding, "Fans who despise umpires are simply sowing their democratic right to protest against tyranny." Charlie Comiskey chimed in to say: "All is fair in war and baseball."

Despite the real dangers involved, several umpires became fixtures. Since counterbelligerence was an ump's best self-defense, it was no accident that most of the best umpires were Irish.

♣Tim Hurst was the most ornery of these. An uncouth man, he governed a game by the force of his personality and sometimes the force of his fists. No wonder Hurst had more physical confrontations with players than did any of his peers.

Hurst had learned to use his fists as a child when he labored as a slate picker in the coal mines of Ashland, Pennsylvania. To earn a few extra dimes, he also participated in the impromptu boxing matches that the miners often staged for their own amusement. After battling on equal terms against the toughest of the Irish miners, Hurst was totally unafraid to match punches with baseball players.

Players were quick to mimic Hurst's thick Irish brogue just to hear him spout his own heavily accented curses. Even so, they were reluctant to push him too far. When Kid Elberfeld reacted to a close call by repeatedly shoving Hurst, the umpire retaliated by using his protective mask to flatten his assailant with one mighty blow. Hurst was subsequently fined one hundred dollars and suspended for seven days, but he refused to ameliorate his behavior.

When he was accosted by an angry fan after a game, Hurst used his wire mask to the same effect. Then when a policeman tried to intervene, Hurst delivered a duplicate blow. On another occasion, when an irate fan threw a beer stein at Hurst, the umpire ducked, picked up the stein, and hurled it back at the fan. Unfortunately, the heavy mug struck another fan in the head, creating a wound that needed six stitches to close. The fans then rioted, forcing the police to quickly arrest Hurst and jail him. Hurst bailed himself out that night and also paid a league-imposed hundred-dollar fine.

After one game in which the Pittsburgh bench jockeys had mercilessly abused him, Hurst invited Jake Stenzel, Pink Hawley, and Denny Lyons to meet him under the stands to settle their dispute with punches. Despite being outnumbered three to one, Hurst took them all on at once and pounded them each into submission. He relented only when Nick Young, the president of the NL, chanced to arrive on the scene.

"What's this?" asked Young.

"Somebody dropped a dollar bill, Uncle Nick," Hurst replied with an innocent grin, "and I said it was mine."

Hurst shunned spikes and chose to wear dress shoes on the field. During an especially heated argument, Clark Griffith, manager of the New York Highlanders, stomped on Hurst's feet. At first the umpire didn't notice the holes in his shoes, but when he did, he entered New York's dugout, helped himself to a cup of water, then put the cup down and knocked out Griffith with a sudden right cross. For this latest KO, Hurst was suspended for five days.

Hurst's riotous career ended on August 3, 1909, when he called Eddie Collins out on an attempted steal even though the second baseman had obviously juggled the throw. Collins and Hurst, two temperamental Irishmen—one a graduate of Columbia University, the other a son of a coal miner—went jaw to jaw, until the umpire committed the ultimate insult by spitting in the player's face.

When the game ended, the police had to escort Hurst to safety as thousands of fans stormed the field throwing beer bottles at the ump. Although Hurst later privately apologized to Collins, he refused to voice his regrets with a public statement. Hurst's only self-defense was this: "I don't like college boys."

When Hurst also refused to file a report to the league, he was fired.

Through it all, Hurst's judgments were grudgingly respected by players and managers throughout the league. In total agreement with his admirers, Hurst often wore a large "B" on the front of his cap. Why? "Because," he said, "I'm the best."

♣John Gaffney's modus operandi was the antithesis of Hurst's. Instead of bullying anybody who dared disagree with him, Gaffney controlled games with his unsurpassed knowledge of the rulebook, his tact, and his diplomacy. Born in Roxbury, Massachusetts, of Irish immigrants, the grim-lipped, fierce-eyed Gaffney also had a terrific rapport with Irish players.

"I have studied the rules thoroughly," Gaffney once said. "I keep my eyes wide open, and I follow the ball with all possible dispatch. With the players I try to keep as even tempered as I can, always speaking to them gentlemanly yet firmly. I dislike to fine, and in all my experience have not inflicted more than $300 in fines, and I have never found it necessary to order a player from the field. Pleasant words to players in passion will work far better than fines."

He was called the "King of Umpires" but also managed the NL's Washington Nationals from 1886 to 1887. When a regularly scheduled ump failed to show one day, Gaffney's fairness was so widely unquestioned that opposing teams were happy to have him work games involving his own team.

Connie Mack declared Gaffney to be the greatest balls-and-strikes umpire in the history of the game. "He was perfect," Mack said. "He would follow a ball all the way from the pitcher, and when he made his decision, he would say that the pitch was one-eighth of an inch outside, or inside, or too high, or too low. And he was always right. There has never been another umpire like him."

♣John Kelly was a weak-hitting catcher for four teams before becoming still another important Irish umpire. Like Gaffney, he oversaw ball games with his gregarious personality and intimate familiarity with the rules. "Honest John" had another element in his game plan that Gaffney lacked—pleasing the fans by being a homer. In 1884, for example, home teams won more than two-thirds of the games Kelly worked.

Like Gaffney, Kelly had a stint as manager, and similarly presided over several of his own team's games in emergencies. In 1887, the champions of the NL (Detroit) and the American Association (St. Louis) engaged in a best-of-fifteen series, won by Detroit. During this series, Gaffney and Kelly worked together, temporarily becoming the first two-man umpiring crew in history.

♣Another record was set by a pair of Irish umps. In June 1897, Mike McDermott forfeited a game to New York after the Pittsburgh players incited a riot over a close call. Three days later, Jim McDonald forfeited a game to Philadelphia when the Pirates reacted to an unfavorable call by deliberately stalling until a threatened rain squall washed over the field.

This was the only time in major league history that a team forfeited two games in one week.

♣Equally as Irish, Jack Sheridan was more Hurst than Gaffney, once punching a player—Emerson "Pink" Hawley—for being overly abusive. Too bad Sheridan lacked Hurst's KO power, because Hawley retaliated by delivering a knockout punch of his own.

However, Sheridan is generally credited with being the first umpire to locate the destination of pitches by crouching behind the plate and peering over the catcher's shoulder. Before Sheridan, umps stood straight up, with the result that pitches in the lower part of the strike zone were routinely called balls. This was another reason why batting averages were so inflated during this period.

Sheridan also shunned the use of a chest protector, priding himself on avoiding being struck by foul tips due to his own quickness and agility. And on the rare occasion when he wasn't quite quick or agile enough, Sheridan never grimaced, rubbed the spot, or gave any indication that he'd been nailed.

♣Charlie Sweeney had enjoyed a six-year career in the various major leagues. A slick fielder who divided his time between second and third, Sweeney's career terminated when he murdered a man during a drunken bar fight. The charge was manslaughter and it earned him a private room in San Quentin.

But by 1898, Sweeney had done his time and was hired by the California League as an umpire. On June 1, 1898, he adjudicated a game between San Francisco and San Jose. Despite his many questionable calls, none of the fans in attendance dared to shout, "Kill the umpire!"

♣Hank O'Day wasn't much of a pitcher (1884–90), with a lifetime mark of 73-110. But of all the major league umpires on record, O'Day had the longest active playing career. Not that having been a bona fide pro did anything to brighten O'Day's dark personality. Fellow ump Bill Klem called O'Day a "misanthropic Irishman." O'Day had no friends, no hobbies, no family, and no interests other than his career.

O'Day was involved in several historic plays, one of them being his ejection of Connie Mack from a game in 1895. Mack was so furious that a bevy of policemen had to drag him off the field. During his entire playing and managing career, which stretched from 1886 to 1950, this marked the only time that Mack was banished from a game.

Another of his peers, Frank "Silk" O'Loughlin, had this to say about O'Day: "He is one of the best umpires, maybe the best today, but he's sour. The abuse you get from the players, the insults from the crowds, and the awful things they write about you in the newspapers take their toll."

BECAUSE IT WAS always open season on the umpires, a great many umps were happy to quit the game and find other employment. Oftentimes, when the regularly scheduled umps experienced travel difficulties or suddenly walked away from their jobs, each team was required to supply a substitute—one second-string player worked balls and strikes, while his equivalent on the opposing team worked the bases. However awkward this situation was, it was assumed that the respective favoritism of both ersatz umps would cancel each other out, so the protests on close plays were minimal.

Sometimes things got downright deadly.

In a game between amateur teams in Newbern, Alabama, a player, Sidney Gooden, vociferously protested a call by the umpire, Richard Lee Jr. The dispute escalated until Gooden knocked Lee to the ground. The ump's father, Richard Lee Sr., rushed from the stands with a bat in hand and attempted to assault Gooden. But the local police intercepted and arrested Senior before he reached Gooden. Even as the police escorted the elder Lee from the playing field, Gooden grabbed another bat, ran up behind the ump's father, and, taking a mighty swing, struck a fatal blow to his head.

Pandemonium reigned, replete with rioting and gunfire. When the dust had settled, two other men had been killed, one by Junior—who fled the scene but was soon hunted down by the local sheriff's bloodhounds.

An umpire's lot was certainly not a happy one.

Chapter Fourteen

More Irish Record Setting

When anyone asks me about the Irish character, I say
look at the trees. Maimed, stark and misshapen, but
ferociously tenacious.

—*Edna O'Brien*

THE SEASONS OF the waning nineteenth century featured an Irish
grab bag of surprises.

♣Duke Farrell was a journeyman catcher who averaged 86 games
per season over the course of an eighteen-year career spent with eight
different teams. Constantly battling weight problems, Farrell registered a more than respectable lifetime batting average of .275. Indeed,
hitting was his forte, and he'd led the American Association in home
runs (12) and RBIs (110) back in 1891.

To the surprise of his peers, when behind the plate for the
Washington Senators on May 11, 1897, Farrell threw out eight of
nine erstwhile base stealers—a record that still survives.

Six years later, Farrell caught Cy Young's perfect game—the first
in American League history.

♣Another unlikely event occurred on April 21, 1898, when a

Phillies pitcher named William "Frosty Bill" Duggleby hit a grand slam in his first major league at-bat—another feat that has never been duplicated. Duggleby lasted eight years, over which he compiled a record of 93-102 and otherwise hit .165.

♣On the next day, April 22, Baltimore's James Jay Hughes pitched a no-hitter on the same day as did Cincy's Ted Breitenstein, marking the first time that two no-hitters were thrown on the same day.

NEXT TO THE Orioles, the Cleveland Spiders had the largest population of Irish players, and manager Pat Tebeau was the only skipper who was eager to duplicate Baltimore's unruly tactics. Whenever and wherever Baltimore faced off with Cleveland, the game always featured high spikes, hard tags, beanball wars, and bloody fights. Even before the games commenced, hostile hometown fans would assault the opponents with rocks, bottles, and garbage as the bad guys entered the ballpark. When the visitors chanced to win the game at hand, the fans would often storm the field to attack the players and the umpire.

No surprise, too, that the Orioles were up to some of their old tricks—and devised a few new ones.

Baltimore's groundskeeper, Thomas Murphy, opened his own bag of tricks. In the days before rosin bags, pitchers used dirt to dry their hands, so, much to the annoyance of visiting pitchers, Murphy sprinkled soap flakes around the mound. The Orioles pitchers, of course, were forewarned which spots to avoid.

During a midseason game in 1897, there was a runner on first when Jack Doyle stepped out of the batter's box as though he had called time, causing the pitcher to stop his delivery. But Doyle never did actually signal for the official stoppage, and the balk sent the runner to second, whereupon a base hit by Doyle scored the tying run.

If a batter didn't try enough to avoid getting hit by a pitch, the umpire was empowered to deny him the free pass to first base. On July 18, 1897, John McGraw twice stepped in front of a pitch, but umpire Jim McDonald refused to award him first base.

However, Hugh Jennings, Baltimore's shortstop, was much craftier, successfully gaining first via being hit by a pitch, for a record total of 46 times that season.

While McGraw specialized in taunting opponents, sometimes he turned his attention to any teammate who had made what he deemed to be a bad play. Most of McGraw's intrasquad curses were directed at Willie Keeler.

After a game in which Keeler had failed to throw home to prevent an important run, McGraw challenged him in the clubhouse. With both of them stark naked, the two teammates began to fight. Jack Doyle, also sans clothing, grabbed a bat as the combatants fell and continued their struggle on the floor.

"I'll break the head of anybody who interferes," barked Doyle. "And I'll also lay five-to-four odds that Mugsy is the first to give up." McGraw, tough as he was, lost this round to Keeler.

Sometimes the Orioles outsmarted themselves. In a game against Louisville, Pete Browning looked to tag up and score from third on a fly ball to right field, but felt Baltimore's third baseman McGraw climbing over his back. Even so, Browning tagged up, scored, then jumped to his feet and laughed as he pointed back to McGraw, who stood red-faced at third, still holding Browning's unbuckled belt.

During another game, an opponent stroked a line drive that rolled between Keeler in right and Steve Brodie in center field. Keeler ran down the ball, turned, and threw it back toward the infield. Unfortunately, the ball Keeler unloosed nearly collided with the extra ball that Brodie had plucked from the deep grass and also heaved in the same direction.

SOMETIMES IRISH PLAYERS on other teams tried to duplicate Baltimore's antics—and suffered dire results.

♣Morgan Murphy was catching for St. Louis and Boston's Fred Tenney was the hitter when a runner attempted to steal second. As Murphy cocked his throwing arm, Tenney stepped squarely in front of him. But as Murphy unleashed his throw, he exaggerated his follow-through so that his elbow bashed Tenney's jaw.

The runner was safe, but Tenney was knocked cold.

♣On July 31, 1897, Brooklyn's Bill Kennedy was so incensed at a call made by Hank O'Day that he threw a ball at the umpire. However, Kennedy neglected to call time, the ball missed O'Day, and the winning run scored.

♣Sometimes subterfuges worked to perfection—as when Chicago's Jimmy Ryan swung and missed a pitch in the dirt. As the catcher scrambled to retrieve the ball, Ryan used his bat to tap it out of reach and allowed a runner on second to easily advance to third.

♣Morgan Murphy of the Phils would make a name for himself again. Turns out he was as quick with his mind as he was with his elbows, arranging several elaborate systems designed to steal the opposing catcher's signs.

A cohort was positioned at the window of a rented room that over-looked the playing field. The spy used binoculars to read the sign, then employed various modes to communicate the message—perhaps a flapping newspaper, window shade, or drapery for a breaking pitch, or no visual aid whatsoever for a fastball.

In Philadelphia, Murphy oversaw the burying of a box with a vibrating buzzer in a far corner of the third-base coach's box. The spy would relay the forthcoming pitch to the coach through the appro-priate vibration, whereupon the coach had a designated hand signal to inform the hitter.

Perhaps that's why Ed Delahanty hit .422 at home that year and only .335 on the road en route to a league-leading .410 average.

What became known as the "Morgan Murphy system" was

finally uncovered by another clever Irishman, Cincinnati's shortstop, Tommy Corcoran.

ANTI-IRISH NONSENSE WAS still the order of the day in Chicago.

Cap Anson continued to battle his Irish players. After the White Stockings finished ninth in 1897, 34 games behind Boston, Anson was convinced that his Irish players had colluded with each other, and had even been encouraged by the Irish owner of the team, A. J. Spalding, to deliberately lose games so that he would get canned.

And their conspiracy succeeded.

According to Anson, "underhanded work looking toward my downfall was indulged in by some of the players. . . . The ringleader in this business was Jimmy Ryan, between whom and the Club's President the most perfect understanding seemed to exist, and for this underhanded work Ryan was rewarded later by being made the team captain, a position that he was too unpopular with the players to hold."

The new manager was another Irishman, Tom Burns, but the German players on the team did indeed rebel when he named Ryan captain. After the Germans threatened a sit-down strike prior to the season's opener, Burns capitulated and Ryan was replaced by Billy Lange, of bona fide German descent.

Although the White Stockings made a jump to fourth place in 1898, the ethnic divide was never bridged and the Irish and Germans were at loggerheads throughout the season.

THE RULES OF the game remained surprisingly confused.

♣In June 1897, Charlie Ganzel was catching and batting in the eight-hole for Boston, while Chick Stahl was hitting third and playing right field. But Stahl was showing flu-like symptoms and after drawing a walk early in the game, he had an urgent need to visit the bathroom. The Beaneaters' manager asked his opposite number if Ganzel could serve as a "courtesy runner" for Stahl. This would allow Stahl to return to action if or when he recovered. Bill Barnie commanded the Brooklyn Bridegrooms and was happy to give his permission, especially since Stahl was a fleet-footed twenty-five-year-old rookie and, at thirty-five, Ganzel was on his last legs, and rarely stole a base. Since both managers were agreeable, this temporary substitution was legal.

Another unexpected development occurred two years later, near the end of the 1899 season. Because the Cleveland Spiders were by far the worst team in the National League (finishing at 20-134, 84 games in the hole), their per-game home attendance dwindled to around two hundred as the season dragged on. As a result, the league's schedule was altered so that Cleveland was able play all road games during August and September.

The preponderance of Irish players on the roster gave the erstwhile Spiders a more appropriate nickname—the Wandering Micks.

HOWEVER, THE MOST unexpected and startling event of the period came in the winter of 1898 when a complicated business deal sent manager Ned Hanlon, along with several of the Orioles' best players, to Brooklyn, leaving John McGraw to manage the decimated remains of Baltimore's teams of glory.

Among those changing uniforms were Willie Keeler, Hughie Jennings, Joe Kelley, Dan McGann, and three pitchers who were 20-plus game winners. Because of a popular acrobatic vaudeville act called Hanlon's Superbas, the Brooklyn Bridegrooms were now dubbed the Superbas, and with a squad that included fourteen Irish players (including such great Irish names as Daly, Dunn, Farrell, Hughes, McGuire, and best of all, Brickyard Kennedy), they easily won the pennant by eight games over Boston.

In his initial employment as a full-time manager, McGraw also did a superb job bullying, threatening, and cajoling the left-for-dead Orioles to an admirable record of 82-62 and a fifth-place finish.

AS THE NEW century approached, here's how several sons of Eire continued to meet the standard of excellence established by their predecessors.

In 1898 Willie Keeler made what was generally deemed by contemporaries to be the greatest catch ever seen in the game at the time. The left-handed Keeler sometimes played shortstop, but was at his natural position in right field in a game at Washington when the batter struck a low line drive that was hooking toward the seats. Keeler raced to the stands and snatched the ball with his left hand, his momentum carrying him headfirst into a barbed-wire fence that separated the fans from the playing field.

His uniform was caught on the barbs and he hung suspended off the ground. Despite the bloody scratches and punctures, Keeler waved away the trainer, stanched the bleeding with handfuls of dirt, and refused to be removed from the game.

What made the play even more meaningful was that the Orioles were already so far behind that the game was hopelessly lost. Still, this highly dramatic example of Keeler's all-out, all-the-time hustle was nothing unusual.

♣Keeler was the batting leader in 1897 (.427) and 1898 (.385), with Ed Delahanty succeeding him in 1899 (.410).

♣The leading home run hitters in 1897 and 1898, respectively, were Hugh Duffy (11) and Jimmy Collins (15).

♣Several of the top pitchers at the end of the century all had Irish roots—Kid Nichols, Amos Rusie, Joe Corbett, Bert Cunningham, Doc McJames, and Joe McGinnity.

WITH THE ARRIVAL of the twentieth century, not even the most astute baseball watcher had the slightest idea what would be in store for what was already the national pastime.

However, one prominent citizen did offer an explanation for the past, present, and future popularity of the game. Dr. S. B. Talcott's official title was Superintendent of the State Lunatic Asylum in New York.

"I believe," he said, "baseball is a homeopathic cure for insanity. It is a kind of craze in itself, and gives the lunatics a new kind of craving to release them of the malady which afflicts their minds."

PRESENT-DAY INTERVIEW

Barry Enright describes his bright red facial hair as "evidence that I have an Irish ginger aspect." Indeed, both of his parents were born in Ireland, although they moved to Scotland in the 1980s because of the Troubles.

Born twenty-five years ago in Stockton, California, Enright measures a sturdy 6'3" and 220 pounds. He is blessed with an arsenal that includes a low-90s fastball, a crackling slider, and a bottom-heavy change-up. In his rookie season of 2010, his 6-7 record with Arizona was ameliorated by a nifty 3.91 ERA.

He has a friendly, modest way about him, but was perplexed by his shaky start in 2011—he went 0-2 with a gargantuan 6.65 ERA. Yielding homers has been his major bugaboo, but he avows that his delivery mechanics are perfect.

"I always seem to struggle early in every season," he says. "I get too passive when I should be challenging hitters. I guess I have to learn to trust my stuff more. It seems every hit I've given up has been with two outs. It's frustrating that I can't shut the door."

Enright has visited the Emerald Isle, but he was only two years old at the time. "But I certainly do identify myself as being Irish."

St. Patrick's Day falls in spring training, so Enright says he treats himself to a Guinness that evening . . . unless he is starting the next day.

Part III

A New Century

Chapter Fifteen

The Delahanty Brothers

They're the product of the vacant lots
All game as bloodied banties,
And, holy smoke, ain't there a bunch
Of baseball Delahantys.

—From a song of the day

THE PLAYING CAREERS of Ed, Joe, Tom, Frank, and Jim Delahanty bridged the two centuries, leaving a baseball family legacy un-
matched, except, perhaps, for the DiMaggio brothers.

♣Tom was born in 1872, making him five years younger than the
oldest and best of the brothers. At 5'8" and 175 pounds, he was also
the smallest. He started his career with a local semipro team in his
hometown of Cleveland, and by 1894, Tom was enjoying a productive
season playing second base for Peoria in the Western Association. Ed
nagged the Phillies to sign Tom for the last few weeks of the NL, but
management refused, claiming Tom was too young and inexperienced.

However, when Philadelphia's second baseman was injured, Tom
was called upon to replace him. Tom had a single and a strikeout in
four at-bats while fielding flawlessly at second. In the same game, his

big brother was 0 for 4, and committed three errors at third base. However, Ed was a star, so his misplays were excusable, while Tom's brief performance convinced the Phillies that his own skills in the field still weren't up to par.

After his release, Tom joined Atlanta in the Southern League, before finishing the season with Detroit in the Western League. He played so well in the minors that Cleveland picked him up as a utility infielder for the 1895 campaign. But Tom was in over his head—batting .204 and making twelve errors in sixteen games.

After being sold to Pittsburgh for $200, Tom went 1 for 3 and booted one ball at shortstop. His second one-game major league season ended when Pittsburgh sent him to Toronto in the Eastern League.

There was one more big league game in his portfolio—a double and two RBIs in four at-bats for Louisville in 1897. Even so, when Tom was guilty of botching two of the three balls hit to him at shortstop, he wound up back in the Western League.

But his 1897 major league appearance was noteworthy more for what Tom said than for what he did. Louis Sockalexis, a Native American, was in his rookie season of what would be an alcohol-shortened three-year career with Cleveland. Tom, apparently forgetting all of the NINA signs he must have seen in his childhood, had this to say about Sockalexis: "The league has gone to hell now that they've let them damn foreigners in." Tom must have also overlooked the fact that Sockalexis finished that 1897 season with a gaudy .338 batting average.

Tom finished out his career by variously playing minor league ball in Youngstown, Ohio; Marion, Indiana; Grand Rapids, Michigan; Wheeling, West Virginia; and Denver, Colorado. His best season by far was 1902, with Denver in the Western League, where he hit .350. But he was already thirty years old and irrevocably categorized as a good-hit, no-field infielder. In 1906, Tom made a brief comeback with Williamsport of the Tri-State League in order to play one last game with his brother Joe.

For his twelve seasons in the high minors, Tom compiled an admirable .295 batting average. However, in his nineteen major league games, Tom could only manage a .239 average.

The fraternal joy of the Delahanty siblings turned to grief on July 2, 1903, when it was discovered that big brother Ed was dead.

Big Ed had been at it again with his multiple contract signings. He was still under contract with the NL Phillies when he received a $4,000 advance for signing an additional contract with the NL Giants. Shortly thereafter, Delahanty accepted a $1,600 advance for signing still another contract, this one with the Washington Nationals in the new American League.

When all the ink had dried, the Washington ownership reimbursed Philadelphia and New York, and Delahanty played the 1902 season with the Nationals. As part of the interleague agreement, Delahanty was forbidden to set foot in Philadelphia under threat of being arrested.

In any event, Delahanty batted .376 for his latest team, thereby becoming the first player to lead both the NL and the AL in hitting.

But he couldn't sit still. He was going to jump teams once more and go back to the Giants in New York.

Leaving a hotel in Detroit after a road game, Ed boarded a train bound for New York City, and got drunk en route. When he couldn't find his own sleeping berth, he began to insult and then assault several passengers who were already bedded down in berths that he variously claimed were his. Delahanty's behavior was so outrageous that he was put off the train at a station in Fort Erie, Ontario.

This all ended very, very badly, as this gruesome news report attested:

From the *Boston Journal*, July 10, 1903:

Ed. Delahanty's Body is Found Below Falls
Identification of Unfortunate Ball Player Who Had Been Put
Off Train and Had Walked Off Open Draw.

Niagara Falls, N.Y., July 9—The body of a man found
in the river below the falls this morning was identified at
Drummondville this afternoon as that of Ed. Delahanty, the
Washington American League ball player, who was drowned off
the International Bridge last Thursday night.

M. A. Green, a stockholder in the Washington team, who is a
friend of the Delahanty family and who came on here to search for
the body, made the identification from the dead man's teeth, two
crooked baseball fingers, also from clothing he wore.

One Leg Torn Off.

One of Delahanty's legs was torn off, presumably by the propeller
of the steamer Maid of the Mist, *near whose landing the body was*
found. The body is now in the morgue at Drummondville, and Mr.
Green will probably arrange to ship it to Washington tonight.

Frank Delahanty of the Syracuse team and E. J. McGuire, a
brother-in-law from Cleveland, are here investigating the death
of the player. They do not believe that Delahanty committed suicide
or that he had been on a spree in Detroit. In the sleeper on the
Michigan Central train on the way down from Detroit, Delahanty
had five drinks of whiskey, says Conductor Cole, and became so
obstreperous that he had to put him off the train at Bridgeburg at
the Canadian end of the bridge. Cole says Delahanty had an open
razor, and was terrifying others in the sleeper.

Walked Off Open Draw.

When the train stopped at Bridgeburg, Cole did not deliver
Delahanty up to a constable as the Canadian police say he should
have done. He just put him off the train.

After the train had disappeared across the bridge, Delahanty
started to walk across, which is against the rules. The night
watchman attempted to stop him. But Delahanty pushed the man
to one side. The draw of the bridge had been opened for a boat, and
the player plunged into the dark waters of the Niagara.

Delahanty's relatives hint at foul play, but there is nothing in the case, apparently, to bear out such a theory.

His brothers grieved, but also collectively vowed to honor Ed's memory by continuing to play the game that he, and they, so dearly loved.

♣Next in line was Joe Delahanty, three years Tom's junior. An excellent outfielder, Joe was deemed to have inherited Big Ed's hitting genes. The proof was Joe's domination of several minor leagues with his big bat: .469 in Allentown, Pennsylvania; .344 in Fall River, Massachusetts; .311 in Paterson, New Jersey. Equally comfortable in the outfield or at third base, Joe was probably the best fielder in the family. He played 1,423 games for a total of fourteen minor league teams in fourteen seasons and finished with a lifetime average of .303.

Duplicating his hitting prowess in the big league was something else. His minor league numbers earned him a brief showcase with St. Louis in 1907, wherein he hit .318 in 22 plate appearances spread out over seven games. During the next two seasons, Joe was the Cardinals' starting right fielder, but top-notch curveballs drove his average down to .255 and then .214.

After a few more stops, in New Orleans, Memphis, Buffalo, Williamsport, Montreal, and Toronto, Joe returned to Cleveland, living a bachelor's life and working as a lithographer.

In 269 National League games, Joe compiled a meager .238 average.

♣Billy was the only Delahanty sibling who never played in the bigs. Born in 1880, he was a more than capable infielder for teams in the Ohio and New York state leagues. However, although the Dodgers were planning to promote him to Brooklyn, while the paperwork was under way, his career was terminated when he was seriously beaned at the plate.

♣The youngest of the crew was Frank, called "Pudgie" to mock the 160 pounds that adhered tightly to his 5'9" frame. He played the outfield and first base for a familiar circuit of minor league teams before breaking in with the American League's New York Highlanders in 1907. Although he was a ball-gobbling fielder, Frank was a weak hitter. Throughout his six years with New York and Cleveland of the American League as well as Buffalo and Philadelphia of the Federal League, Frank's cumulative batting average was a paltry .226.

♣Because of his fair complexion and boyish looks, Jim Delahanty was called the "Yellow Kid," after a popular cartoon character. Jim fielded various positions in both the outfield and the infield like a savvy veteran, did some emergency pitching, and was no slouch with a bat in his hands. Like Tom and Joe before him, Jim made the rounds of numerous minor league stops—the highlight being a league-leading .379 average with Hartford in the Colonial League.

When Jim reached the majors with Chicago in 1907, he remained among the elite for the next thirteen years (including two seasons with the Federal League). Having outgrown his Yellow Kid status, he was described by contemporaries as "a tobacco-chewing tough guy" with an agreeable sense of humor.

Jim was at his best in the 1909 World Series with Detroit, when he surpassed Ty Cobb and Honus Wagner by pounding out a .346 average. Two years later, Jim batted .339 and totaled 94 RBIs. However, in 1912, Jim was unfairly blamed for a players' strike that resulted when Ty Cobb was suspended for going into the stands and attacking a fan who had loudly cursed the ferocious Georgia Peach. Even though Jim was innocent of the charge, he was branded as a lying troublemaker and the Tigers waived him.

Clearly the second-best Delahanty, Jim had a highly respectable .283 lifetime batting average in the major leagues. After Ed's untimely death, it was Jim who had the longest ride. His retirement from Beaumont in the Texas League in 1916 ended the Delahanty era, which had begun in 1887.

"With me gone," said Jimmy, "there is no one to take my place."

Chapter Sixteen

A New League

Being Irish, he had an abiding sense of tragedy, which
sustained him through temporary periods of joy.
—*William Butler Yeats*

THE MOST SIGNIFICANT happening in the new century actually
began on October 12, 1899. That's when Ban Johnson, president of
the American Association, changed the name of his organization to
the American League. Ever ambitious, Johnson aimed to begin operations in time for the 1901 season.

The National League unwittingly aided Johnson's game plan in
March 1900, when they decided to drop four of its weakest franchises
and go with eight teams. The owners of the discarded Baltimore
Orioles were paid $30,000 as recompense, while the suddenly defunct
teams in Cleveland, Louisville, and Washington each received
$10,000. (The National League's new lineup of St. Louis, Pittsburgh,
Philadelphia, New York, Cincinnati, Chicago, Boston, and Brooklyn
would remain intact for fifty-three years, until the Boston Braves
relocated to Milwaukee.)

SEVERAL SIGNIFICANT IRISH players from the deleted teams had their contracts claimed by holdover franchises, and in 1900 plied their trade in new uniforms.

♣John McGraw found himself in a St. Louis uniform. Although he hit .344, he was profoundly unhappy to have to play and live away from the east coast.

♣Wilbert Robinson was likewise shifted from Baltimore to St. Louis. "Robby" served as a stout backup catcher (.248) as well as a cheerful presence in the clubhouse.

♣Aussie-born Joe Quinn went from Cleveland to St. Louis but was soon traded to Cincinnati. The slick-fielding second baseman batted a combined .270.

♣With Boston, Bill Dinneen reversed the 14-20 record he had previously recorded in Washington.

♣Just two seasons removed from a 28-win season with Louisville, Bert Cunningham had a sore arm and managed only four victories in Chicago.

♣A romantic Irish player was Danny Murphy, who turned down a generous offer from the Giants because he couldn't bear the thought of being separated from his childhood sweetheart. Murphy finally did sign with the Giants, but then went AWOL after playing in only twenty-two games. The I'm-here/I'm-there pattern was repeated the following season when Murphy's playing season lasted only nine games. However, after being traded to Philadelphia, Murphy went on to hit over .300 six times during his outstanding tenure with the Phillies.

Despite the more recent influx of other immigrant groups into the country and into the NL, nearly 38 percent of the 202 players who participated in the 1900 season still had Irish roots. Chicago headed the list with thirteen Irishmen, and Brooklyn's roster included a dozen. The most non-Irish squad was Cincinnati's, with only six sons of the Emerald Isle.

The financial rewards for virtually every player had skyrocketed by 1900. Salaries averaged $2,000 at a time when the average worker was fortunate to earn $700 a year. Also, the elite players were able to find lucrative off-season employment as well as an increasing number of commercial endorsements. For instance, Ed Delahanty and Napoleon Lajoie had been paid several hundred dollars to permit their likenesses to be used in advertisements for Stuart's Dyspepsia Tablets.

Indeed, as the game became increasingly popular, baseball players were no longer shunned in proper society. Teams were now welcomed in top-flight hotels around the league. Fathers of well-educated, highly respectable daughters no longer forbade them to consort with ballplayers. Contributing to this universal acceptance was the fact that 25 percent of NL players active in the 1900 season had attended college for various periods of time. This compared favorably with other men in their age group, of whom only 5 percent had received some form of higher education.

The only meaningful rule change that greeted the new century was the reshaping of home plate. Replacing the diamond-set square that was only twelve inches wide, the new base was a five-sided, seventeen-inch slab of rubber that significantly widened the available strike zone. Batting averages and home runs plummeted.

However, the antics and achievements of several Irish players were unaffected by money, popularity, or new rules.

Even when they were teammates with the Orioles, Jack Doyle

and John McGraw never got along and frequently traded punches. Indeed, McGraw once had to be restrained by Ned Hanlon from attacking Doyle with a bat. "Otherwise," said McGraw, "I would have happily broken his jaw."

Nicknamed "Dirty Jack" because of his vicious play and ready fists, Doyle was also infamous for once having thoroughly thrashed umpire Tommy Lynch during a game.

By 1900, McGraw played for St. Louis and Doyle was a Giant. Early in the season, Doyle flashed his high spikes at McGraw while he was sliding into third; the cuts on McGraw's shins were so severe that he was out of action for several weeks.

In the ultimate irony, after retiring from baseball, Dirty Jack served a two-year stint as police commissioner in Holyoke, Massachusetts.

On June 6, representatives from all eight NL teams met in New York to discuss the formation of a players' union. Thirteen of the twenty-three players in attendance were Irish. The percentage would have been higher except that John McGraw and Jimmy Ryan were absent due to schedule conflicts. The group agreed on two procedures: to reject Samuel Gompers's offer to affiliate with his American Federation of Labor, and to meet at a future date to formulate bylaws in conjunction with several lawyers.

As they did with the players' previous union, NL bigwigs scoffed at this latest example of players' solidarity.

♣On July 7, Kid Nichols pitched the Beaneaters to an 11–4 win over Chicago. At the time, Nichols was thirty years and ten months old, which made him the youngest pitcher ever to record 300 lifetime wins—an achievement that still stands.

♣The most influential Irish player of the early 1900s, the "Iron Man" Joe McGinnity, was celebrated for his durability on the mound. Over the course of his career he completed 314 of his 381 starts, and was a league leader in innings pitched four times. In 1903, he'd start both games of a doubleheader—three times in a single month. Even so, McGinnity's nickname came from his off-season job—working in his father-in-law's iron foundry.

After compiling a 28-16 mark in his rookie season with the 1899 Orioles, McGinnity's 28-8 record was a critical factor in helping Brooklyn repeat as NL champs, and he was voted into Cooperstown in 1946.

THE YEAR 1901 saw the launch of the new American League, with these new rules:

- No player could be suspended for more than ten days regardless of his transgression.
- Clubs pay all the medical bills for injured players.
- Should a team fold, its players would become free agents after ten days.
- Players could not be sold or sent to a minor league team without their written permission.
- The league's reserve clause would be in effect for only three years after an initial contract is signed.
- Players bound by the reserve clause could not have their original contracted salaries reduced.
- Any salary disputes would be resolved by binding arbitration.

As you can imagine, with these player-partial rules and generous funding, the AL ignited a bidding war for several elite players. Bids by the new franchises in Baltimore, Chicago, and Milwaukee to John McGraw, Jimmy Collins, and Hugh Duffy, respectively, were clinched when they were all offered the chance to be player-managers.

Iron Man McGinnity moved from Brooklyn to the resurrected

Orioles, and on September 3, 1901, pitched complete games in both halves of a doubleheader—beating Milwaukee 10–0 before losing 6–1.

♣Moving from the Boston Beaneaters to the AL's Chicago White Stockings was catcher Billy Sullivan, a poor hitter but the best fielder and handler of pitchers in the game. Also, Jim "Nixey" Callahan, a two-time 20-game winner for Chicago's NL team, moved across town to join the AL's White Stockings.

♣All told, approximately 25 percent of the new league's players were of Irish persuasion.

♣Moreover, six of the AL's charter franchises were managed by Irishmen: Baltimore (McGraw), Boston (Collins), Chicago (Clark Griffith, who led the White Stockings to the pennant), Cleveland (Jim McAleer), Milwaukee (Duffy), and Philadelphia (Connie Mack). Only the fortunes of Detroit and Washington were in the hands of non-Irishmen.

Mike O'Neill's parents hailed from County Galway, and he was followed into the major leagues by three brothers:

♣Jack O'Neill caught for three teams from 1902 to 1906, and was noted for his glove, not his bat—as attested by his lifetime average of .196.

♣Steve O'Neill was another backstop, playing for four teams from 1911 to 1928. He hit over .300 from 1920 to 1922, and with Stan Coveleski formed the "coal miners" battery when Cleveland won the 1920 World Series. After he hung up his spikes, Steve managed in the big leagues for fourteen years without ever experiencing a losing season, and led the Detroit Tigers to a World Series championship in 1945.

♣Jim O'Neill was the youngest, an infielder for Washington in 1920 and 1923. Injuries limited him to 109 games, but he still registered a lifetime batting average of .287.

Together, the O'Neills were one brother short of the Delahantys.

Chapter Seventeen

Mr. Mack

Cornelius Mack;
Neither the Yankees nor years
Can halt his attack.
                    —*Ogden Nash*

BEFORE 1900, FOUR Irish managers combined to lead their respective teams to eleven pennants combined—Ned Hanlon, Bill McGunnigle, Mike "King" Kelly, and Charlie Comiskey—but the excellence of Irish skippers was even more pronounced in the first decades of the twentieth century:

♣Jimmy Collins won AL pennants in Boston in 1903 and 1904.

♣Under the direction of Bill Carrigan, the Red Sox won two more pennants, in 1915 and 1916.

♣Hughie Jennings steered Detroit to the top of the AL from 1907 to 1909.

♣Pat Moran's Phillies were NL champs in 1915, and he duplicated his success with Cincinnati in 1919.

♣Miller Huggins, beginning in 1918, had the good fortune to manage Babe Ruth and Lou Gehrig to three World Championships.

♣Kid Gleason managed the stained White Sox into the World Series in 1919.

♣And in 1905, *all* of the eight NL franchises were managed by Irishmen.

Alas, not every Irish manager was destined for greatness, but their sheer number was indicative of the Emerald Age of players who then moved to the bench: Frank Selee (a .598 career winning percentage), Bill McPhee, Jimmy McAleer, Hugh Duffy, Fred Dwyer, Joe Kelley, Nixey Callahan, Kid Nichols, Frank Tenney, Fred Clarke, Deacon McGuire, Roger Bresnahan, Billy Sullivan, Bill Dahlen, "Rowdy Jack" O'Connor, Hank O'Day, Joe Tinker, Johnny Evers, Wilbert Robinson, "Sunset Jimmy" Burke, "Scrappy Bill" Joyce, Tommy Dowd, John McCloskey, and the Irish-born Patsy Donovan.

However, there's no question that one of the most accomplished managers in the entire history of the game, along with John McGraw, was Connie Mack. Between them, they would win eighteen pennants and eight world championships.

But no one managed as long as Mack.

BORN TO IMMIGRANT parents, Connie Mack was forced to quit school at the age of fourteen in order to help support his family. The need was great because of his father's failure to fully recover from an injury suffered while fighting for the Union in the Civil War. As a result, Michael McGillicuddy took to drinking and was unable to work.

Fortunately, Mack was quick to discover that he could earn decent money playing baseball, and he quickly advanced through local amateur teams, to semipro and minor league outfits, before debuting with the Washington Senators in 1886.

Along the way, he shortened his family name to make it fit in box scores.

While he was never more than a competent hitter (.246 over

eleven major league seasons), Mack was a good-fielding catcher who was especially valued for his intelligence and his creativity. And his six-decade-plus career on and off the field encompassed the transition from baseball's pioneer era to the modern era.

In Mack's rookie season with the Senators, the amenities available to players were both crude and costly. Players were responsible for transporting their uniforms (for which they paid thirty dollars), shoes, bats, gloves, and personal belongings. Before games, they changed their attire in the third-rate hotels where they slept, two to a bed. They then either walked or rode in a horse-drawn omnibus to the ballpark—for the ride the players were charged fifty cents for every round trip.

"The locker room in the Washington ball park," said Mack, "had no showers or bathroom facilities other than a sort of barrel-like pool sunk into the ground and filled with water. The water would stay there for a week without being changed. After a while they outgrew the barrel and put in little individual tin pans. On the other side of the locker room a sink was put in with three or four spigots from which we would fill our pans. I anticipated the shower bath by filling the pan and emptying it over my head."

By the time Mack retired from the game in 1950, each player had his own bed on the road, there were showers in the locker rooms, and equipment men were responsible for cleaning, packing, and transporting the uniforms and other paraphernalia to the train, bus, or airport.

When his catching skills began to erode, Mack served as player-manager of the Pittsburgh Pirates in the National League (1894–96), never finishing higher than sixth.

Although he was only thumbed from a game once in his entire career, Mack had more nonconfrontational yet petulant ways of demonstrating his displeasure with umpires who he felt made erroneous calls.

Back when he managed the Pirates, the umpires had no masks of their own and depended on the catcher's handing over his mask after the third out was recorded. But, during a game in Baltimore, Mack was upset with a call by George Weidman—and just as the Pittsburgh catcher was offering his mask, Mack ran onto the field, grabbed the mask out of the ump's hands, and silently stormed back to the bench. Wilbert Robinson was catching for the Orioles and gave Weidman a spare mask so the game could resume.

As ever, the loopholes in the existing rules were fully exploited by a generation of Irishmen—few of them more imaginative than Mack—who forced the powers that be to make adjustments.

Mack routinely stationed a boy on the grandstand roof, charging him to retrieve the many foul balls that landed up there. But Mack would secretly provide the boy with several balls that had been stored overnight in an icebox in his office. When the opponents were due to bat, the boy would climb down to the field and give the frozen balls to the umpire in lieu of the live ones that had landed on the roof. For several weeks, nobody could understand why so many solid shots off opponents' bats resulted in weak ground balls.

Eventually, Mack's deception was discovered, and in 1896 a new rule required that the home team provide the umpire with a dozen new balls *before* every game.

But at least one of Mack's more subtle hornswoggles was never discovered. Harry Jordan was an overly sensitive rookie pitcher with the 1894 Pirates. Known in the trade as having "rabbit ears," Jordan would quickly lose his composure when an opposing team's bench jockeys began riding him. Jordan started his abbreviated major league career against the Cleveland Spiders, one of the most venomous harassers of opponents in the game.

Mack's solution was characteristically simple: he simply spread the word that Jordan was deaf. The Spiders didn't bother to waste their breath and Jordan hurled a complete-game win, the only one of his career.

Mack continued to wear his uniform during his stint with the Pirates, and often coached at third base. From this vantage point, he would habitually wait until one of the Pirates hit a high pop-up to the infield, so high that two of the infielders strained to catch sight of the ball. Then Mack would call out the name of another infielder who wasn't close to the play—"McCauley's got it!"—while the ball dropped safely.

In 1901, Mack was instrumental in delivering financial backers, a ballpark, and several players to the new American League, enabling them to field a team in Philadelphia. He was rewarded for these efforts by being named treasurer, manager, and part owner of the Philadelphia Athletics.

Mack became a genius when he commanded the Athletics. Behind a hot-hitting lineup as well as a great pitching staff, the A's won the 1902 AL pennant by five games over the St. Louis Browns. When the A's returned to the top of the AL's final standings in 1905, they were bested by McGraw's New York Giants in the second World Series ever played.

This version of Mack's Athletics would be the first of three powerhouse teams that he would be solely responsible for assembling and managing. As each group aged, Mack assiduously stocked his roster with younger players.

Connie Mack, Mrs. Mack, Miss McGillicuddy,
and Mrs. G. Colby
(Library of Congress)

Mack's appearance was a stern one, with his bushy black eyebrows imparting an unforgiving cast to his flashing brown eyes, and his thin lips tightened in a perpetual grimace. His players always called him "Mr. Mack," while he referred to them by their given names or sometimes even their middle names; for example, Charles Albert "Chief" Bender was invariably "Albert."

Mack was a confirmed teetotaler, who once said, "I'd die before I took a drink." Mack traded away Joe Jackson, one of the best natural hitters he had ever seen, because of Shoeless Joe's fondness for alcohol, as well as his dull awareness of the game's intricacies.

More than for sheer talent, Mack prized players who were disciplined in their personal lives, and who were also self-motivated and intelligent on the field. Even so, Mack was not above seeking help from more dubious sources.

Baseball players were (and still are) addicted to numerous superstitions. Hitters would expect a game full of base hits if they found a hairpin or saw a wagon loaded with empty barrels. The best guarantee of a hit, though, was to rub a hunchback's hump before stepping into the batter's box. Conversely, witnessing a funeral procession or being stared at by a cross-eyed person would ensure a hitless game. The only antidote for these jinxes was to quickly spit in a hat.

It's not surprising that players treasured their good luck charms, which generally included one or several of the following: the badge from a retired detective, a hotel key, a peach pit, a short length of trolley wire, a horse chestnut, the minute hand of a watch, or the rook from a chess set.

Pitchers had their own set of superstitions. Starting a game by striking out the first batter would certainly lead to a loss. Hurling a shutout was believed to bring such misfortune that some pitchers deliberately allowed the opponents to score in lopsided games.

So it was no surprise when one of Mack's outfielders, Rube Oldring, brought a short, overweight, pale-faced, hunchbacked teenager to the ballpark on October 2, the last day of the 1909 season. The Athletics had lost three straight games, which had cost them the pennant, and which even Mack blamed on several turns of bad luck. The A's were in Washington for a doubleheader, and Oldring asked Mack if the fifteen-year-old boy could tend the bats.

Mack, in dire need of good luck in any form, readily agreed.

The lad's name was Louis Van Zelst, and his affliction originally resulted from a bad fall that twisted his spine when he was eight. Born in West Philadelphia, he'd spent the last few years as a good luck mascot for all of the varsity teams at the University of Pennsylvania. "Little Van" was familiar to Oldring only because he and several of his teammates lived near Penn.

Louis Van Zelst
(*Frank Russo*)

In any case, Van Zelst did an excellent job during the twin bill, fetching the bats from and returning them to the bat rack in perfect order. All done with a smile and a cheerful disposition. Lo and behold, the A's won both games.

Impressed on all counts, Mack invited Little Van to be the team's batboy and mascot for the 1910 season—a one-year tryout that lasted for six years. Van Zelst was soon fitted for a uniform and put on the payroll, and he tended to the bats during every home game and an increasing number of road games.

The players responded with warmth to his enthusiasm, and to his ability to perfectly mimic Eddie Plank's nervous routine on the mound. Eddie Collins invited Little Van to his wedding. When they were on the road, Jack Coombs made sure the batboy was settled in his hotel room or Pullman berth. The players contributed generous bonuses after the three World Series the Athletics won during Van Zelst's tenure with the team. On Sundays, Jack Barry took him to Mass. Before one game, Mack empowered Van Zelst to take the lineup card to the umps gathered at home plate. But when Mack gave him the chance to coach first base during a game in New York, umpire Tom Connolly nixed the plan.

Although he was occasionally afflicted with painful back spasms, Little Van's sunny disposition was never eclipsed. He would sidle up beside a batter in a slump and say in his thin, fragile voice, "Better rub my back."

Van Zelst was diagnosed with Bright's disease late in the winter of 1915, and he died two months later.

By 1910, Mack's second great team was in place, stocked with Irishmen.

♣Eddie Collins played a flawless second base and hit .324. With his boyish face and crooked-toothed smile, Collins set the standard at his position for the next sixteen seasons. Collins was a college boy, and had even got into a game in '06 while still technically an amateur; Collins was officially listed in the box score as "Sullivan." By some measures, he is considered the greatest second baseman ever, and he was inducted into Cooperstown in 1939.

♣Jack Barry played shortstop. An excellent contact hitter who excelled at executing bunts and hit-and-run plays, Barry hit .289 and combined with Collins to form the most adept double-play tandem in baseball at the time.

♣Harry Davis, a fine glove man, was the regular first baseman but was occasionally spelled by John "Stuffy" McInnis, nicknamed as a boy because of the calls of "That's the stuff, kid" that greeted his plays on the diamond.

♣At third was Frank Baker, who would gain the nickname "Home Run" after swatting a pair of round-trippers that won games in the 1911 World Series.

From 1910 through 1914, Mack's A's won four pennants and three World Series.

When McInnis became the full-time first baseman in 1911, his incredible range and steady hitting perfectly complemented Collins, Barry, and Baker. Indeed, because of their combined salaries, this quartet was famously branded the "$100,000 infield."

In 1914, Collins hit .344, McInnis .314, and Baker .319 while also leading the AL with nine homers, and Barry batted .242. Noted baseball maven Bill James has called this particular group the greatest infield in the history of baseball.

But then the appearance of the latest (and last) challenger to the existing pair of major leagues compelled Mack to dismantle his second superteam.

THE FEDERAL LEAGUE was financed by three men who had made their respective fortunes by selling oil, ice, and baked goods. Starting as the Columbia League, a minor league outfit, in 1912, the name change accompanied the declaration that the eight extant teams now considered themselves to be of major league caliber. Four of these teams competed directly with AL or NL franchises in Chicago, St. Louis, Pittsburgh, and Brooklyn. The other four were situated in Baltimore, Buffalo, Indianapolis, and Kansas City.

A salary war similar to the financial uproar created by the Players' League back in 1890 attracted several noteworthy Irish players to the upstart organization. Bill McKechnie abandoned the New York Yankees, Jack Quinn left the Boston Braves, Davy Jones fled Detroit, and Ad Brennan and Mickey Doolan quit the Phillies.

Although Mack's team lost only one player—Danny Murphy, a .300-hitting spare outfielder—the A's were faced with the prospect of radically increasing their payroll to prevent their stars from leaving. However, in so doing, the Athletics were at great risk of not only losing money but also of having to declare bankruptcy.

Mack's only recourse was to fill the coffers by dismantling his

team, and then start all over. Eddie Collins was sold to the Chicago
White Sox, and Frank Baker went to the Yankees in exchange for a
bundle of money. Then early in the 1915 season, Jack Barry was sold
to the Boston Red Sox. McInnis was the only holdover, but he was
traded to the Bosox in 1917.

Despite the deep pockets of its backers, the Federal League failed
to attract sufficient paying customers to last. After their initial 1914
season, they instituted an antitrust suit against both the AL and the
NL. However, the suit languished on the calendar of a federal judge
named Kenesaw Mountain Landis (who was destined to become the
commissioner of baseball after the Black Sox scandal of 1919). The
delay sealed the doom of the Federals.

Meanwhile, on July 7, 1914, the Baltimore franchise in the
International League couldn't compete at the gate with the FL's
Baltimore entry, prompting the Orioles' owner-manager, Jack Dunn,
to keep his team afloat by selling his best players. For the bargain-
basement sum of $10,000, Dunn offered Mack three players, includ-
ing a moonfaced pitcher named George Herman Ruth.

The local sportswriters had already dubbed Ruth "Dunn's Baby"
or "Babe," and he had impressed John McGraw during an exhibition
game between Baltimore and New York. Since Dunn was a onetime
teammate of McGraw's, he promised to give McGraw and the Giants
the first chance to buy Ruth if and when that option became available.
Only three months later, however, and for reasons of his own, Dunn
came to Mack.

Mack pleaded poverty, but referred Dunn to the Red Sox, who
were agreeable. Because of the broken promise, McGraw never forgave Dunn.

Turning down this particular deal was one reason why many
baseball watchers deemed Mack to be a cheapskate and even a miser.
Yet this image was disputed by an anecdote related by one of Mack's
longtime scouts, Harry O'Donnell.

One time Mr. Mack asked me to scout a team way out in the bushes and report back on its best player. When I saw him later I said, "That outfit ain't got anybody you could use, just nobody."

Mr. Mack said, "That's not what I sent you to do. Go back and get me a report on the best player they have."

So I went back. The guy was strictly Class C but I reported on him.

"Fine," said Mr. Mack, and paid the club owner, a widow who, I learned later, had to have the money to keep going, $5,000 for a useless prospect. He took that way to give her enough to keep the club.

Mack never changed his attire in his later years in the dugout—coat and tie and either a straw hat or a bowler—no matter how high the summertime temperature climbed. He'd sit in the middle of the bench, with his right hand holding his scorecard and his pencil, his left elbow resting on his knee, and his chin cupped in his left hand. Never moving, not even visiting the restroom or the water cooler. To coax a ball fair or foul or into or out of an outfielder's glove, Mack would occasionally use some body English. In an especially critical situation, he would rock back and forth on the bench.

After the 1915 season, four Federal League teams—Pittsburgh, Buffalo, Brooklyn, and Newark—were purchased lock, stock, and players by a combination of several AL and NL owners. In addition, the owners of the FL's St. Louis Terriers were permitted to buy the AL's St. Louis Browns, and the sale of the Chicago Cubs to the owners of the Chicago Whales was also allowed.

For the next seven seasons, Mack's Athletics wallowed in last place. The lowlight of this dismal stretch was the 1919 season, when they finished 36-104 with a .257 winning percentage, the lowest in the post-1900 history of the major leagues.

♣The A's next resurgence began in 1925 with the presence of three key Irish players—Jimmy Dykes, "Easy" Jim Poole, and Chick Galloway—plus half-Irish Mickey Cochrane. By 1927, Mack was renowned as the "Tall Tactician" and returned to public prominence with his picture (in coat, tie, and straw hat) gracing the cover of *Time* magazine. Two years later, the A's vaulted to the top of the game—winning the pennant and beating the Cubs in the World Series.

The 1929 season also included the most unlikely of happenings: Connie Mack actually cussing one of his players. Lefty Grove was notoriously temperamental and nothing stoked his anger more than errors committed by his fielders. During one game, he reacted to a pair of booted ground balls by lobbing meatballs to the next few hitters.

Back in the dugout, Mack and Grove engaged in a heated disagreement. The argument grew so heated that Mack was led to say, "And to hell with you, too, Robert." This marked the first and only time in his entire sixty-four-year career that any player ever heard Mack cuss.

Grove's reaction was to laugh, return to the mound, and win the game.

The Athletics' dominance continued in 1930, this time when they overcame the Cardinals in what was already being called the Fall Classic. The following season, the Cardinals returned the favor, marking the end of the A's dynasty by winning the seventh game of the series.

In 1932, Philadelphia had an excellent 94-60 season, only to finish a distant thirteen games behind the Ruth-Gehrig Yankees.

By the end of the 1932 season, the Great Depression was firmly established, and making an honest buck was a difficult task for anybody, much less a pro baseball team. Consequently, to save his franchise, financial considerations once more forced Mack to start breaking up his third (and last) elite team.

He traded away most of his great players, including a few headed for the Hall of Fame. As for the A's, they were only headed for last place—which is precisely where they finished in ten of Mack's remaining eighteen seasons in the command seat.

When he was in his seventies, Mack would often go home after the first game of a doubleheader played in Philadelphia and listen to the nightcap on the radio. But throughout the game, he'd constantly pace his living room and try to soothe himself by jingling the change in his pants pocket.

Here's how Red Smith described Mack in his most senior seasons: "Toward the end he was old, sick and suddenly a figure of forlorn dignity bewildered . . . as the baseball monument he had build crumbled away."

He was nearly eighty-eight when he finally retired. "I'm not quitting because I'm too old," he insisted. "I'm quitting because I think the people want me to."

Mack sold his beloved A's to Arnold Johnson after the 1954 season, and shortly thereafter the franchise was moved to Kansas City.

Connie Mack passed away on February 8, 1956, at the ripe old age of ninety-three.

During his fifty-three years managing the Pirates and the Athletics, Mack amassed 3,731 wins and 3,948 losses—both all-time records that will never be surpassed.

In addition to winning nine pennants and five World Series, Mack left a lasting legacy that is all about intelligence, loyalty, resourcefulness, and, most of all, dignity.

PRESENT-DAY INTERVIEW

She's ninety-seven years old, confined to a wheelchair, and is the only one of Connie Mack's eight offspring still among us, but Ruth Mack Clark's mind is still vibrant and very much alive.

"It's true that I never had much of a sense of Irish history," she says, "but my mom's maiden name was Hoolihan so I do know that I'm more than slightly Irish. There's a family tree somewhere, probably up in the attic. Yet I recall that Dad's folks came from County Kerry. In any case, what my parents emphasized about our heritage was to always stick up for the Irish people."

While she does stick up for her father's reputation as a gentlemanly manager who never went on the field to argue with umpires and never let a cussword pass his lips, Clark can't help being totally honest. "When he strongly disagreed with an umpire's call," she says, "he would wait until the game was over, then linger in the tunnel leading from the field to the dressing rooms. That's when Dad would let the umpires have it in no uncertain terms. Yes, Dad was mild-mannered, but he was also a fierce competitor."

However, by the time he returned home from any given game, Mack was totally even-keeled. "Even during his last few years when the Athletics were a very poor team, we couldn't tell by his demeanor whether they had lost or won the game. It always amazed me how he could hold himself together after the most agonizing losses."

There was one occasion, though, when Mack's postgame behavior was unusual. "He was just bubbling over with enthusiasm as soon as he walked in the door," Clark recalls. "He couldn't wait to tell us how the team was so many runs behind before making a remarkable comeback to beat the Yankees. The Yankees!"

"I was sitting behind my parents and watching a game in the 1951 World Series between the Yankees and the Giants," she says, "and I happened to clap my hands with glee when the Giants scored a run. Dad quickly turned to me and said, 'Don't you ever forget that you're an American Leaguer.'"

Among Clark's most poignant memories is a special pregame celebration during the 2000 season in Oakland. "The A's were honoring Dad," she remembers, "and Art Howe was the team's manager. Well, as he escorted me onto the field he was dressed up like Dad with the suit, necktie, celluloid collar, and straw hat. Not only did he look like Dad, but having him at my side almost felt like Dad was there. It had me in tears. The only blemish on the occasion was that the Yankees won the game."

"If I was allowed to," Clark added, "I would have hated the Yankees."

Chapter Eighteen

Take Me Out to the Ball Game

Katie Casey was baseball mad.
Had the fever and had it bad.

Nelly Kelly was sure some fan,
She would root just like any man.

THERE WAS A new song in the air early in the new century—"Take Me Out to the Ball Game." The lyrics were scribbled on a scrap of paper in 1908 while Jack Norworth was riding a subway in New York. He was a vaudevillian who had never attended a baseball game, and neither had his partner, who soon composed the melody.

Nor was he Irish, but he certainly felt the need to use the lyrical nature of an Irish girl's name to hook the listener. One modern sportswriter, Frank Deford, has even made the whimsical proposal that Katie Casey was the metaphorical daughter of that mighty slugger of the Mudville nine.

The chorus, of course, has become familiar to men, women, and children of all ages, yet the rest of the song remains obscure:

Katie Casey was baseball mad,
Had the fever and had it bad.

Just to root for the home town crew,
Ev'ry sou [penny]
Katie blew.
On a Saturday her young beau
Called to see if she'd like to go
To see a show, but Miss Kate said "No,
I'll tell you what you can do:"

Katie Casey saw all the games,
Knew the players by their first names.
Told the umpire he was wrong,
All along,
Good and strong.
When the score was just two to two,
Katie Casey knew what to do,
Just to cheer up the boys she knew,
She made the gang sing this song:

In 1927, Norworth revised the lyrics to embody the same baseball passion in another Irish lass:

Nelly Kelly loved baseball games,
Knew the players, knew all their names.
You could see her there ev'ry day,
Shout "Hurray"
When they'd play.
Her boyfriend by the name of Joe
Said, "To Coney Isle dear, let's go,"
Then Nelly started to fret and pout,
And to him, I heard her shout:

Norworth went on to pen several other pop hits, including "Shine on, Harvest Moon." His original hit was first played at a minor league game in 1934, a year before several major league ball clubs made the communal singing of the chorus part of the in-game routines. Several humbuggers have objected to this inclusion of the song in the traditional seventh-inning stretch, their main point being the absurdity of fans who are already in the ballpark asking to be taken to the "old ball game."

IN THE EARLY 1900s, as ever, Irishmen were setting records and making news—of both significant and dubious kinds.

1902

Two Irishmen made historic contributions during the 1902 season.

♣Nixey Callahan hurled the AL's first no-hitter on September 20.

♣And back on June 3, hard-hitting pitcher Mike O'Neill not only won 18 games with the St. Louis Cardinals, but also blasted the first-ever pinch-hit grand slam.

1903

♣An Irish pitcher had a huge hand in helping the Boston Red Sox win the first World Series ever played.

Bill Dinneen won three of the Sox's five victories in the best-of-nine format, capping his performance by shutting out Pittsburgh, 3–0, in the deciding game.

1904

♣Dan McGann, a hard-hitting outfielder for the Giants, stole five bases in a game played on May 27. This feat would stand alone as a NL record until 1974, when Davey Lopes matched McGann.

♣On May 14, Cubs outfielder Jack McCarthy sprained his ankle when he stepped on the large hand broom the umpire used to sweep off home plate. Henceforth umps were instructed to use pocket-sized whisk brooms.

♣The Red Sox were for sale, and John "Honey Fitz" Fitzgerald (grandfather to John, Robert, and Edward Kennedy) put together a syndicate that made a generous bid to take over the team. But the president of the American League, worried that he'd never be able to control the notoriously independent Irishman, nixed any deal. Seven years later, a group of Irish-backed investors, but without Fitzgerald, finally purchased the franchise.

1905

♣On September 14, the two Irish members of the Cubs' immortal double-play combination, shortstop Joe Tinker and second baseman Johnny Evers, got into a vicious fistfight on the field during an exhibition game in Indiana. Tinker took exception to Evers's stranding several of his teammates in the hotel lobby when he sped off by himself in a taxi that was supposed to take them to the ballpark.

While Tinker and Evers continued to team up for routinely sensational twin killings until 1913, they didn't speak to each other for thirty-three years.

♣On September 27, 1905, good ol' Bill Dinneen pitched a no-hitter against the White Sox.

Later, Dinneen became one of the most respected umpires in AL history. He called balls and strikes for five other no-hitters, making him the only individual in major league history to pitch a no-hitter *and* call one as a plate umpire.

♣He went on to tie the record set by another Irishman, Tommy Connolly, by officiating in eight World Series.

1906

♣Overseen by owner Charles Comiskey, the White Sox not only won their first World Series, but were also major league baseball's most profitable franchise. "I started with fifty dollars back in 1877," Comiskey boasted, "and look where I am now."

Indeed, he was the baseball king of Chicago, with both major political parties frequently begging him to run for mayor. Comiskey's response to this importuning was always the same: "I'd rather win a pennant than an election."

His transformation from a rowdy, confrontational, crank-rousing ballplayer to a prominent civic leader was remarkable, but for the next twelve years he would be a pillar of respectability.

♣To circumvent the prohibition against playing ball on Sunday, the Brooklyn Superbas charged no admission fee on the Sabbath, requiring fans to purchase team programs instead. Even so, on June 16, president Charles Ebbets, along with Ned Hanlon and Joe Kelley, the Irish managers of the Superbas and the visiting Cincinnati Reds, were arrested. A local judge quickly dismissed the charges, the arrestees were set free, and the game resumed.

♣Charles "Red" Dooin was with the Phillies in his eighth year as a major league catcher. Tired of having his shins repeatedly bruised by foul tips, Dooin rigged up a pair of papier-mâché guards that he wore under his stockings when behind the plate and in the batter's box. His peers derided him for being a sissy.

1907

♣An Irishman was indirectly involved with the major league's initial in-season suicide: Jimmy Collins had coached the Boston Pilgrims during a woeful 49-105 season in 1906. In lieu of being fired, Collins was suspended at season's end and replaced by Chick Stahl, who was expected to function as the team's player-manager.

In his heyday, Stahl was a fine hitter, batting .354 in his rookie season (1897) with the Boston Beaneaters. He jumped to the Boston Pilgrims in 1901 without missing a beat or many base hits. In 1906, Stahl hadn't missed a game and hit a disappointing .286, yet his lifetime average was still .305.

Stahl's plan was to become a part-time player and concentrate on his managerial duties. But, at the conclusion of spring training, as the Pilgrims made their way to Boston, several players noted that Stahl seemed to be depressed. So much so that he raised the possibility of killing himself. Then, on March 28, prior to an exhibition game in West Baden, Indiana, Stahl died after drinking four ounces of carbolic acid.

The note he left was addressed to his teammates: "Boys, I just couldn't help it. You drove me to it."

Nobody concerned was able to specify Stahl's motivation, especially since he was always a carefree, live-it-up kind of guy who had girlfriends stashed all over the country. Perhaps the team's inferior play in spring training was the cause. Perhaps there was a woman involved.

The mystery was never solved.

♣Because of his Irish roots, Roger Bresnahan's nickname was "Duke of Tralee" after the small town in County Kerry that his parents hailed from. He was also a splendid receiver behind the plate and a good enough batsman (.279 over seventeen years) to eventually be honored in the Hall of Fame.

Bresnahan's most troublesome problem was the number of foul tips, wild pitches, and sliding base runners that kept his shins bruised and himself out of action for weeks at a time. Red Dooin's inadequate papier-mâché shin protectors gave Bresnahan the idea to fashion something more substantial. He eventually adapted equipment worn by wicket keepers during cricket matches and came up with a pair of effective and serviceable shin guards.

He wore them for the first time on April 11, the Opening Day of the 1907 season, and endured the ridicule of his peers. But Bresnahan's makeshift shin guards worked and were soon copied by other major league catchers.

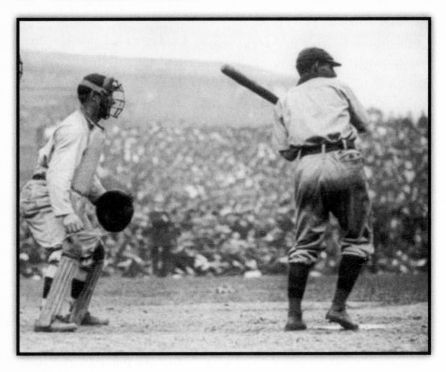

Roger Bresnahan catching for the Giants, 1908

♣At 5'6" and 140 pounds, Miller Huggins looked more like a lep-rechaun than a full-sized Irishman. If he also hit like a lightweight (.265 and only nine home runs over thirteen seasons), Miller was adept at drawing walks and stealing bases, and was a slick glove man at second base for the Reds and Cardinals.

Imagine the hometown fans' surprise and elation when Huggins led off a game on June 19, 1907, by clouting a homer against the almost invincible Christy Mathewson. Indeed, the fans showed their appreciation after the game by presenting Huggins with a pair of shoes, a gold watch, a five-pound box of chocolates, a scarf pin, and a Morris chair.

Years later, the "Mighty Mite" would earn admittance into baseball heaven (Cooperstown, 1964) by managing the powerhouse Yankees of the 1920s.

1908

♣John "Jiggs" Donohue of the Detroit Tigers led the AL's first basemen in fielding percentage, assists, and putouts from 1905 to 1907, and his 1,846 putouts in 1907 remains the major league standard.

On May 31, 1908, Donohue set a single-game record when he registered twenty putouts in a nine-inning game.

♣Mike "Turkey" Donlin won the 1908 opening game for the Giants at the Polo Grounds with a dramatic home run. What was more dramatic, literally, about that event, is that Donlin had hit .334 in 1906, but left in '07 with his wife, Mable, to go on the vaudeville circuit to play the lead role in a short comedy titled *Stealing Home*. A critic from *Variety* loved his performance, writing, "Mike Donlin as a polite comedian is quite the most delightful vaudeville surprise you ever enjoyed."

Appropriately for a stage actor, on July 30, 1908, after drawing a walk, Donlin began yelling to the umpire that the pitcher had dallied more than the allowed twenty seconds between pitches. The umpire, a fellow Irishman named Jimmy Johnstone, thumbed Donlin from the game. Donlin quickly ran to the clubhouse, changed into his civilian clothes, and was able to keep a dinner date with his wife.

So far as is known, no other hitter has ever been ejected from a game for protesting his receiving a free pass.

However, Donlin made much more money on the stage than he did on the ball field, so he went back in front of the footlights in 1909. Donlin returned to the diamond on a part-time basis in 1911 and completed his career with a superlative .333 batting average.

Donlin is still another Irish player who rightfully belongs in Cooperstown.

♣In 1908, an Irishman who did make the Hall of Fame, albeit in 1957, accomplished something no other player had up to that point.

Sam Crawford, one of the greatest sluggers of the dead-ball years, became the first player to lead both leagues in home runs in his career.

He led the NL with 16 in 1901, and then the AL with 7 in '08. Not astonishing numbers, except for their time.

What is astonishing, however, is that Crawford retired in 1915 as the all-time leader in triples (309)—still the record, and more than double the number accumulated by such speedsters as Mays, Rose, and Brock.

SEVERAL IRISHMEN WERE involved in the foreshadowing of one of the most controversial games in history. The setup contest took place on September 4, 1908, when the Cubs visited the Pirates.

Pittsburgh was batting in the bottom of the ninth with two outs, the bases loaded, and the score tied. That's when Owen Wilson lined a single to center that apparently scored Fred Clarke from third with the winning run. But the runner on first, following the usual practice at the time, instead of running to touch second base, made an abrupt left turn and headed for the dugout.

Johnny Evers, the Cubs' ever-alert second baseman, got his hands on the ball and tagged the untouched base to register the third out on a force play.

However, the only umpire on duty was the perpetually unhappy Hank O'Day, who had already left the field. When apprised of Evers's deed, O'Day claimed that because the run scored before the third out was registered, the run counted and the game was over. According to the rulebook at that time, however, O'Day was mistaken. Even so, an appeal to the National League president, Harry Pulliam, supported O'Day.

Nineteen days later, the Giants and the Cubs were locked in a tight race for the pennant and faced off for a critical contest in New York. The score was 1–1 in the home team's half of the ninth inning with two outs and Harry "Moose" McCormick the runner on first.

Fred Merkle was the batter, a light-hitting rookie who was making his first start of the season only because the Giants' regular first base-man was injured. But Merkle lined a single to right that moved the potential winning run, in the person of McCormick, to third.

Next up was New York's veteran shortstop, Al Bridwell, who noticed that Merkle was taking an unusually long lead off first base. Thinking that Merkle was on the verge of making a foolish attempt to steal second, Bridwell waved to him to drastically shorten his lead off first. Bridwell then proceeded to drill a line drive into center field that scored McCormick and apparently ended the game.

It should be noted that the Giants' clubhouse was situated in distant center field, and that the fans at the Polo Grounds were in the habit of storming the field to touch, congratulate, or perhaps cuss the players immediately after the end of every game. So strategic dashes to the safety of the clubhouse were routine—and before he placed a foot on second base, that's precisely what Merkle did, even as the ball was still rolling toward the distant fence.

The two umpires, Hank O'Day and Bob Emslie, were also quick to abandon the field.

But Johnny Evers noticed that Merkle had failed to touch second, and that a force play was still in order. Evers screamed for the Cubs' center fielder to retrieve the ball and throw it to him.

The plot thickened, however, when the Giants' third-base coach—none other than "Iron Man" Joe McGinnity—saw what Evers was up to, ran onto the field, intercepted the ball, and hurled it over the left-field bleachers and into the street. Undeterred, Evers came up with another baseball from the Cubs' bench, tagged second, and declared that the run didn't count.

Chicago's player-manager, Frank Chance, then pulled the umpires back onto the field. Since O'Day was the senior umpire, an appeal was lodged, claiming that not only should the game still be tied, but that also, since McGinnity had interfered with a live ball, and since thousands of fans were running riot on the field, the game should be forfeited to the Cubs.

O'Day demurred, saying that he'd have to consult the league office before making a definitive ruling. A few hours later, safe in his hotel room, O'Day declared the game to have ended in a 1–1 tie.

A further appeal to NL president Henry Pulliam led to three days of deliberation, after which O'Day's decision was upheld and the game was officially declared a 1–1 tie. In making this judgment, Pulliam claimed to see no inconsistency with the nearly identical circumstances of the September 4 game and the game of the twenty-third. According to Pulliam, on both occasions he was merely supporting O'Day's reporting of facts.

Since New York and Chicago ended the season tied for first place, the disputed game was replayed on October 4. On the mound for the Giants was the formidable Christy Mathewson, but the Giants hatched a plan that was sure to give them even more of an edge: since McGinnity's aching arm made him a noncombatant, and Chance always hit well against Mathewson, McGinnity was supposed to bait Chance into engaging in a fight that would get both of them ejected. However, despite being cursed, physically pushed, and even having his toes stomped by McGinnity, Chance was too smart to be suckered in and the plan was foiled.

The Cubs won, 4–2, with Chance getting a key hit. Since Chicago won the pennant by a game over New York, what the newspaper branded "Merkle's Bonehead" play was extremely costly. In any event, the Cubs went on to sweep the Tigers in the World Series.

But neither McGraw nor the Giants blamed Merkle for the critical loss. Instead, they put the onus on O'Day. Merkle went on to play another eight years for McGraw's Giants, plus nine more seasons with the Dodgers, the Cubs, and the Yankees.

Bridwell, though, always felt that if he hadn't shortened Merkle's lead, second base would have been touched, and the Giants would have won both the game and the pennant.

♣Meanwhile, in the American League, the White Sox's Ed Walsh pitched a still-unequaled twentieth-century record of 464 innings en route to becoming the last major league pitcher to win forty games in a single season. Walsh's primary weapon was his spitball.

How good was this pitch?

Here's what Hall of Famer Sam Crawford had to say about Hall of Famer Walsh: "I think that the ball disintegrated on the way to the plate and the catcher put it back together again. I swear, when it went past the plate it was just the spit that went by."

1909

This season had some highlights—and lowlights—for some Irish ballplayers and officials.

♣Mike Powers was nicknamed "Doc" because he attended medical school during the off-seasons and succeeded in earning his degree. On the field he was a sturdy, if light-hitting, catcher with Connie Mack's Athletics. On April 12, the opening day of the A's season, he was so intent on tracking a foul pop-up that he failed to notice how rapidly he was approaching a railing. The impact was significant enough to cause Powers severe abdominal pain. After being rushed to a hospital, exploratory surgery discovered an intestinal blockage that required the removal of most of his intestinal tract. Powers died on April 26.

It was commonly believed that the Irishman's demise was the first on-field fatality in major league history.

♣The Iron Man's arm finally began to rust. After averaging 344 innings for each of his ten seasons, and after being the pro game's leading winner five times, the thirty-nine-year-old Joe McGinnity was released by the Giants on February 27. But if he no longer had the powerhouse stuff to dominate major league hitters, McGinnity could still crank up his fastball to pitch effectively for thirteen more seasons in the minor leagues—winning twenty games six times. When he was fifty-five, McGinnity worked 85 innings as pitcher-manager and part-owner of a team in Dubuque, Iowa.

The end came in 1929, when McGinnity failed to recover from a bad fall.

More indicative of his mastery than his lifetime major league record of 246-142 is McGinnity's 2.66 ERA. Joe McGinnity is another proud Irishman to grace the Hall of Fame.

♣If Arlie Latham's coaching abilities were not highly regarded by many of the Giants, John McGraw valued his old teammate's willingness to help out in emergencies. Back in 1887, Latham had stolen 109 bases for the St. Louis Brown Stockings in the American Association, but he had hung up his spikes in 1899. However, when the Giants were hamstrung by several injuries to starting players, McGraw activated Latham.

The onetime infielder played two games at first base, went hitless in two at-bats, and was used twice as a pinch runner. It was in the latter capacity that on August 18, during the late innings of New York's 14-1 win over Philadelphia, Latham surprised everybody in the ballpark by taking off for second on the first pitch.

By virtue of this not-so-instant replay of his youthful successes, the forty-nine-year-old Latham is still in the books as being the most elderly major leaguer to ever steal a base.

♣NL president Harry Pulliam was a hard worker whose resourcefulness was echoed in his personal motto: "Take nothing for granted in baseball."

Even so, Pulliam wilted under the pressure of adjudicating the disputed Merkle's boneheaded game. Immediately after his decision ordering the game to be replayed, Pulliam took several months' leave. Although he returned for the start of the 1909 season, Pulliam's depression never lifted.

On July 29, 1909, while seated in his lodgings at the New York Athletic Club, Pulliam shot himself in the heart and died the next day.

There were no games played when he was buried on August 1.

1910

♣During his active career (1889–1907), Jimmy McAleer was a quick-footed center fielder with a slow bat. After retiring, he became a manager of the St. Louis Browns for eight years before assuming the same position with Washington in 1910.

McAleer is credited with convincing William Howard Taft to pioneer what became a treasured tradition when, on April 14, the president stood in his field-side box and tossed the official game ball to the home team's catcher, on Opening Day in D.C.

♣Jimmy Archer, a catcher for the Cubs, was one of the last major league players to be born in Ireland (Dublin, May 13, 1883). While making the requisite journey through the minor leagues, Archer usually spent his off-seasons in Toronto working for a barrel maker. But a misstep in the winter of 1903 caused Archer to fall into a vat of boiling sap and seriously burn his throwing arm. As the injury slowly healed it became increasingly evident that Archer's biceps were permanently contracted. However, instead of being a hindrance, the shortening of the muscle had the surprising effect of adding considerable zip to his throws to second base even when he released the ball from a squatting position.

As a result, Archer was always among the league leaders in assists by catchers—and led the National League in that category in 1912. Late in July 1910, Archer secured an honored place in the record books when, in a nine-inning game, he threw out seven hopeful base stealers.

♣On October 9, an Irish third baseman was a featured player in the most hotly contested competition for a batting title the game has ever seen.

Because of his shin-seeking spikes and hair-trigger temper, Ty Cobb was hated by virtually all of his opponents and most of his teammates. On the last day of the 1910 season, Cobb was hitting .385, and Cleveland's Napoleon Lajoie was the runner-up with .376. Cobb opted to sit out Detroit's last two games to ensure that his average would not fall, but Cleveland was playing a doubleheader against St. Louis so Lajoie anticipated getting anywhere from 8 to 10 at-bats.

The Browns so detested Cobb that John "Red" Corriden was

instructed to play way, way back at third whenever Lajoie came to the plate, and the rookie gladly obliged. Lajoie took advantage of the situation by dropping six bunts toward third base that Corriden had no chance of fielding. In Lajoie's other at-bats, he smacked a sharp single to left field, and was also awarded a bogus hit when the shortstop made a wild throw on a routine ground ball.

Lajoie finished at .3840947, second best to Cobb's .3850693.

Chapter Nineteen

Faustian Bargain

I don't think there's any point in being Irish if you don't
think the world is going to break your heart eventually.
—Daniel Patrick Moynihan

AFTER THE GIANTS failed to win three consecutive World Series
(1911–13, the first and last to the A's), pitcher Christy Mathewson
claimed that the Giants were "a team of puppets worked from the
bench by a string." And John McGraw was the puppetmaster, who
deprived his players of any personal creativity and initiative. As a result, the Giants lacked self-confidence and were liable to make mis-
judgments and boneheaded plays at critical moments.

No wonder that McGraw finished second to Connie Mack on
a pair of significant lists: career wins (3,582 to 2,763) and World
Series won (5 to 3). However, McGraw bested his contemporary in
two other important categories: pennants won (10 for McGraw to
9 for Mack) and lifetime winning percentage (.586 to .484). In addition, McGraw's teams suffered only four losing seasons, compared to
twenty-five for Mack.

The extenuating circumstances here are critical, however, since McGraw's Giants were always backed by owners who had much more financial resources than Mack ever had available. Consequently, McGraw was never compelled to break up any of his championship teams for monetary reasons; Mack had to do it three times.

Even so, there are also a host of similarities between these two Irish managers who dominated baseball up through World War I.

McGraw first saw the light of day in Truxton, New York, the first of seven children born to an Irish immigrant and his second wife. An incurable fever decimated the family in the winter of 1884–85, when John's mother, one half sister, and three siblings perished. Jobs were hard to come by, and those that were available paid meager wages. It was therefore understandable that McGraw's father had no patience for his son's frittering away his time playing baseball and insisted that the boy spend more time earning money. When the old man became abusive, the twelve-year-old boy ran away from home and was raised by a kindly neighbor, Mary Goddard.

During his years as part of Goddard's household, McGraw took on several jobs that allowed him to save money to buy baseballs and the magazines that chronicled the doings of his heroes.

After proving to be the best player on his high school team, McGraw began climbing the ladder of amateur, semipro, and minor league teams until he reached the American Association's edition of the Baltimore Orioles in 1891. Over the course of his sixteen-year major league career, McGraw compiled a .334 batting average, topping out at .391 in 1899. Moreover, his skill at drawing walks ranks his lifetime .466 on-base percentage (a retroactive stat) third of all time, behind only Ted Williams (.482) and Babe Ruth (.474).

McGraw functioned as player-manager for both the Orioles (1899, 1901–2) and the Giants (1902–6) before going to the bench and the coaching lines full-time. His move from Baltimore in the AL to the NL's New York franchise was a controversial one: in July 1902, McGraw was under suspension due to one of his frequent rowdy confrontations with umpires, so he simply jumped leagues—taking Joe McGinnity, Dan McGann, and Roger Bresnahan along with him.

McGraw certainly didn't restrain his umpire baiting for his new employers. "Kickers are born and not made," he said, using the period term for arguing. McGraw went so far as to claim that his habitual "kicking" gained his team fifty additional runs per season.

Despite his game-time persona, McGraw was always a soft touch when approached by down-and-out former players. It was estimated that sob stories extracted at least $2,000 every year from him.

McGraw was also celebrated for his loyalty. On September 22, 1904, he inserted into the Giants lineup two aging ex-teammates who happened to be Irish.

Ed Brouthers was forty-six years old, had been retired for eight years, and went hitless in four at-bats as the Giants lost to the Reds, 7–5. At age fifty-three, "Orator Jim" O'Rourke hadn't played in eleven years, but caught the entire game and cracked a solid single in his four trips to the plate. The game was otherwise meaningless since the season was just about over, with the Giants winning the pennant by a margin of thirteen games over Chicago.

Many years later, McGraw demonstrated his loyalty on several other occasions, finding jobs for old Irish stars like Brouthers, Mickey Welch, and Amos Rusie as night watchmen and press box attendants at the Polo Grounds.

Sometimes McGraw's benevolence had to necessarily take a more surreptitious turn, as when he tried to help Arthur "Bugs" Raymond, an outstanding spitball pitcher with a penchant for drinking too much and too often. Raymond's career peaked in 1906 when he won 18 games and showed a 2.47 ERA for McGraw's Giants. But to McGraw's dismay, Raymond simply couldn't stay on the wagon. Levying significant fines on Bugs whenever he broke training or simply vanished from a ballpark did not deter him. If he was broke, Raymond would go into a bar, pull a baseball from his pocket, autograph it on the spot, and then drink to his heart's content.

"After he's had a night out," said Christy Mathewson, "you shouldn't get too close to Bugs because his breath could stop a freight train."

Unbeknownst to Bugs, McGraw was sending the fine money to Raymond's wife. But the spitballer only lasted parts of two more seasons in pro baseball, compiling a record of 10-15, after which he returned to his hometown of Chicago and did some pitching and umpiring in semipro leagues.

Raymond was found dead in a hotel room on September 7, 1912, his skull fractured and his brain filled with blood as a result of a pair of fights he had been in a few nights earlier. Raymond was only thirty and, while McGraw mourned his premature ending, Mugsy also said this: "That man took seven years off my own life."

Combined with his ruthless attention to detail and his understanding of the day-to-day vicissitudes of the game, McGraw's fidelity to current and former players made him a respected and admired figure in the clubhouse. Fred Snodgrass played under McGraw's direction for eight years (1908–15) and later offered this testimony:

> Sometimes Mr. McGraw would bawl the dickens out of me, as he did everybody else. Any mental error, any failure to think, and McGraw would be all over you. And I do believe he had the most vicious tongue of any man who ever lived. Absolutely! Sometimes that wasn't very easy to take, you know.
>
> However, he'd never get on you for a mechanical mistake, a fielding error or failure to get a hit. He was a very fair man, and it was only when you really had it coming to you that you got it. And once he'd bawl you out good and proper . . . then he'd forget it. He wouldn't ever mention it again.

Even after Snodgrass dropped an easy fly ball that cost the Giants a game in the World Series of 1912, McGraw added $1,000 to his next contract.

McGraw's largesse reached beyond down-at-the-heels ex-teammates and his current players. At the end of each season, McGraw would arrange for the Giants' used uniforms to be presented to the baseball team at the Auburn Prison in upstate New York.

Perhaps he was motivated by a belief that Auburn could easily have been his youthful destination but for baseball and the grace of God.

Nor was McGraw's appreciation of players' talents dimmed by the major leagues' institutional racism. While vacationing in Warm Springs, Georgia, prior to spring training, McGraw chanced to witness an amateur team practicing on a diamond near his hotel. His critical eye locked on to Charley Grant, a second baseman for a powerful black pro team in Chicago who was currently employed as a bellhop at the same hotel where McGraw was staying. McGraw marveled at Grant's polished moves and decided that the young man was big-league ready.

Since Grant had straight hair and sharp features, McGraw concocted a scheme that he hoped would enable the young man to play for the Giants. Grant agreed to adopt the alias of Chief Tokahoma along with a bogus ancestry that included a fictional mother who was said to be living in Lawrence, Kansas.

But Charles Comiskey smoked out the ruse. "This Cherokee of McGraw's," said Comiskey, "is really Charley Grant, the crack Negro second-baseman, fixed up with war paint and a bunch of feathers. If McGraw tries to keep this so-called Indian, then I'll either put a Chinaman on third base or whitewash a colored player."

McGraw did sign Grant to a contract, but left him in Hot Springs after swearing that he'd be summoned to the big leagues sooner rather than later. Sadly, the summons never came.

In 1913, McGraw actually did sign a player who was believed to be 100 percent authentic Native American, but who was really one-quarter Irish. James Francis "Jim" Thorpe's grandmothers had Sac, Fox, and Potawatomi blood, his mother's father was French, and his paternal grandfather was Irish. At the time, Thorpe was generally considered to be the best athlete in the world.

McGraw signed Thorpe to a $5,000 contract more for his value as a gate attraction than as an attempt to improve the Giants roster. Indeed, Thorpe seldom played during the next three seasons, achieving a combined batting average of only .195 in 66 games.

After being sold to Cincinnati, Thorpe did have one historic at-bat in the major leagues. On May 2, 1917, the Reds' Fred Toney and the Cubs' Hippo Vaughn both pitched nine innings without yielding a hit. There was one out in the top of the tenth, and the Reds had runners on second and third via walks, when Thorpe hit a swinging bunt back to Vaughn. The ball was neatly fielded and thrown to catcher Art Wilson, but the ball bounced off his chest protector even as a run scored. Toney held the Cubs hitless in the home half of the tenth, and Thorpe was credited with the only RBI in the famous Double-No-Hit game.

After another go-round with the Giants and a brief sojourn with the Red Sox, Thorpe's major league career terminated after the 1919 season. For the next several years he played minor league baseball, as well as professional football and basketball.

Thorpe battled alcoholism after his active career was over, and died at age sixty-four of his third heart attack.

McGraw's modest rebellion against the prevailing racial prejudice is further demonstrated by what his players saw on March 15, 1918, when they arrived at the ballpark in Marlin, Texas, before a scheduled spring training workout. McGraw was already there, in uniform, hitting grounders and fly balls and offering instruction to more than a dozen black youngsters.

McGRAW WAS LIKEWISE ahead of his time in being a micromanager of nearly everything that happened on the field. He called for every pitchout, pickoff throw, stolen base, hit-and-run, sacrifice bunt, and suicide or safety squeeze. In addition, McGraw often bypassed his catchers and called every pitch.

Despite Christy Mathewson's complaints, McGraw's wire-pulling tactics have become the norm for the modern manager.

Before he started gaining weight—eventually nearly doubling the 120 pounds he weighed as a rookie—McGraw loved to occupy the third-base coaching box. From there he'd leap about, click his heels, clap the glove he started wearing after he split a finger trying to bare-hand a wicked foul line drive, shout at the umpire and at the opposing pitcher, and run to the plate to pat the shoulder of each hitter as he stepped into the batter's box.

Opponents claimed that McGraw's antics were designed to distract the pitcher, intimidate the ump, and stoke up the cranks. More often than not, McGraw's raucous efforts were successful.

During the off-season, McGraw sometimes played to smaller but even more appreciative audiences. After King Kelly set the precedent, numerous baseball celebrities became well-paid attractions on the vaudeville stage. In the 1912 off-season, McGraw was paid $3,000 per week for fifteen weeks to tour under the auspices of the B. F. Keith circuit. For delivering anecdotes, personal reminiscences, and brief monologues on the secrets of inside baseball, McGraw was the highest-remunerated vaudeville performer of the day.

All too frequently, though, McGraw's off-field behavior wasn't quite as socko at the box office. During a mini-vacation in Hot Springs, Arkansas, McGraw joined forces with a local sharpie to take on all challengers in pitching silver dollars into a basket on the hotel grounds. Tossing coins came almost as easy to McGraw as tossing baseballs, and the hustle netted about $2,300 before the police appeared to charge them with unlicensed public gambling. After each of them posted a two-hundred-dollar bond and delivered some ultrafriendly words and an autographed baseball, the local judge dismissed the charge.

McGraw needed more than some blarney and his signature to

get off the hook in October 1920, when he was indicted for violating the Volstead Act. He had purchased several bottles of bootleg liquor when his erratic driving caused a policeman to stop his car and inspect the contents of the backseat. It took hundreds of dollars in lawyers' fees plus the intervention of several hotshot New York politicos to save McGraw from serving time.

Like Connie Mack, McGraw took to wearing a coat and tie and remaining bench-bound in his later years. Another similarity was their superstitious nature, including a vulnerability to the supposed benefits of human good-luck charms.

In late July 1911, a thirty-year-old, 6'2", husky farm boy from Marion, Kansas, introduced himself to McGraw at the Planter's Hotel in St. Louis. "Mr. McGraw," the young man said in his slight German accent, "my name is Charles Victor Faust . . . and a few weeks ago I went to a fortune-teller who told me that if I joined the Giants and pitched for them that they would win the pennant."

McGraw was doubtful, but he understood that good ballplayers came in all ages, shapes, and sizes and could turn up anywhere at any time. So McGraw arranged for Faust to undergo a pregame tryout before the next day's game.

Faust showed up in his Sunday-go-to-meeting suit, accepted a glove from McGraw, and then went over signals for the six different pitches he claimed to have in his arsenal. After agreeing with each sign that McGraw flashed him, Faust went into an elaborate windmill windup with his pitching arm whirling in several circles before he delivered the pitch. However, no matter what signal McGraw gave, every pitch was exactly the same—a high school–caliber not-so-fastball.

"How's your hitting?" McGraw asked.

"Pretty good," said Faust.

"We're having batting practice right now," said McGraw, "so get a bat and go up there. I want to see you run, too, so run it out and see if you can score."

The joke soon spread to the Giants players. When Faust dribbled a meatball to the shortstop, the ball was intentionally fumbled as the hopeful player turned first, slid into second, slid into third, and finished with a flourish by sliding into home—tearing up his suit pants in the process.

But the Giants won the subsequent game, 9–0, so McGraw put Faust in a uniform and sat him on the bench the next day. With Faust repeating his pregame tryout routines, New York also won the remaining three games in the series, but McGraw had had enough. He instructed Faust to go back to the hotel, where a player contract and a train ticket to Chicago were supposedly waiting for him. The Giants then headed for the train station, leaving Faust in St. Louis, prior to their losing two of three games to the Cubs.

When the Giants returned to New York, Faust was waiting for them at the Polo Grounds. McGraw was quick to issue him another uniform and allowed him to warm up before the game—which New York won. The Giants were 4-0 with Faust on hand, and 1-2 in his absence. That was good enough for McGraw to become a believer.

From then on, Faust was in uniform and loosened his arm before every game, sincerely believing that he was going to pitch for the Giants on that *particular* day. Win followed win, leading the Giants to begin referring to Faust as "Victory."

McGraw made sure Faust had enough money in his pocket to afford a daily shave, haircut, and massage, as well as three square meals in upscale restaurants. To earn his keep, Faust sometimes assisted the Giants batboy, Dick Hennessey, and sometimes pitched batting practice, but mostly hung around and radiated good luck.

There were thirteen daily newspapers in New York and they competed with each other to present feature stories about the Giants' new mascot. With such perpetual publicity, Faust was soon offered, and accepted, $400 per week to wear a nondescript baseball uniform and appear six times a day on a vaudeville stage. His act consisted of incredibly clumsy and inept imitations of Ty Cobb,

Christy Mathewson, and Honus Wagner. And the audiences loved him, as well.

While Faust was absent, the Giants lost four straight games, prompting Faust to abandon the stage and show up at the Polo Grounds. "I've got to pitch today," he informed McGraw. "You fellows need me." And after Faust entertained the fans before the game with his exaggerated windup, the Giants broke their losing streak.

Late in the season, with the Giants well on their way to winning the pennant, McGraw sent Faust to the mound in the top of the ninth in a hopelessly lost home game against the Boston Braves. The leadoff batter hit a long double, the pitcher bunted him to third, and another long fly ball scored a run. Mike Donlin was laughing so hard that all he could manage was a feeble groundout to third. Even though the Giants made three legitimate outs in the last half of the inning, Faust was granted a turn at bat. He nudged a grounder back to the pitcher, and the Braves tossed the ball around the infield while Faust chugged around the bases until he was tagged out at home.

During the last inning of the regular season, Faust had another chance to pitch—this time against Brooklyn. The Dodgers hitters took mighty swings but went down without reaching base. In the bottom half of the ninth inning, Faust was sent to home plate in real time. He was deliberately (but gently) hit by a pitch, allowed to steal second and third, then scored on an infield out as the fans laughed and cheered.

With Faust on hand, the Giants went 39-9, prompting Connie Mack to opine that Faust was as valuable an asset to New York as Van Zelst was to his Athletics.

The two teams met in the 1911 World Series, with the A's winning in six games. Several of McGraw's players sincerely believed that they had lost only because Victory had been outjinxed by the more experienced Little Louie.

Faust was hugely disappointed by McGraw's failure to include him among the Giants' starting pitchers. In the off-season, Faust worked on pitching with his left hand to make himself twice as good. In fact, during spring training with the 1912 Giants, Faust yielded only four runs in pitching a complete game against an amateur team.

The Giants broke out of the gate with a sterling record of 54-11. McGraw, however, wanted nothing more to do with the traveling sideshow, and Faust was sent back to Kansas, never to return to the big leagues. The Giants cruised to the pennant, only to lose the World Series to the Red Sox.

After the 1914 season, Fred Snodgrass was in Seattle on the last leg of a barnstorming tour when Faust came to his hotel room. "I'm not very well," said Faust. "But I think if you could prevail on Mr. McGraw to send me to Hot Springs a month before spring training, I could get in shape and help the Giants win another pennant."

Snodgrass said that he would indeed speak to McGraw.

But Faust, responding to a summons from "Lulu," his imaginary girlfriend, left the hotel and walked all the way to Portland. He was in a daze when the police found him and wound up being committed to an insane asylum, where he perished of tuberculosis in 1915.

If McGraw's employment of a handicapped mascot was nothing new, he does deserve credit for several legitimate innovations. In 1909, he signed Arlie Latham, who had enjoyed a seventeen-year career playing first, as the game's first-ever full-time coach.

Latham was a notorious practical joker, earning the nom de diamond of "the Freshest Man on Earth." McGraw's idea was that Latham's pranks would keep the team loose and entertained. But several of the players couldn't stand Latham's wisecracking presence, nor his ill-advised instructions on the base paths. Fred Snodgrass once referred to Latham as "probably the worst third base coach who ever lived." Another player was so irate when Latham attempted to give him a hotfoot that he beat the older man to a bloody pulp in a hotel lobby.

Speaking of coaches, McGraw frequently brought Wilbert

Robinson to spring training to operate as the game's first pitching coach.

And in 1921, when McGraw added Hughie Jennings to his staff, the Giants became the first team to employ three coaches.

Besides hiring Latham, McGraw did make his share of monumental mistakes. During a spring training game in 1919, Babe Ruth clouted a stupendous home run over the palm trees in center that traveled at least five hundred feet. Everybody else on hand gasped in wild wonder, except for McGraw. Evidently nursing a lingering case of sour grapes, McGraw was not impressed.

"If he plays every day," groused McGraw, "the bum will hit into a hundred double plays before the season is over."

♣Lefty O'Doul was a converted pitcher who played the outfield for the 1928 Giants. In his first full season as a hitter, O'Doul batted an impressive .319, but once again McGraw was unimpressed. According to McGraw, the thirty-one-year-old O'Doul was too old, too slow, and too much of an Irish goof-off. So O'Doul was dealt away.

The very next season, with the Phils, O'Doul led the National League in hits (254) and batting average (.398). Three years later, he would repeat as the NL's best hitter, with a .368 average for the Dodgers.

Overall, O'Doul's lifetime mark of .349 places him among the most deserving players *not* in Cooperstown.

O'Doul achieved everlasting fame in other ways, however. As a baseball ambassador he is considered the driving force behind the game catching on in post–World War II Japan. As manager of the San Francisco Seals, he coached a young Joe DiMaggio, and his Lefty O'Doul's Restaurant and Cocktail Lounge—and his Bloody Mary—are Bay Area institutions. He is such a favorite son of San Francisco that a bridge over McCovey Cove bears his name.

Lefty O'Doul Bridge
(Wally Gobetz)

Perhaps Ruth and O'Doul are the exceptions proving the rule that John McGraw was an excellent judge of talent. Even more important, his aggressive, creative game plan always got the best out of his players, which goes a long way to explain why McGraw's teams won ten pennants and five World Series.

Two years after he left the game, and forty-one days short of his sixty-first birthday, John McGraw died in 1934, from complications resulting from prostate cancer.

McGraw's managing career extended for thirty-three seasons and his lifetime winning percentage of .589 ranks him third behind another pair of Irishmen, Joe McCarthy at .614 (more on him later) and Frank Selee at .598.

Irish winners.

Chapter Twenty

Scandal and War

... in recognition of his bravery and skill in hurling
bombs ...

*—Recommendation for awarding the
Canadian Military Cross to Billy O'Hara*

BY 1911, IRISH players were no longer the most successful ethnic
group in the major leagues.

Playing professional baseball was now a thoroughly respectable
career choice. Along with an increased number of Germans, Poles,
and players born below the Mason-Dixon Line, the huge success
of college-educated Christy Mathewson even made the game an
acceptable option for middle-class WASPs. At the same time, as the
influence of the Irish proliferated in urban areas, politics and law
enforcement became more accessible to Irish lads.

That's why only 17 percent of players in the major leagues in 1911
were Irish.

However, America's diamonds still retained an emerald hue, since
thirteen of the sixteen teams were managed by Irishmen.

Considering how much, and for how long, Irish players had dominated the game, it would be only natural to assume that any anti-
Irish bias was extinct.

Not so.

Reprising the Anson-era White Stockings, the Boston Red Sox were also divided by fierce ethnic rivalries. The ostensible origin of this latter division dated back to 1910, when an Irish rookie joined the team. His name was George Lewis, but he used his Irish-born mother's name, Duffy, as his handle.

Duffy Lewis was cocky for a mere rookie, and he vociferously objected to the hazing to which veterans traditionally subjected all rookies. Lewis's uppity attitude quickly earned the enmity of such important Boston players as Tris Speaker and Joe Wood.

Before long, the team split into two factions: The Irish Catholic contingent was led by Lewis and catcher Bill Carrigan, while the so-called Masons followed the leads of Speaker, Wood, and manager Jake Stahl. Jimmy McAleer was the team's president, but despite his Irish heritage he did his best to appear neutral.

After running away with the 1912 AL pennant and then besting the Giants in the World Series, Boston's internal antagonisms led to their fourth-place finish in 1913, forcing McAleer to take a stand. McAleer proved to be a green-blooded Irishman when he canned Stahl and replaced him with Carrigan. By 1915, the Red Sox beat the Phillies to reestablish themselves as the best team in the game.

Speaker was subsequently exiled to Cleveland and Wood's sore arm caused him to miss the entire 1916 season, and with that the Red Sox further demonstrated the value of their newly found harmony by repeating as World Series champs.

STILL, MAKE NO mistake, the Irish imprint on the game in the 1910s was strong, with plenty of surprising developments to go around.

1911

♣Irish-born Jack Doyle, aka "Dirty Jack," whose reputation for assaulting umpires was legendary, had once beaten umpire Thomas Lynch to a bloody pulp; on the lighter side, he'd wrestled Bob Emslie to the ground and attempted to snatch the ump's toupee off his bald dome.

Incredible it was, then, that in 1911, Lynch, now the head of the National League's umpiring staff, hired Doyle after receiving good reports on Dirty Jack's performance as a minor league arbitrator. By then, two umps per game was the norm, and they almost always traveled and worked in tandem. For some reason, Lynch paired Doyle with Emslie. Imagine the league-wide astonishment when the two former antagonists worked well together.

"Emslie and Doyle got along like Damon and Pythias," noted the erudite Mathewson. "This business makes strange bed-fellows."

♣A newsworthy rookie was pitcher Marty O'Toole, for whose services Pittsburgh paid the St. Paul Saints the record-breaking sum of $22,500. Considering that he had posted a 91-36 record since 1908 while pitching for various minor league teams, O'Toole seemed like a bargain.

Unfortunately for the Pirates, O'Toole was 3-2 in 1911, and his 159 walks issued led the NL. After two more lackluster seasons, O'Toole reverted to civilian life with a lifetime 27-36 record in the bigs.

1912

♣A pair of Irish brothers were instrumental in solidifying the NL's showcase franchise in Brooklyn. Charles Ebbets had plans to build a new 30,000-seat stadium. On January 2, 1912, he had even purchased a suitable parcel of land near busy Bedford Avenue. All that Ebbets required to make his latest dream come true was more money. His solution was to arrange for his Dodgers partner, Henry Medicus, to sell his 50 percent share of the team to brothers Steve and Ed McKeever and turn most of the money over to the building fund.

The stately, yet cozy, Ebbets Field opened for business in 1913.

♣The most bizarre game in baseball history took place on May 18, 1912, and involved a host of replacement Irishmen.

Blame Ty Cobb for igniting the situation when, on May 15, he leaped into the stands at the Polo Grounds and thrashed a fan who had been verbally abusing him. AL president Ban Johnson suspended Cobb and hit him with a $5,000 fine.

Cobb's Detroit Tigers teammates felt that it was the fan who had crossed the line and Cobb's reaction was justified. To protest the punishment, his teammates voted to go on strike and not play in a home game against the A's. Detroit's owner was aghast at the prospect of having to pay a large fine if the Tigers failed to field a team. So he instructed manager Hugh Jennings to sign a bunch of local amateur players and put them in the lineup.

Among these substitutes were Aloysius Travers, Jim McGarr, Patrick Meaney, and Jack Smith (born John Coffey). Also summoned into action was forty-eight-year-old Jim McGuire, one of Detroit's coaches. Travers pitched a complete game, but gave up a record 26 hits as the A's prevailed, 24–2. The Tigers regulars resumed their rightful places on the field two days later.

♣Toward the end of the 1912 season, Eddie Collins set a more positive post-1900 record that still stands when he stole six bases in one game.

To prove that this feat was not an aberration, Collins did an encore fifteen days later.

1913

♣The genesis of the long, fractious, and even bloody rivalry between the Brooklyn Robins/Dodgers and the New York Giants occurred during a party hosted by John McGraw on October 12, 1913. Just two days before, the Athletics had beaten the Giants in the World Series, the third consecutive championship lost by New York.

The get-together was billed as a reunion of McGraw's old Oriole teammates, and among the guests was Wilbert Robinson. Robbie had been the primary catcher of those potent Orioles teams and was currently serving as the Giants' third-base coach.

Despite the apparent bonhomie, McGraw was still rankled by his team's profound lack of success in these postseason competitions. McGraw was especially embittered by the down-to-the-wire nature of the Athletics' most recent triumphs—four of them by one or two runs.

After multiple toasts to past Orioles glories, McGraw suddenly turned on Robinson. All of the losses in the recent series resulted from Robinson's coaching mistakes: waving runners home only to see them thrown out at the plate, and not waving them home when they could easily have scored.

Robinson responded by claiming that McGraw had made more mistakes than anybody. Whereupon McGraw fired Robinson on the spot.

Before he stormed off the premises, Robinson emptied a glass of beer over McGraw's head.

Within weeks, Robinson was hired to manage the Brooklyn franchise, a position he held until 1931—finally retiring one year before McGraw did.

During the intervening eighteen seasons, the fierce competition between the two managers and their respective teams established a precedent of Giants-Dodgers animosity that still exists.

1914

♣On July 17, 1914, an incident occurred in the Polo Grounds that confirmed to true believers the transcendent nature of the Irish race.

After making a spectacular running, diving catch of a long line drive, John "Red" Murray was struck by lightning. Although he was knocked unconscious by the bolt, Murray was unharmed and finished the game.

♣That same year also bore witness to the implacable

contentiousness that has frequently been associated with the Irish. Over the course of the season, Johnny Evers set a record that wouldn't be equaled for forty-six years (by Jim Piersall), when he was ejected from seven ball games.

♣The 1914 season saw the inauguration of another hopeful major league—the Federal League. The charter members of this new organization were Baltimore, Brooklyn, Buffalo, Chicago, Indianapolis, Kansas City, Pittsburgh, and St. Louis. The resources of the Federal League's wealthy backers were demonstrated by their being able to plan, finance, and construct eight new ballparks during the three months prior to the opening of the season.

Most noteworthy among the Irish players who opted to join the new league were Jack Quinn and Joe Evers. The former won the first-ever FL game when he pitched the Brooklyn Tip-Tops (named after a hugely successful bakery in the borough) to a win over the Chicago Whales. The latter leaped at the chance to be player-manager of the Whales.

Other significant Irish league jumpers included Jim and Frank Delahanty, Bill McKechnie (a future Hall of Famer who would win four pennants and two World Series with various teams), and Al Bridwell (who had played shortstop for many of McGraw's best teams in New York).

♣Certainly the most marginal of the FL players was a John McGraw, who pitched two scoreless innings in the one game in which he appeared. His birthplace in Intercourse, Pennsylvania, led to numerous jokes that *this* John McGraw was the illegitimate son of *the* John McGraw.

♣To take advantage of the outstanding reputation of Irish players, the decidedly non-Irish Leopold Christopher Hoernschemeyer took the name of Lee Magee. He had been a serviceable outfielder for the Cardinals who couldn't resist the temptation to become a player-manager in the upstart league.

However, since there were now three professional teams in

Chicago and St. Louis, something had to give. And, after completing two financially disastrous seasons, the Federal League folded.

1917

♣Several Irishmen played prominent roles in a memorable ball game held on June 23, 1917.

Babe Ruth took the mound for the Red Sox against the visiting Washington Senators. The first batter he faced was Ray Morgan, who looked at four pitches that the umpire, one Clarence "Brick" Owens, judged to be out of the strike zone. Babe, however, took exception to every call and his abuse of Owens became more vehement with each pitch—until finally Owens thumbed him from the game.

Ruth's immediate reaction to his banishment was to charge Owens and punch his jaw with what was fortunately only a glancing blow.

Ernie Grady Shore was called in from the bullpen to replace Ruth, and right away, Morgan was thrown out trying to steal second base. Shore then proceeded to retire the next twenty-six hitters he faced.

Ruth was fined one hundred dollars, suspended for ten days, and obliged to make a public apology, while Shore was originally credited with pitching a perfect game. Shore's accomplishment remained on the record books until the 1970s, when an alteration of the relevant criteria reduced the official status of his gem to a "shared no-hitter."

1919

♣Only three Irishmen were directly involved in the 1919 Black Sox scheme: a small-time gambler named Joseph "Sport" Sullivan; Fred McMullin, a marginal player who demanded to be cut into the action when he overheard the guilty parties discussing the particulars of the deal; and, it must be said, team owner Charles Comiskey, who provided the motivation for the catastrophe that nearly destroyed the game.

When other teams were providing their players with $4 or $5 per diem, Comiskey would only pay them $3 even though the White Sox were perhaps the most profitable franchise in all of baseball. This may seem a trifling matter, but in terms of today's buying power $1 would be the equivalent of $13. The White Sox had reason to grumble every time they paid for a meal on the road.

Comiskey also loved to flaunt his extravagant lifestyle, which included a vacation complex in Wisconsin called Camp Jerome. During the course of any given summer, he would invite sportswriters and business executives there to enjoy unlimited quantities of booze and food. But when outfielder Oscar "Happy" Felsch asked Comiskey if he could possibly spend a few off-days in Camp Jerome, Comiskey huffed and said, "No ballplayers allowed."

Before a July 4 game in Detroit, Felsch made an unsuccessful bid to convince his teammates to go on strike against "that bastard" unless Comiskey raised their per diem. For several reasons, the unhappy Felsch needed little convincing to join the coterie of Black Sox.

Joe Jackson was one of the best hitters in the game, but he was a poorly educated country bumpkin; Eddie Collins was the game's premier second baseman and was a college graduate. Comiskey paid Jackson $6,000; Collins made $14,500.

The players on the bottom of the payroll believed that those of their teammates who had attended college were favored with better contracts. This apparent disparity led to bitter feelings between the two groups. The feud was so divisive that, even though Eddie Collins was the team's captain, none of the other underpaid infielders let him touch the ball when they played catch to warm up between innings.

Soon after the seven Black Sox dumped the series to Cincinnati, the nefarious plot was no longer a secret. Sportswriters strongly hinted that the series had been rigged, as did players around both leagues. In private, even Comiskey admitted that he was well aware of what had transpired. Yet he was reluctant to help the ensuing investigations, whose findings would certainly damage his own business.

IN THE MINDS and hearts of all Americans, the Great War in Europe was much more important than baseball.

Once the big guns started firing, many Irish baseball players made significant contributions to the Allies' efforts from 1914 to 1918.

♣None, however, were as vital as that made by Billy O'Hara. A native of Toronto, O'Hara was a strong-armed outfielder who otherwise failed to distinguish himself with the 1909 Giants and 1910 Cardinals. He was, however, a quite capable player with the Toronto Maple Leafs of the International League.

When Britain declared war on Germany, O'Hara was quick to enlist in the Royal Flying Corps, where he was eventually reprimanded when he crashed in a noncombat mission. If he couldn't be a flyer, then O'Hara wanted to serve in the infantry, so he transferred to the 24th Canadian Battalion.

O'Hara noted that a standard-issue hand grenade was about three times the weight of a baseball but roughly the same size and shape. The officially sanctioned way to throw the grenade was with an underhanded lobbing motion that greatly limited range and accuracy. O'Hara's impulse was to launch the hand bomb with the same overhand action as he used when throwing baseballs. This innovation dramatically improved the effectiveness of the device and he was asked to teach the proper form to his fellow infantrymen.

This critical alteration, along with a courageous attack on a well-fortified German trench at the Battle of the Somme in 1915, won O'Hara the much-coveted Military Cross "in recognition of his bravery and skill in hurling bombs."

After the armistice, O'Hara tried to escape his memories of the gruesome carnage by living as a trapper in the frozen wilderness of northern Ontario. He didn't return to civilization until 1927, when he managed his hometown Maple Leafs.

Billy O'Hara baseball card
(*Gary Joseph Cieradkowski*)

In the wake of the Great War, and spurred by Babe Ruth's home run heroics with the Yankees, American League attendance was up by 40 percent in 1920. Indeed, with 1,289,422 paying customers witnessing their home games at the Polo Grounds, the Yankees were the first pro team to draw over one million fans.

America wanted to forget, move on, and watch baseball.

Chapter Twenty-One

They're All Good Irish Names

Jennings and McGann, Doyle and Callahan.
Hanlon, Scanlon, Kirk and Donlin,
Joe McGinnity, Shea and Finnerty,
Farrell, Carroll, Darrell and McAmes.
Connie Mack and John McGraw
All together shout hurrah!
They're all good Irish names.
                    —From a baseball song of the day

DURING THE ROARING Twenties, as the Irish had more opportunities to improve both their social and economic standing, the percentage of Irish players in the major leagues declined. However, by decade's end, there were still more than sixty Irishmen in the major leagues.

But first, a woman of Irish descent made the record books.

♣On August 14, 1922, Lizzie Murphy played two innings at first during an exhibition game between the Red Sox and an AL allstar team. Murphy was already an experienced semipro player, and although she never came to bat in this particular contest, she became the first woman to play in any manner of game that featured major league players.

The occasion was a benefit for the family of Tommy McCarthy, he of Hall of Fame and Heavenly Twins fame, who had died the week before, yet several of her temporary teammates were not happy about sharing their sacred turf with a female. On a routine grounder to third, the throw to Murphy was deliberately sent high and wide in an attempt to embarrass her—but she made the catch and recovery in time for the out.

In 1928, Murphy played a complete game with the Cleveland Colored Giants of the Negro League.

For extra income and respect, Lizzie famously produced her own baseball card.

Baseball card of Lizzie Murphy
(Warren Athletic Hall of Fame)

Back to the boys, among the solid performers of the 1920s were:

♣"Jumping" Joe Dugan, who played a sure-handed third base on five pennant-winning Yankee squads. Dugan would laugh about being a mere .280 hitter in a lineup that was known as "Murderers' Row." Dugan also joked that he was once fined for breaking up a rally when he hit a single after the five previous hitters had produced two doubles, two triples, and a home run.

♣Jimmy Dykes played the hot corner for two of Connie Mack's pennant-winning teams in Philadelphia. During his twenty-two-year active career, Dykes hit over .300 five times, with a high of .327 when the A's won the World Series—in which he batted .421. He retired with 2,256 hits and a lifetime average of .280. Although Dykes didn't talk much, he was a practical joker who handed out exploding cigars like they were candy. Upon retiring, Dykes went on to manage in the big leagues for another twenty-one seasons.

♣Marty McManus was a career .289 hitter in fifteen seasons as a utility infielder. Among his specialties were stealing bases, fooling base runners with the hidden ball trick, and showing good hands and great range on the field. Twice McManus finished in the top twenty in American League MVP voting. From 1944 to 1948 he managed the South Bend Blue Sox in the All-American Girls Professional Baseball League.

♣Joe Judge was a contact hitter who hit .298 over twenty years, and was such an outstanding glove man at first base (an astounding lifetime fielding percentage of .993) as to draw favorable comparisons with Frank Chance (.987). Judge hit over .300 nine times, with a high of .324 in 1924, when Washington won the World Series.

♣"Long" Larry McLean stood 6'5" and was the tallest catcher in major league history. His thirteen-year stint began with the Red Sox (1901) and ended with the Giants (1915). McLean was a heavy drinker, which led to his suspension by John McGraw. In 1921, McLean suffered an untimely demise when he was shot dead in a brawl with a Boston saloonkeeper.

The same time frame also saw the peak seasons of several Irish players who were destined to be admitted into the Hall of Fame—one of them under a cloud of controversy.

♣Chief among these was Gordon Stanley "Mickey" Cochrane, universally regarded as the best catcher of the era. If his fielding was merely adequate, Cochrane made his mark with a bat in his hands. His lifetime average of .320 is the highest ever for a catcher. Cochrane hit lefty and was so fast that Connie Mack often put him in the leadoff spot. He was the AL's MVP in 1928 and 1934 and played in four World Series competitions. In 1999, the *Sporting News* listed the 100 greatest players in major league history, ranking Cochrane No. 65.

And, even though his father was a native of Ulster in Northern Ireland, Cochrane would often deny the fact that he was indeed Irish.

♣Harold Joseph "Pie" Traynor matched Cochrane's lifetime .320 batting average, and played his entire seventeen-year career with the Pittsburgh Pirates. Besides his prowess at the plate, Traynor was acclaimed as being the greatest-fielding third baseman of his time, and in 1969, he was officially installed there on Major League Baseball's all-time team.

Webbed pockets and oversized gloves give modern infielders a huge advantage on the field. In Traynor's day, the primary purpose of gloves was to protect a fielder's hand. Indeed, Traynor's gloves were so small that backhanded snares of grounders were extremely rare, forcing him to field these hot shots barehanded.

♣Speaking of exceptional fielders, Bob O'Farrell's name heads the list of great-fielding catchers in the 1920s. During his twenty-one years in the majors, O'Farrell frequently led the National League's backstops in putouts or assists, and was the NL's MVP in 1926. He is perhaps best remembered for throwing out Babe Ruth when Ruth attempted to steal second base with two out in the last of the ninth and the Yankees trailing by one run in the seventh game of the 1926 World Series.

♣Harry Heilmann was one of the greatest hitters ever. Although some birth record research shows an Irish mother, there's no question that his lifetime batting average of .3416 was surpassed by only five other Irish players: Lefty O'Doul at .349, Ed Delahanty's .345, Billy Hamilton with .344, and Dan Brouthers at .3421—and is twelfth-best all-time. Yet Heilmann outdid his countrymen by hitting over .390 four times, with a high of .403 in 1923.

During his seventeen seasons with (mostly) Detroit and Cincinnati, he was also the first to hit a home run in every existing major league ballpark.

Although he was primarily a line-drive hitter, Heilmann could also hit with power. His 183 lifetime homers included a prodigious shot in Detroit on July 8, 1921, that traveled 610 feet.

In 1999, Heilmann was ranked No. 54 in the *Sporting News'* list of the 100 greatest players ever.

♣George Kelly was called "High Pockets" because he stood 6'4". A longtime first baseman for the New York Giants, from 1915 to 1932, Kelly led the NL with 23 home runs in 1923, and twice paced his peers in RBIs. Despite these fancy numbers, as well as his .297 lifetime batting average, Kelly's admittance into the Hall of Fame in 1973 was contentious. That's because he was voted in by a Veterans Committee that featured two influential former teammates, Frankie Frisch and Bill Terry.

Noted baseball historian Bill James went so far as to brand Kelly as "the worst player in the Hall of Fame."

Lost in the shadow of Mack and McGraw, yet another adequate Irish player excelled when put in charge of men on the field.

♣William Boyd McKechnie was the first manager to win World Series titles with two different teams, beginning with the 1925 Pirates and later with the '40 Reds, and remains one of only two managers to win pennants with three teams, winning the NL in '28 with the Cardinals. For that, the "Deacon," as he was known, made Cooperstown in '62.

Unfortunately, the Black Sox scandal spilled over into the new decade.

With the resumption of play in April 1920, the cultural differences that caused so much turmoil on the White Sox roster were exacerbated by the all-but-public awareness of the scandal.

The Clean Sox were led by Eddie Collins and John Francis "Shano" Collins (his nickname being a diminutive of the Irish form of his first name, Sean), but the Black Sox continued to do business with gamblers as the 1920 season unfolded.

Indeed, prior to a game in Cleveland, Fred McMullin contacted some high-echelon gamblers in St. Louis to arrange another deliberate loss. When the other Black Sox refused, McMullin threatened to spill the beans to the cops. The Sox lost the game in question when Joe Jackson misplayed an easy fly ball and another player made a wild throw that enabled Cleveland to score.

A grand jury was convened on September 20, 1920. Even though the White Sox were only two games behind the league-leading Cleveland Indians and were about to finish the season with three games against the lowly St. Louis Browns, Comiskey suspended the seven implicated players.

Comiskey then made the grand gesture of paying manager Gleason and the ten Clean Sox $1,500 each, the sum representing the difference between the losers' and the winners' shares in the 1919 series.

Despite all that happened, Comiskey resumed his miserly ways. The 1921 White Sox were an unmitigated disaster, finishing in seventh place with a dismal record of 62-92. The team's only good news was provided by Dickey Kerr, who pitched to a 19-17 record. Kerr then asked Comiskey to increase his next contract by $500, but was rudely refused.

Kerr was so irate that he left the Sox in favor of managing several minor league outfits. During this time, Kerr converted the nineteen-year-old Stan Musial from an inferior pitcher into a hard-hitting outfielder.

The White Sox wouldn't return to the World Series until 1959.

Returning to the highlights of the 1920s:

♣On July 21, 1921, Roger O'Connor's career home run record was broken by a Mr. Ruth.

♣The final score of what was arguably the most poorly played major league ball game was 26–23. The date was August 25, 1922, and the Cubs outlasted the Phillies. The box score listed 51 hits, 23 walks, and ten errors. When the Cubs tallied fourteen runs in the fourth inning, Marty Callaghan batted three times, producing two hits and a strikeout.

♣William Edward "Wild Bill" Donovan was frequently in the wrong place at the wrong time. He had been an accomplished pitcher, winning 25 games for Brooklyn in 1901, another 25 (while losing only four) for Detroit in 1907, and then had the misfortune to manage the hapless 1915–17 Yankees—before the Babe arrived in the Bronx.

On December 10, 1923, Donovan was the manager of the New Haven franchise in the Eastern League, when he and the team's general manager, George Weiss, boarded the Twentieth Century Limited in New York to travel to baseball's winter meetings in Chicago. Since Weiss was younger than Donovan, he let his manager have the lower berth while he climbed to the upper. But there was a major accident along the way, in which Weiss suffered minor injuries but Donovan was killed.

♣Less than a year later, a pair of Irishmen survived a potential betting scandal with their lives, but not their careers, intact. Jimmy O'Connell was a substitute outfielder for the Giants and Albert "Cozy" Dolan one of the team's coaches. With one series left to play in the 1924 season, the Giants, at home against Philly, were neck-and-neck with the Dodgers.

During pregame warm-ups on September 27, 1924, O'Connell approached John "Heinie" Sand, Philadelphia's shortstop. The two men were well acquainted since they had played against each other for several years in the Pacific Coast League.

"How do you feel about the game?" O'Connell asked Sand.

"We don't feel," was Sand's response. "We're going to beat you."

O'Connell then said this: "I'll give you five hundred dollars if you don't bear down too hard."

"Nothing doing," said Sand.

When O'Connell reported the dialogue to Dolan, his partner in the proposal, the coach said, "Well, Jimmy, forget it."

The Giants won the game, but Sand wasn't done talking. Within a few hours, O'Connell was summoned to the office of Commissioner Landis, where the guilty player readily admitted his part in the scheme.

O'Connell further claimed that the idea was Dolan's, and that several other Giants had agreed to contribute money to the pot.

After hearing the fervid denials of the three players implicated by O'Connell, Landis issued his ruling. Both O'Connell and Dolan were suspended and then barred from the game, and no penalty was imposed on the others.

♣A few months later, there was better news for the Irish. On the basis of their arrangement of a highly successful European tour of an all-star team, John McGraw, Hughie Jennings, and Charlie Comiskey were awarded silver medals by the French Baseball Federation for promoting baseball in France.

A few Irish big leaguers were, well, big. Really big.

♣The biggest battery in the history of the major leagues made its debut on July 12, 1928. Starting behind the plate was 265-pound Frank "Shanty" Hogan, a veteran who was always battling his weight. When one of his managers gave him a list of acceptable foods, Hogan arranged a secret code with the waitresses in his favorite eateries. If he ordered "spinach," for example, he would be served potatoes.

On the mound was a 260-pound pitcher, Garland "the Pitching Pachyderm" Buckeye, who in the off-season was gainfully employed as an offensive lineman for the Chicago Cardinals. Whereas Hogan survived for thirteen seasons in the big leagues, Buckeye's poor control limited him to 108 games in five seasons and made this appearance his last in the majors.

The team that fielded this oversized duo? The New York Giants.

♣Now an umpire, Bill Dinneen was the victim in another first-time event when, in the middle of the 1928 season, he was literally bitten by a player whom he had just called out on strikes. The perpetrator of this misdeed was Bob "Fats" Fothergill, who came by his nickname by carrying well over 250 pounds on his 5'11" frame. Despite his excess poundage, however, Fothergill was an outstanding hitter, completing his career with a .325 batting average. Through it all, Fothergill was constantly trying to lose weight. In the several weeks prior to biting Dinneen, Fats's latest crash diet included daily visits to Turkish baths and wearing a rubber suit when warming up before games. No wonder his nerves were jangling. After getting tossed out of the game by Dinneen, Fothergill had this to say: "That's okay. That was the first bite of meat I've had in a month."

ONE OF THE greatest Irish players of all time got his big break near the end of the decade:

♣Joe Cronin's mother was born in Athlone, County Westmeath, and his father in County Cork. No wonder Cronin had what was described as "Irish blue eyes" to go with his dirty blond hair and jutting jaw.

Cronin had spent parts of the 1926 and 1927 seasons with the Phillies fielding his shortstop position with grace but batting a mediocre .257. By 1928, Cronin was playing shortstop for the Kansas City Blues in the International League and not hitting at all.

Midseason, Cronin was appropriately the beneficiary of what he later referred to as "the luck of the Irish."

That's when he was ordered to "go upstairs and see Joe Engel."

Cronin had no idea that Engel was a scout for the Washington Senators and was convinced that the Blues were going to demote him to a lower minor league. Imagine Cronin's surprise and delight when Engel said that he'd been called up to the bigs and handed him a train ticket.

As Engel would later report: "I knew I was watching a great player. I bought Cronin at a time he was hitting .221. When I told Clark Griffith what I had done, he screamed, 'You paid $7,500 for that bum? Well, you didn't buy him for me. You bought him for yourself. He's not my ballplayer—he's yours. You keep him and don't either you or Cronin show up at the ballpark.'"

To add more green-tinted good fortune to the mix, Cronin did report to Clark Griffith's office on July 16 and the first face he saw there was that of the owner's secretary and niece, Mildred Robertson. As a joke, Joe Engel had told Mildred that he'd hunt up a husband for her on this latest scouting trip.

By 1930, Cronin had established himself as the game's premier shortstop and a sure future Hall of Famer. With this confirmation of his ability to support the owner's daughter in the manner to which she was accustomed, Mildred and Cronin were wed in 1933.

Chapter Twenty-Two

The Alert Irishman

I'm going up with real Irish now.
—*Joe McCarthy, on moving from New York to Boston*

JOE MCCARTHY WAS so lucky, he won even when he lost.

He'd been a flashy-fielding infielder during his fifteen-year minor league career yet hadn't gotten a whiff of the majors because he couldn't hit curveballs. In fact, he rarely hit well enough to break into the starting lineup with bush-league teams in Louisville, Toledo, Buffalo, and Wilkes-Barre. No wonder McCarthy's nickname was "Utility Joe."

But there was never any doubt about McCarthy's baseball IQ. Nor did his flashing blue eyes, his stubborn jaw, or his pasty complexion leave any question as to his ethnicity. Newspapers often hailed the fielding gems of "the alert little Irishman" and commented on his "Hibernian" intensity. Moreover, in the off-seasons he often toured with a vaudeville company, where he showed himself to be a "clever dancer" and usually played the role of an Irish policeman in comedy skits.

At the tender age of twenty-six, he became player-manager of

Pennsylvania's Wilkes-Barre Barons. By 1919, McCarthy had been promoted to the command seat of the Louisville Colonels in the American Association, where he won the pennant in 1921.

On May 6, 1923, McCarthy welcomed a celebrated guest to a home game against Columbus, an ex-Oriole, now the Reverend Billy Sunday. Without benefit of a contract, Sunday umpired a few innings, played the field for the Colonels, and grounded to the pitcher in his only at-bat. Despite the egregious illegalities, Columbus didn't bother to lodge a protest since they won the game.

After piloting Louisville to another AA pennant in 1925, McCarthy finally got the call to manage the cellar-dwelling Chicago Cubs. The first notice of his hiring in the *Chicago Tribune* emphasized that McCarthy had never played in the major leagues. This rather snide reference gave fans all over the league license to barrage McCarthy with loud cries of "Busher!" every time he stepped onto the field.

In his rookie season with the Cubs, McCarthy made the same flawed personnel decision that John McGraw had previously made—cutting Lefty O'Doul. Even though the twenty-five-year-old O'Doul had just hit .375, clouted 22 homers, and registered 191 RBIs in the tough Pacific Coast League, McCarthy echoed McGraw in claiming that he wasn't ready for the big leagues.

Four years later, O'Doul was with the Phillies when he pinch-hit a game-winning home run in the bottom of the twelfth. McCarthy was manning the third-base coaching box as O'Doul presented him with a one-figured salute in passing.

Despite misjudging O'Doul, McCarthy managed the Cubs into the first division in 1926, and into the World Series three seasons later. And the team's performance against one of Connie Mack's superteams would eventually lead to McCarthy's bad-luck-turned-good happenstance.

The Cubs were down two games to one but had an 8–0 lead going into the bottom of the seventh inning and had their ace on the mound. The subsequent disaster was quick and merciless as the A's slugged base hits all over the field.

The Phils not only won the game, 10–8, but their ten-run inning set a World Series record that still stands. To make a bad situation even worse, the very next day Philadelphia tallied three runs in the bottom of the ninth to win the close-out game by a score of 3–2.

The Cubs' owner, Philip Wrigley, was so embittered and embarrassed that nearly one year later, even though his team was battling the St. Louis Cardinals for the pennant, he wanted to can McCarthy. Bill Veeck Jr. was Chicago's general manager and he strongly disagreed with his boss. After several furious arguments that got nowhere, Wrigley and Veeck decided that McCarthy's future would be decided by a coin toss.

As apparently bad luck would have it, Wrigley made the right call and McCarthy was immediately fired.

Within weeks, however, McCarthy was chosen in 1931 to manage the game's showcase franchise—the New York Yankees.

Ruth, Gehrig, Tony Lazzeri, "Long Bob" Meusel, and Co. formed a powerhouse team and there were widespread doubts among New York's sportswriters that the tight-lipped McCarthy had the charisma to gain his new players' respect. Ruth, in particular, was dubious about the hire. The Sultan of Swat taking orders from a guy who had never played in the majors?

The Yankees had gone through two caretaker managers after Miller Huggins died suddenly in the fall of 1929. So this McCarthy fellow was the fourth manager Ruth had experienced in little more than a year. Besides, the Babe was convinced that he would manage the team as soon as his playing days were done. As far as he was concerned, McCarthy's main duty was to keep the command seat warm until Ruth took over. But the more success that McCarthy had, the more Ruth grew to hate him.

Plagued by a rash of injuries, the Yankees finished the 1931 season in second place, a whopping 13½ games behind Philadelphia. But the following season, much to McCarthy's delight and Wrigley's despair, the Bronx Bombers swept the Cubs in the World Series.

By 1934, Babe Ruth was washed up—"only" hitting .288, belting 22 homers, and drawing 103 walks while whiffing 63 times—and wound up embarrassing himself with the Boston Braves in the 1935 season. But Gehrig, Lazzeri, and Bill Dickey were still potent hitters, and in 1936, the Yankees added Joe DiMaggio to the lineup.

McCarthy subsequently guided the Yankees to a record-setting four consecutive World Series triumphs (1936–39), which included another satisfying sweep of the Chicago Cubs.

McCarthy was now established as a full-fledged genius, and his players were amazed at their skipper's acumen, especially his attention to the smallest details. Here's Lou Gehrig's testimony: "Joe could look at the dents in a catcher's glove and see how effective a pitcher was with his curve ball. He also noted the velocity of foul balls that went back to the screen as a way of gauging the speed and hop of a pitcher's fastball."

As much as possible, McCarthy also had left-handed throwers playing left field and righties playing right field. That's because throws from righties always had a natural left-to-right curve (and vice versa for lefties), so a throw home from properly armed corner outfielders would swerve toward the field and not toward foul territory. McCarthy reasoned that even a slightly more accurate throw could be the difference in a close play at the plate.

When McCarthy activated the steal sign, the hitter would casually reset his feet a few inches farther away from the pitcher, forcing the catcher to likewise shift back. This slight adjustment meant that the catcher's subsequent throw attempting to nail the runner would be a few inches longer.

Unlike the famous Irish bench battlers of the past, McCarthy was not an arguer. He famously said, "Try not to find too much fault with the umpires. You cannot expect them to be as perfect as you are."

In addition, McCarthy made minor adjustments in the Yankees' uniforms. He insisted that the bill of their caps be squared off and that the jerseys be tailored slightly larger than required. His reasoning here was that the cap would make his players seem more intimidating, while the oversized uniforms would make them appear bigger and stronger than they really were.

According to Joe DiMaggio, "Never a day went by that you didn't learn something from Joe McCarthy."

Even Joe Page—a brilliant reliever whose late-night habits and alcoholism were anathema to McCarthy—couldn't avoid praising the Yankees skipper: "I hated his guts, but there was never a better manager."

Nor was McCarthy reluctant to ask for divine help. On a Sunday morning before the Yankees were to play the Red Sox, the managers of both teams happened to attend the same church service. When Joe Cronin lit two candles at the altar, McCarthy had one of his players light three candles. The ensuing game was won by New York by the score of 3–2.

For McCarthy, attitude was equally as important as talent.

Although the Yankees eventually won the 1937 pennant by thirteen games over Detroit, they suffered a four-game losing streak in midseason. After McCarthy vigorously vented his displeasure, one of his players—a utility outfielder named Roy Johnson—was overheard saying this to a teammate: "What, does he expect us to win every game?"

Instead of confronting Johnson, McCarthy immediately sought out general manager Ed Barrow. "I don't care who you get," said McCarthy. "Just get him out of here." And Johnson was gone.

McCARTHY'S EXPERT HANDLING of the Yankees extended into the following decade, most memorably in Game 4 of the 1941 World Series, when his lineup took full advantage of one of the most famous plays in baseball history. The Yanks led the series two games to one, but trailed 4–3 in the top of the ninth. On the mound for the Brooklyn Dodgers was Hugh Casey, and his battery mate was another Irishman, Mickey Owen. There were two outs, the bases were empty, and Tommy Henrich was in a 1-2 hole when he swung and missed Casey's next pitch.

Game over? Series tied at two-all?

Not so.

The pitch got past Owen, and Henrich was safe at first. In short order, this miscue was followed by a single by DiMaggio, a double by Charlie Keller, a walk to Bill Dickey, and a double by Joe Gordon.

New York had tallied four runs and won the game 7–4 to take a commanding 3–1 lead in the series. The *New York Times* labeled the catastrophe "Flatbush's Darkest Hour."

Owen was universally blamed, even though Casey's disastrous pitch was most likely a slippery, hand-to-handle spitball.

Night fell early in Brooklyn on the very next day when the disheartened Dodgers could only manage four hits and one run as the Yankees closed out the series.

The Yankees copped another pennant in 1942, only to lose in the Fall Classic to the St. Louis Cardinals. McCarthy's pinstriped gang returned the favor the following season. But in 1944 and 1945, many of his best players were wearing GI gear.

McCarthy led this motley crew to a pair of first-division finishes and a combined record of 164-142. Even when dealt a bad hand, the master had not lost his touch.

But there would be trouble afoot when Larry MacPhail was named the Yankees president after the 1945 season. Known in the trade as "Loud Larry," he had become universally known as a meddling, blustering, self-promoting alcoholic used to being surrounded by sycophants who treated his every word as gospel. It was hate at first sight for McCarthy and his new Irish boss.

Still, with his team restored following the end of World War II,

MacPhail expected the Yankees to cruise to another pennant. But injuries to DiMaggio limited the Yankee Clipper's playing time and his performance. Except for his dismal .265 batting average in the last year of his career, Joe's .290 mark in 1946 was the lowest he ever hit. Nor did MacPhail help the cause when he sold the team's best pitcher to the Red Sox with the Yankees trailing Boston by only three games. And although the Yankees won 87 and lost only 67, they finished in third place, seventeen games behind the red-hot first-place Red Sox.

MacPhail would brook no extenuating circumstances and McCarthy was canned.

McCarthy's tenure with the Yankees lasted sixteen years and featured eight American League pennants, seven world championships, and a winning percentage of .627, plus an astounding success rate of .698 in World Series competition. No surprise that he wasn't unemployed for very long.

Joe Cronin had significant successes as a manager. Functioning as player-manager of the Washington Senators, he'd led the team into the World Series in 1933 (losing to McGraw's Giants). And in 1946, Cronin's Bosox made it to the series, extending the Cardinals to a seventh game before succumbing. But Cronin was weary of managing, and he'd also gained too much weight to feel comfortable wearing a uniform in public.

A disappointing third-place finish in 1947, plus widespread criticism that "Jolly Joe" had kowtowed to his players—particularly Ted Williams—convinced Cronin that he'd be better off serving as the Red Sox's general manager. And since McCarthy had taken a year off to regenerate his interest and his motivation, the hire was a no-brainer.

McCarthy was delighted not only to return to big-league action, but to have the chance to live and work in Boston.

At age seventy-one, McCarthy hadn't forgotten any of the details that had been so instrumental in his successful seasons in New York, but his enforced idleness had made him significantly more malleable. Indeed, a manager needed to be highly flexible to deal with Williams. As it turned out, Williams and McCarthy quickly bonded when they discovered their common dislike of reporters. Short monosyllabic answers and downright snubs characterized the routine responses by both player and manager to what they regarded as reporters' intrusive and ignorant questions.

Even with Williams in his corner, however, the Red Sox were unable to reach the top of the American League. In 1948, they lost a one-game playoff for the pennant to Cleveland, and the following year they finished one game behind the Yankees.

Cronin offered no help in his new administrative position. While the Red Sox's core roster remained mostly intact, Cronin constantly tinkered with the team's supporting cast. In his eleven years as Boston's GM, the trade-happy Cronin engaged in twenty-seven deals—twelve with Washington. It was hard even for McCarthy to recognize his players without a scorecard.

The combined frustrations exacerbated the most severe of McCarthy's bad habits—drinking White Horse Scotch too much and too often. By 1949, he was taking an occasional nip during games from a flask guarded by the trainer. McCarthy's inebriations caused him to miss an increasing number of games—absences that were reported to be caused by gastric disturbances, the flu, and other temporary illnesses.

By early June 1950, McCarthy was ready to quit baseball. In a lengthy conversation with Cronin, McCarthy was advised to ease off the booze and was convinced to keep his job. But neither suggestion had lasting effects. McCarthy cited health problems in announcing his retirement from the game on June 24. Cronin quickly replaced him with another Irishman, Steve O'Neill.

Gaining control of his untoward consumption of alcohol, McCarthy lived a genial retirement with his beloved wife, Elizabeth, in their beloved "Yankee Farm" outside Buffalo. Surviving his 1957 induction into the Hall of Fame by twenty years, McCarthy died at ninety in virtual anonymity.

McCarthy's overall accomplishments were good enough for him to be ranked with John McGraw and Connie Mack as one of the greatest managers in the history of the game.

And this exalted triumvirate of extraordinary Irishmen were soon to be a quartet—joined by another elite manager who likewise had significant roots in the Emerald Isle.

Chapter Twenty-Three

Homer in the Gloamin'

Roamin' in the gloamin' on the bonnie banks o' Clyde.
Roamin' in the gloamin' wae my lassie by my side.

—*Harry Lauder*

WHILE MCCARTHY'S YANKEES ruled the game in the 1930s, other Irishmen also provided headlines on the sports pages.

♣On June 7, 1932, pitcher John Quinn was forty-eight years old. When he belted a double that day, he became (and still is) the oldest major leaguer to produce an extra-base hit.

By August 14, Quinn was forty-nine and working out of Brooklyn's bullpen. After he pitched two scoreless innings in relief, the Dodgers won the game in the bottom half of the tenth, making Quinn the oldest pitcher in major league history to be credited with a win.

♣The ownership of the Red Sox changed hands on February 2, 1933, when one Irishman (Robert Quinn) sold the team to an All-American WASP (Tom Yawkey) and another Irishman (Eddie Collins).

♣Charley O'Leary had been a good-field, no-hit shortstop until his retirement in 1913. On September 30, the last day of the 1934 season, O'Leary was a coach for the St. Louis Browns and thought to be fifty-two years old. Just for the fun of it, O'Leary was activated and entered the game as a pinch hitter, whereupon he singled and eventually scored. Subsequent research, however, has discovered that O'Leary was actually fifty-nine at the time, making him (and not Jim O'Rourke) the oldest player both to hit safely and score a run in a big league game.

♣Larry MacPhail was always an audacious, fast-talking, Barnum & Bailey kind of guy. After working his way up through the minor leagues, MacPhail was the general manager of the Cincinnati Reds on May 25, 1935, when he proposed and arranged for the first night game in major league history. Due to more of MacPhail's persistent efforts, President Franklin Roosevelt was prevailed upon to throw the switch that activated the several banks of lights.

Three years later, MacPhail was general manager of the Dodgers, and his latest brainstorm was to take the baseballs used for a home game on August 8 and dye them dandelion yellow. Johnny Mize hit the first and only yellow home run, and the extra balls were used in three games during the 1939 season.

♣Kitty Burke was an Irish lass who loved her hometown Cincinnati Reds. She was there on July 31, 1935, when the Reds over-sold admission to a night game against St. Louis. Since there were more fans than seats, ropes were set up a few feet from the foul lines to contain the standees.

Paul Dean was on the mound for the Cardinals and, during the game, Miss Kitty ducked under the restraining ropes, grabbed a bat, and ran to home plate. Dean went along with the gag and lobbed a pitch that Burke grounded back to him. Burke was barely halfway to first base when Dean's easy toss beat her to the bag.

Everybody on hand had a good laugh except Frankie Frisch, the Cardinals' manager. He stormed out of his dugout and petitioned the umpires to count Burke's grounder as an official out that should be charged to the Reds. His protest got nowhere.

♣In 1934, brothers Wes and Rick Ferrell were one of the few familial pitcher-catcher combos in baseball history. For five years in Boston uniforms they toiled, and both are in the Red Sox Hall of Fame. After being traded, Rick hit a home run off Wes in a game in 1938.

A seven-time all-star, Rick would go on to a Hall of Fame career, playing in the most games as a catcher in the AL until Carlton Fisk broke his record in 1988.

Wes was a good pitcher, but just as good a hitter. Several baseball historians consider him one of the best-hitting pitchers ever, and his hitting and pitching were both good enough to at least get him on the ballot for the Hall.

♣On September 9, 1935, Joe Cronin was denied a sure base hit by a heads-up play by Odell Hale, the third baseman of the Cleveland Indians. Cronin smashed a liner that was hit too hard for Hale to glove. In fact, the ball struck Hale squarely in the forehead, then caromed on a fly over to shortstop Billy Knickerbocker, who made the easy catch.

♣Mickey Cochrane was positively the best catcher the Irish have ever produced. But his brilliant, Hall of Fame career ended with sudden tragedy.

The Tigers were playing the Yankees on May 25, 1937, and, in his last at-bat, Cochrane had smacked a home run off Bump Hadley, New York's feisty veteran pitcher. Since batting helmets had yet to be invented, a simple brushback pitch would suffice as retaliation.

But Hadley was a spot starter who desperately wanted to impress his manager, Joe McCarthy, with his toughness and his willingness to intimidate hitters. Hadley's control was always shaky. And his get-even pitch struck Cochrane squarely above his left ear, fracturing the catcher's skull and ending his brilliant career.

♣During his fourteen seasons in the majors, Michael "Pinky" Higgins played third base for the A's, Red Sox, and Tigers. In June 1938, Higgins made the record book by hitting safely in twelve consecutive at-bats.

♣Bill McGowan was another in the long line of outstanding Irish umpires, and was elected to the Hall of Fame in 1992. His domain was the American League, where he worked in 2,541 consecutive games from 1925 to 1954. His nickname of "Number One" was reinforced by his being called upon to be the home plate ump in the first ever All-Star Game—1933—and by his being awarded arbiter responsibilities in eight World Series.

In addition to his fairness, diligence, dramatic calls, and overall acumen, McGowan was celebrated for his compassion. On numerous occasions, whenever a good-natured hitter was mired in a deep slump, McGowan was willing to turn a called strike into a ball. And the hitter need not be Irish!

THE MOST MOMENTOUS incident in the 1937 All-Star Game involved a pair of Irish players who were both destined for the Hall of Fame.

♣The catcher for the National League was Charles Leo Hartnett of the Chicago Cubs, who was called "Gabby" because he was notoriously shy and reluctant to speak. Despite his reticence, Hartnett was an extraordinary fielder equipped with a cannon-arm that negated the ambitions of even the most proficient base stealers. Hartnett was no slouch at bat, as demonstrated by his .297 career batting average.

Nor did Hartnett lack a wry sense of humor: Before a 1931 exhibition game between the Cubs and the White Sox, Hartnett was photographed signing an autograph for Al Capone. Baseball Commissioner Kenesaw Mountain Landis was upset by the widely distributed photo, especially as the Black Sox scandal still lingered in the public's awareness. In response to a telegram from Landis that chastised Hartnett and prohibited him from duplicating the misdeed, Gabby's telegraphed response was: "OK, but if you don't want me to have my picture taken with Al Capone, you tell him."

After hitting .344 in 1935, Hartnett was named the NL's MVP. During his twenty-year career, he would be selected to six All-Star Games.

But in the 1937 midseason contest, Hartnett was behind the plate, with Dizzy Dean on the mound and Earl Averill in the batter's box. Dean repeatedly shook off Hartnett's signal for a curveball, insisting on throwing a fastball. Which Dean did, with disastrous results.

♣Earl Averill was a full-blooded Irishman as well as a superb center fielder and batsman. He was in the midst of a thirteen-year career and a .318 lifetime batting average. Like Hartnett, Averill would eventually become a six-time all-star.

But on that fateful summer's day in 1937, Averill's eyes widened with delight when he zeroed in on Dean's fastball. He cracked a vicious line drive that chanced to hit Dean's left foot with such force that the pitcher's big toe was fractured.

Turned out that Dean returned to action much too hastily, the gimp in his delivery injured his pitching arm, and he never regained his dominant form.

Some twenty-five years later, Averill was arrested while boarding a plane en route to Detroit for an Old Timers' Game. It seems that he wanted to use his own bat in the game, and carried it in a gun case.

THE 1938 SEASON ended on one of the most famous walk-off home runs of all time—the Homer in the Gloamin'. And hit by none other than Irish Hall of Famer Gabby Hartnett.

On September 28, 1938, the Cubs were a half game behind the Pirates at the start of game two of a three-game series at Wrigley Field, a ballpark that disdained artificial lighting until the 1960s. Dusk was falling in the bottom of the ninth, score tied 5–5. The umps ruled this would be the last inning.

Hartnett came up with two out, and on an 0-2 count, he hit the ball into the left-center bleachers. The fans went crazy; the Cubs were in first, and would finish there. The only sour note was a World Series loss to the Yankees.

Still, as the song said, for one day, Cubs fans and Irishmen everywhere rejoiced.

When the sun has gone to rest,
That's the time we love the best.
O, it's lovely roamin' in the gloamin'.

Chapter Twenty-Four

A Real Casey

I played for Casey both before and after he was a genius.
—*Warren Spahn*

ON SEPTEMBER 17, 1912, Charles Dillon Stengel initiated his fourteen-year active career with four singles, one walk, two stolen bases, and two RBIs in the Dodgers' 7–3 win over Pittsburgh.

His mother was Irish, his father was German, and Stengel was all mischief. His wide-set eyes, prominent ears, and flexible lips would soon make Stengel's absurdly mugging antics the delight of newspaper photographers.

Since all players with even a drop of German blood were called "Dutch," that was the rookie's first nickname. However, he soon gained fame and notoriety as "Casey" either because he was perpetually talking about the pleasures available in his hometown of Kansas City, Missouri, or because his powerless bat was sarcastically compared to the epic swings of "Casey at the Bat."

Between his minor league seasons, Stengel enrolled in dental school, just in case his baseball career never succeeded. Stengel said that he "never liked pulling teeth," and after hitting .317 at the tail end of the 1912 season, he abandoned dental school.

Bill Dahlen was the manager of the Dodgers and even though the lefty-swinging Stengel played in 124 games in 1913 (batting .272), he rarely was allowed to face southpaw pitchers. Then, with Brooklyn finishing in sixth place, 34½ games behind the pennant-winning Giants, Dahlen was replaced by onetime Orioles catcher Wilbert Robinson.

As ever, "Robbie" was such a good-natured soul that the team was renamed the Brooklyn Robins. On the bench, Robinson was fond of regaling his players with tales of the good old days, and of his various hunting and fishing expeditions. Sometimes Robinson would forget to give signals to his third-base coach. Was the sacrifice bunt on? The steal? The hit-and-run? But Robinson never forgot to continue platooning Stengel.

ROBINSON DECLARED THAT he could do anything that his old catching rival Gabby Street could do and do it even better. Like catching a baseball dropped from an airplane.

Back in 1908, a local sportswriter carried a bag of baseballs to the top of the Washington Monument. The idea was to prove just how good a catcher Charles "Gabby" Street was by seeing if he could catch a baseball dropped from 555 feet. Street missed the first dozen balls but made a nifty catch of the thirteenth.

Street had already made a name for himself as a Washington Senator by catching for the great Walter Johnson, and would later go on to manage the St. Louis Cardinals to two championships in the 1930s (including besting Connie Mack), and then go on to the radio booth alongside a young Harry Caray.

So in March 1915, Robinson and his players chipped in to hire a pilot and a plane. The team's clubhouse man, Don Comerford, was also sent aloft with two baseballs. Robinson circled the area around second base and tracked the flight of the plane. But Comerford's two drops missed the ballpark completely. Comerford was about to give up when he saw a sack of grapefruits stashed in the plane. On the subsequent pass over the field, he dropped the grapefruit.

Down near second base, Robinson moved around trying to get a bead on what he believed to be a falling baseball. "Get away! Get away!" he yelled at the hovering spectators. "I got it! I got it!"

The missile landed squarely in Robinson's mitt and exploded on contact. Robinson was knocked to the ground as the juice and the pulp splashed into his face.

"Help! Help!" he screamed. "I'm bleeding to death! Help me!"

From then on, Robinson was known around the league as "Grapefruit."

And, because of his well-earned reputation as a trickster, Robinson placed the entire blame for his humiliation on Stengel.

AFTER BEING TRADED to Pittsburgh in 1918, Stengel was demoted to part-time duty. Yet whenever the Pirates visited Brooklyn, the fans greeted him with affection, leaving Stengel to search for some way to reciprocate. Much to the distress of every manager he ever had, Stengel was already proficient at catching easy fly balls behind his back, so the Brooklyn fans had seen that trick several times.

But then, during an early-season visit, Stengel took advantage of an unusual happenstance to perform a perfect bit of nonsense.

The Robins' bullpen was located in foul territory adjacent to the right-field wall. After the sixth inning, Stengel paused on his way to the dugout to get a drink of water at the home team's bullpen, only to see Leon Cadore, one of Brooklyn's pitchers, gently holding something in his hands. It was a sparrow that had lost its way.

"Let me have it," Casey said.

Stengel surreptitiously put the bird on top of his head and covered it with his cap.

As ever, the Brooklyn fans greeted Casey as he strolled to the plate with insincere applause and good-natured jeers. Whereupon Stengel tipped his hat and the bird flew away.

Even the umpire had to laugh. But Wilbert Robinson saw nothing humorous about his ex-player's latest stunt. "Hell," groused Robbie, "he always did have birds in his garret."

When he avoided the temptation to act the clown, the 5'10", 175-pound Stengel was an outstanding fielder and a solid hitter. He would exceed .300 five times in his career and retire in 1925 with a lifetime average of .285. But his wacky behavior led to still another trade—this time from the Pirates to the Phillies in 1920.

After training camp, major league teams would generate extra income by barnstorming their way from Florida back to their home city. So it was that the Phils were taking batting practice before an exhibition game in Fort Wayne, Indiana. As usual, the grandstands were already packed with fans anxious to witness major league hitters blast away at half-speed pitches. But there was one leather-lunged yokel sitting near the Phillies dugout, wearing overalls and a shabby straw hat, with a red bandanna tied around his scrawny neck.

"You can't hit, you city loafers!" he shouted. "You call that hitting? Anybody could hit better than that."

After suffering such abuse for several minutes, one of the Phillies finally responded: "You've got a pretty big mouth. You think you could do any better?"

"Dang right I could," said the disgruntled fan.

"Why don't you come out here and try?"

"All right," said the farmer. "I will."

He then proceeded to shuffle onto the field, pick up the first bat he saw, and step into the batter's box. Whereupon he smashed line drives all over the field, and even blasted a few over the fence.

It was Casey Stengel, always willing to entertain a crowd.

The Phillies' manager, Gavvy Cravath, was not entertained a few days later when Stengel wore his uniform backward while taking batting practice. Controlling his anger, Cravath only said this to Stengel: "I'm not surprised. You've done everything else backward down here. You might as well wear your pants that way too."

A last-place finish cost Cravath his job, but under the direction of Billy Donovan the team was still mired in the cellar. Donovan was soon fired and several players were cut, demoted to the minors, or traded.

Even though Stengel was hitting .305, he was dealt to the Giants midway through the 1921 season. Casey responded to his change of address by saying, "Wake up muscles, we're in New York now."

Under the unforgiving management of John McGraw, Stengel limited his frolics and delinquencies to his off-field activities. Casey always had a taste for alcohol, and in his new teammate, "Irish" Bob Meusel (who wasn't Irish), he found a willing barhopping partner. McGraw was suspicious when both players frequently came to games slightly dazed, so he hired a detective to follow them both.

Stengel was quick to recognize that he and Meusel were being shadowed, and he voiced his displeasure to McGraw. "I don't want to share a detective with anyone else," Casey said. "I want one of my own."

Even the crusty McGraw had to acknowledge Stengel's uniqueness when he cracked two dramatic home runs that accounted for the only games the Giants won in the 1923 World Series. Stengel's homers were also the first postseason round-trippers hit in Yankee Stadium.

Still, Stengel was a little too unique for McGraw. Casey's World Series heroics along with his .339 average in the regular season didn't dissuade McGraw from trading him to the Boston Braves.

Stengel had a productive 1924 season with the Braves—hitting .280 in 131 games. But after a dismal performance in 1925—hitting .077 in 12 games—Stengel leaped at the chance to become the player-manager of the Toledo Mud Hens in the American Association.

Stengel's kicking, screaming, crowd-baiting protests earned him several suspensions during his six years in Toledo. Other more embarrassing incidents also marked his tenure with the Mud Hens.

Back then, clubhouses all contained large wooden boxes filled with sawdust that were used as targets for the many tobacco-chewing players. Before one game, Casey noted a slumping Mud Hen entering the clubhouse wearing a brand-new suit and a crestfallen expression. Stengel was in the process of changing into his uniform but, before climbing into his pants, he rushed over to the player, grabbed a bat, and began to demonstrate the proper way to hit curveballs. In his enthusiasm, one of Stengel's instructional swings hit the sawdust box and splattered gobs of gunk all over the player's suit.

Stengel made a hasty exit, went out on the field, and grabbed a fungo bat. But he had forgotten to put his pants on. When several women in the stands started pointing at him and joined in a chorus of loud giggles, Casey was bewildered. "They got some crazy women here in Toledo," he muttered. "What are they hollering about?"

One of Toledo's regular outfielders was John "Jocko" Conlan, a jovial Irishman who was destined to become an outstanding major league umpire. Even though he happened to be standing next to Stengel, Conlan grinned, but said nothing.

Finally Stengel looked down and said, "Why, I haven't got my pants on!" He then screamed at Conlan, "Why didn't you tell me?" as he clipped the player's shins with the fungo bat.

Many years would pass before "Casey the Clown" would prove to be one of the most successful managers in the major leagues and be tagged with a much more respectful nickname—the Old Perfessor. But even that road took time and many stops.

Casey Stengel finally got his shot on the big stage when he became the manager of the hapless Brooklyn Dodgers in 1934. The team never reached the first division during his three-year stint there, even though Stengel utilized every trick he could devise. Foremost among these was the "precision play."

With a runner on third, the plan called for the pitcher to deliberately throw at the batter's head, then yell, "Watch out!" As the hitter ducked out of harm's way, the runner would invariably freeze and be an easy victim of the catcher's pickoff throw to the third baseman. But after a few early successes, the play had to be abandoned when, despite the prearranged routine, the third baseman would also freeze.

Even though his second two-year contract was still in effect, Casey's cumulative record in Brooklyn was 208-251, bad enough to merit a pink slip. Stengel and his wife, Edna, spent the next year cashing the Dodgers' checks, spending time in Kansas City, and traveling to Texas, where he investigated the oil business.

Then in the winter of 1937–38, Stengel invested $43,000 in the decidedly mediocre Boston Bees, who were getting stung at the box office by the Red Sox, their crosstown rivals. Was it pure coincidence that shortly thereafter Stengel became the manager of the Bees?

In any event, none of Casey's tactics or antics could prompt the Bees into the first division. After a semi-respectable 77-75 record that boosted the team into fifth place, Boston spent the next four seasons one step out of the cellar. Stengel sought to lighten the mood with some of his best witticisms:

"Good pitching beats good hitting, and vice versa."

"All right, everybody line up alphabetically according to your height."

"That boy couldn't hit the ground if he fell out of an airplane."

"The secret of managing is to keep the guys who hate you away from the guys who are undecided."

"There comes a time in every man's life and I've had plenty of them."

The local sportswriters eventually grew weary of Stengel's constant joking. Early in the 1943 season (his last in Boston), Stengel was hit by a taxicab and suffered a fractured leg that kept him away from the team for several weeks. The response of one newspaper was to name the taxi driver the Sportsman of the Year in Boston.

It was back to the bushes for Casey.

He soon hooked up with the Milwaukee Brewers of the American

Association. Bill Veeck, the owner of the franchise, was vehemently opposed to the hire. But Veeck was serving with the Marines in the South Pacific and didn't discover the identity of his new manager until after the deed was done.

Even though Stengel's Brewers finished at 102-51 and copped the AA pennant, he was canned as soon as Veeck returned to the States. Not to worry, though, since Casey quickly signed on with his hometown Kansas City Blues in the same league.

As the Blues limped through a pitiful 65-86 season, Casey had this to say to the hostile media: "Please don't cut my throat. I may want to do that myself."

Another firing led to still another job, this one with the Oakland Oaks of the Triple-A Pacific Coast League. He was pleased to live and work in proximity to the Golden Gate Bridge. "I like the idea of bridges," he said. "Everywhere I go they throw in a bridge as part of the service. Every manager wants to jump off a bridge sooner or later, and it's very nice for an old man to know he doesn't have to walk fifty miles to find one."

In 1948, the Oaks won the pennant and prestigious *Sport Magazine* named Stengel the minor league manager of the year. Despite this honor, the New York media was outraged when Casey was chosen to manage the New York Yankees.

What? The clown who made only opponents laugh when he managed the Dodgers?

Turned out that Stengel not only had the last laugh, but his Yankees proceeded to win five consecutive World Series from 1949 to 1953.

Of course, Stengel's pitching staff featured four aces. And the Yankees' powerhouse lineup variously included the likes of DiMaggio, Tommy Henrich, Yogi Berra, Phil Rizzuto, Hank Bauer, Gene Woodling, Johnny Mize, and Mickey Mantle.

"Managing," quoth Casey, "is getting paid for home runs someone else hits."

One critical component of New York's success was Casey's deft maneuvering of his players through his revival of the platoon system, which had fallen out of favor in the previous twenty years. Nor was he afraid to go against the proverbial book—as in the deciding game of the 1951 World Series, when he summoned lefty Bob Kuzava to face a trio of heavy-hitting righties in the ninth with the bases loaded, none out, and the Yankees nursing a 4–1 lead. Kuzava was up to the task, retiring Monte Irvin, Bobby Thomson, and Sal Yvars 1-2-3.

One of Casey's machinations was even more radical.

On September 9, 1950, the Yankees received a letter in which the writer threatened to shoot Phil Rizzuto if the Yankees' shortstop took the field in a game in Boston. The FBI was informed, but Stengel had his own way of dealing with the situation: having Rizzuto and a rookie utility infielder named Billy Martin switch uniforms.

However, the Yankees' success went to Casey's head, and his players came to resent the know-it-all arrogance that he soon manifested. During the 1950 World Series versus the Phillies, the otherwise sure-handed Gene Woodling misplayed a fly ball to left field, which allowed two runs to score and necessitated Stengel's removing Whitey Ford from the game. Stengel then mocked Woodling's difficulty in locating the ball in the Stadium's notorious "sun field" by staggering blindly on his way to the mound. After Allie Reynolds took the ball to end the threat and the series, Woodling screamed at Stengel during the postgame celebration, but Casey's only reaction was to laugh and glug some more champagne.

NOT EVEN STENGEL'S players could untangle his elocutions. According to Rizzuto, "We'd have clubhouse meetings that would last an hour, an hour and a half and he' talk the whole time. If you listened carefully there'd be something useful in there, but he confused a lot of players. Especially the younger ones."

Unfortunately, what everybody within hearing range could understand was Stengel's racial prejudice. In the sixth game of the 1952 World Series, Vic Raschi was pitching to the Dodgers' Roy Campanella when Casey shouted to the mound, "Stick one in that nigger's ear." Stengel's vulgar encouragement for Raschi to bean Campy (which he ignored) was overheard by all the writers in the press box. But no mention of Casey's slur was ever printed.

Moreover, Stengel habitually referred to blacks as "jigs" and "jigaboos." In 1959, the Yankees signed their first black player, catcher Elston Howard. This was Casey's reaction: "Well, when they finally got me a nigger, I get the only one who can't run." But neither the media nor the team's bigwigs gave any indications that Stengel's rampant racism was a problem. As long as the Yankees kept winning, he had a license to say whatever about whomever.

Even though the Yanks won 103 games in 1954, they finished eight games behind Cleveland. But Stengel led them back into the winner's circle from 1955 to 1958, splitting two World Series confrontations each with Milwaukee and Brooklyn.

In addition to all of his series championships, Stengel believed that his most significant legacy would be the development of Mickey Mantle into being—dare he say it?—the best hitter ever.

Mantle, said Stengel, " should lead the league in everything with his combination of speed and power. He should win the triple batting crown every year. In fact, he should be able to do anything he wants to do."

Unfortunately, the Mick's career was blighted by serious injuries as well as a serious drinking problem. Mantle, of course, became an incredible player, but his failure to live up to his manager's lofty expectations led to a touchy relationship between the two of them.

Nothing went right for the 1959 Yankees, and they finished in third place, fifteen games behind the White Sox. But the team rebounded from its worst season under Stengel by cruising to the pennant in 1960. Then came the dramatic World Series against the Pirates, where one of several critical plays was a routine double-play grounder to Yankee shortstop Tony Kubek that took an unexpected hop when it hit a pebble, smashed into Kubek's throat, and enabled Pittsburgh to put together a big inning.

Even though the Yankees outscored the Pirates by 28 runs throughout the series, Bill Mazeroski's dramatic homer in the bottom of the ninth won the seventh game for the Pirates.

Within weeks, Stengel was fired. In twelve mostly glorious seasons in New York, Casey had won ten pennants, seven World Series, and amassed a winning percentage of .623. The only reason provided by the Yankees brass was that he had turned seventy the previous July 30, and was deemed too old to continue being an effective leader of young men.

"They told me my services were no longer required," said Casey, "because they wanted to put in a youth program. . . . I'll never make the mistake of being seventy again."

But Stengel wasn't quite finished in the Big Apple. In 1962 he became the manager of the brand-new New York Mets.

The first player the Mets selected in the expansion draft was Hobie Landrith, a notoriously weak-hitting catcher.

When asked to explain this choice, Casey said, "You have to have a catcher because if you don't, every pitch will roll all the way to the backstop."

One of his new players asked Stengel if he'd ever played the game, to which Casey replied, "Sure I played. Did you think I was born at the age of seventy-one, sitting in a dugout trying to manage guys like you?"

However, if Casey was indeed too old to stay awake throughout several ball games, his crackling wit remained intact. One day during batting practice he pointed to Ed Kranepool. "See that fellow over there?" he asked a reporter. "He's twenty years old. In ten years he has a chance to be a star."

Then he pointed a crooked yellowed finger at Greg Goossen. "Now, that other fellow over there he's twenty, too. In ten years he has a chance to be thirty."

The Amazin's, of course, were lovable losers passionately embraced by jilted Giants and Dodgers fans. As they lost game after game—120 in 1962, 111 in 1963, and 109 in 1964—Stengel's ability to contort his rubber face, hold his liquor, and come up with quotable lines kept the fans and the sportswriters smiling.

"I've been in this game for a hundred years, but I'm seeing new ways to lose that I never knew existed before."

During spring training in 1964, Stengel instructed his coaches to move the workouts to a field that was a short walk from the Mets' normal practice field. "I just want to see if they can play any better on the road."

Late in the 1965 season, Casey had had enough—of traveling, of aching joints, and mostly of losing. "Can't anybody here play this game?"

He never did make the mistake of being seventy again, and lived peacefully in his adopted hometown of Glendale, California, until he passed away a few weeks past his eighty-fifth birthday.

Before he passed away, Casey had the last word: "If anybody wants me, tell them I'm being embalmed."

PRESENT-DAY INTERVIEW

In addition to his slender, undamaged fingers, John Flaherty has a clean-cut, open-faced look that belies his fourteen-year career in the bigs. Over the course of 1,047 games with Tampa Bay, San Diego, Detroit, the Yankees, and the Bosox, Flaherty hit only .252 and clouted 80 homers, but was celebrated for his defensive prowess as well as his exceptional handling of pitchers.

He was mostly a backup player, yet with the Yankees he was in their starting lineup every five days. That's because Randy Johnson so admired his pitch-calling that the tall southpaw demanded Flaherty serve as his personal catcher.

"I can confirm that I'm Irish," Flaherty says. "My father's parents were born in County Kerry, where the family's original name was O'Flaherty. They came to America sometime after World War II, looking to escape the aftermath of destruction and confusion that blighted all of Europe, while also hoping to take advantage of the postwar economic boom in the States."

Born in the Bronx, Flaherty grew up in what he calls "an Irish conclave" swarming with aunts, uncles, and cousins, most of them from County Cork.

The church, of course, was always an important presence in his boyhood, but his ethnic heritage was mostly manifest in his "tough Irish household. If you wanted something, whatever it might be—a baseball glove or bat or ball—you had to earn it. Nothing but the basics of food, clothing, and shelter was handed to us. For sure, there was plenty of love to go around, but the emphasis was always on cultivating a good work ethic. And we were always proud to be Irish."

That meant doing nothing to embarrass the family name. "This became even more important once I started in pro ball and wore my name on the back of my uniform."

Throughout his career, Flaherty seldom experienced any demonstrations of camaraderie with his fellow Irishmen. "Although there was a minor league umpire named Sweeney who occasionally narrowed the strike zone when I was hitting."

On the flip side, Flaherty never observed a hint of anti-Irish bias.

Although he's still in the public eye as a frequent color commentator for the Yankees on the YES Network, Flaherty keeps a low profile. He occasionally addresses local Little League banquets in his adopted hometown in upstate New York, but belongs to no Irish social clubs. Even so, he was voted into the Irish-American Baseball Hall of Fame in 2010.

Shortly thereafter, Flaherty was also selected to receive the Irish-

American Sports Good Guy award at a benefit luncheon to raise scholarship funds for Fordham University undergraduates.

"Both of these awards came as complete surprises," he says, "and I'm honored to be so well thought of."

Flaherty seems too good to be true, but there's nothing phony about him. Here's how he boils down the essence of what his Irish heritage has meant to him: "Always respect other people."

Chapter Twenty-Five

Wartime

The longed-for tidal wave
Of justice can rise up
And hope and history rhyme.
                —*Seamus Heaney*

MANY STAR-QUALITY PLAYERS would eventually enlist in the armed forces, but the first major leaguer to be drafted in 1941 was an Irishman.

♣Hugh Mulcahy pitched for the Phillies, who had been the National League's worst team for four consecutive seasons. No surprise then that Mulcahy had never produced a winning record in Philadelphia and was a two-time twenty-game loser. In fact, his nickname was "Losing Pitcher." Still, he served four admirable years overseas, before returning to play three more years.

As per usual, Irishmen set new records:

♣By 1943, Joe Cronin was only inserting himself in the Red Sox's lineup either in emergencies or as a pinch hitter. Even with his rapidly expanding waistline, however, he still knew how to use a bat. Over the course of the season, Cronin cracked five pinch-hit homers, a single-season major league record that was later tied by Jerry Lynch and Rusty Staub but never surpassed.

Still unequaled are the 25 pinch-hit RBIs that Cronin delivered that year.

♣Charles "Red" Barrett was a control-oriented veteran pitcher for the Boston Braves. Even so, up until August 10, 1944, he'd lost many more games than he'd won. But on that date—a night game in Cincinnati that Boston won 2–0—Barrett made an about-face.

What was extraordinary about that contest was its having been completed in one hour and fifteen minutes, a record-short duration for any game played under the lights before or since. Even more unusual was Barrett's needing only 58 pitches to record the necessary 27 outs—which still stands as a record for a complete game.

Perhaps Jocko Conlan, the home plate umpire, had expanded Barrett's strike zone to help out a fellow Irishman.

Whatever really happened that night, Barrett was suddenly transformed into an ace. The following season, he led the NL with 23 wins and 24 complete games. Barrett's turnaround was rewarded when he was named to the NL's all-star squad in midsummer. However, the gas rationing necessary to the war effort limited traveling and the 1945 All-Star Game was never played.

♣The 1941 season signaled the arrival of one of the finest umpires the game had ever seen—John "Jocko" Conlan. It was Conlan, remember, who neglected to tell Casey Stengel that he'd left his uniform pants in the clubhouse when they were both employed by the Toledo Mud Hens. Conlan had gone on to play two seasons with the White Sox but his glove was full of holes.

In his first full season as an arbiter, Conlan led his National League peers by ejecting 26 players for disagreeing too forcefully with his decisions. When asked to explain his quick thumb, Conlan said, "You've got to have and command respect. Without them, you're nothing."

One rainy day in Conlan's rookie season, Pittsburgh was trailing in the early innings when he resisted Frankie Frisch's demand that he call the game. Frisch was managing the Pirates and he renewed his argument by walking onto the field carrying a large unfurled umbrella. Not only did Conlan dismiss Frisch for the duration, but he made sure that the game was completed despite the downpour.

Over the next twenty-four years, Conlan was involved in several other unique situations. In 1961, Leo Durocher was a coach for the Los Angeles Dodgers and got the heave-ho from Conlan for protesting a close call at home plate that wasn't to his liking. Durocher sought to demonstrate his displeasure by kicking the ground, but accidentally booted Conlan in the shins. The umpire returned the favor and soon the two men were taking turns kicking each other— until Durocher gave up upon realizing that Conlan was wearing shin guards and steel-toed shoes.

Throughout his Hall of Fame career, Conlan was always mindful of his ethnicity. During a game in St. Louis, he banished Pittsburgh's Danny Murtaugh for arguing over a called strike three. But Murtaugh appealed to the Irish heritage that both he and Conlan shared. After all, the Cardinals' corner infielders (Whitey Kurowski and Stan Musial) were Polish, the second baseman (Red Schoendienst) was German, the pitcher (Howie Pollet) was French, and the catcher (Joe Garagiola) was Italian.

"But there are only two Irishmen on the field," Murtaugh pointed out, "and you want to throw half of us out!"

Convinced by Murtaugh's logic, Conlan allowed him to remain in the game.

Conlan was working behind the plate one day when he grew weary of Richie Ashburn's constant barking at his ball-and-strike decisions. "I'll tell you what I'm going to do, Richie," Conlan finally said. "I'm going to let you call your own balls and strikes."

The very next pitch bounced in the dirt several inches in front of the plate, and Ashburn called it a strike. "Richie," said Conlan, "you have just had the only chance a hitter has ever had in the history of baseball to bat and umpire at the same time. And you blew it. That's the last pitch you call. I'm not going to have you louse up my profession."

♣Nine months after Mickey Owen muffed Hugh Casey's spitter to give the Yankees life in the 1941 World Series, Brooklyn's catcher achieved a modicum of redemption when he smacked a pinch-hit home run in the 1942 All-Star Game. His round-tripper represented the only run scored by the National League in losing 3–1. It should also be noted that Owen batted 421 times that season without hitting another homer.

♣That same summer, an unnamed sportswriter in Ireland was both enthused and confused when he witnessed his first baseball game. The combatants were a pair of U.S. Army teams.

Here's how the writer described one particular play: "Kentucky Wildcat has the bat—wallop, wham! The white ball, like a comet, streaks to the outfield. The Wildcat drops the bat like it was electric-heated and hares away to the big blob of whitewash that marks first base. He has reached the first milestone of the four that make a run. The scoring's on the deferred payment system—on installments."

The writer also marveled that, unlike cricket or soccer, the baseball game never stopped for refreshments. "On we go. No halftime or anything like that. No break for tea or a highball. No sir! The game's the thing."

The 1945 season saw the emergence of still another league that dared to challenge the established National and American leagues. The Mexican League actually began operations in 1925 and, in addition to native players, was mostly home to highly talented Cubans and American blacks. But in the early 1940s the organization was taken over by Jorge Pasquel, a hugely ambitious, wealthy Mexican industrialist.

Pasquel set out to woo established big leaguers with promises of large salaries, no taxes, and subsidized living accommodations. The major league's commissioner Happy Chandler ruled that any jumpers would be banned from professional baseball in the States for five years. But Pasquel spent upwards of $50 million to improve living and playing conditions in the Liga Mexicana de Béisbol and managed to entice twenty-two big leaguers to play south of the border, including Mickey Owen.

"I'm perfectly happy here," Owen claimed. "My wife likes Mexico, we just moved into a luxurious modern apartment, and everything is dandy."

However, Ted Williams turned down an offer of $300,000 for three years; Stan Musial spurned $650,000 for a five-year commitment; Phil Rizzuto didn't give a second thought to a proffered deal worth $10,000 and a brand-new Cadillac; and Babe Ruth rejected a whopping $1 million to be the league's president.

NINETEEN FORTY-FIVE PROVED to be the Year of the Irish in Cooperstown as the Old-Timers Committee voted to admit Roger Bresnahan, Dan Brouthers, Jimmy Collins, Ed Delahanty, Hugh Duffy, Hughie Jennings, Mike Kelly, and Wilbert Robinson.

♣ANOTHER IRISH PLAYER in that same year was the not-so-proud possessor of a much more dubious distinction.

Measuring only 5'9" and 150 pounds, Joe Cleary didn't look like a pitcher, but his fastball had a surprising hop and he'd been moderately successful in various minor leagues, posting an 84-84 record.

As on many other teams, the Washington Senators' best pitchers were working for Uncle Sam and the team was desperate to find adequate substitutes. Signing Cleary seemed like a good idea at the time.

On August 4, 1945, in the second game of a doubleheader against the Red Sox, Cleary climbed the mound to start the fourth inning.

The results of his one and only major league appearance were disastrous. He faced eight batters, struck out one, issued three walks, was touched for five hits, and yielded seven earned runs.

His resulting ERA of 189.0 is the highest ever for any pitcher who retired a batter. Cleary first saw the emerald-tinted light of day in County Cork, also qualifying him as the last Irish-born player in the major leagues.

♣However, in May 1946, the Irish influence in the modernization of the game continued to be honored when Johnny Evers, Tom McCarthy, Ed Walsh, Clark Griffith, and Joe McGinnity were enshrined in the Hall.

Even so, with Jackie Robinson's breaking the color line in 1947, the racism of numerous members of the major league community was revealed. In addition to the aforementioned racial prejudice of Cronin and Stengel, another pair of Irishmen shared the same blind spot.

♣Before and after his military service, Hugh Casey was simply the best reliever in the National League—twice setting the pace in saves and in relief wins. While the Yankees bested the Dodgers in the 1947 World Series, Casey had a hand in each one of Brooklyn's victories—winning Games 3 and 4, and saving Game 6.

Born and raised in the deep South, Casey was never able (or willing) to transcend a segregationist mind-set. In 1947, he was furious at having Robinson as a teammate and continually gave the rookie a hard time. Casey was free with the N-word, and when he was on the mound categorically ignored the signals flashed by Roy Campanella. Casey was traded to Pittsburgh after the 1948 season.

Nor was a certain umpire immune from the warped vision of racism. It was common knowledge around the league that Jocko Conlan would quickly eject black players for mildly protesting any of his calls, while allowing white players to stomp around and curse him with impunity. Conlan's racial bias was likewise in evidence when he habitually narrowed the strike zone for white hitters and expanded it for black hitters.

SEVERAL IRISHMEN WERE at the top of their game in the 1940s:

♣George McQuinn was among the best-fielding first basemen of his time, and in 1944, he batted .438 in the St. Louis Browns' one and only World Series appearance. Among his other accomplishments was a 34-game hitting streak to go with a lifetime average of .278.

McQuinn's stats could easily have been better had he reached the major leagues earlier than the late age of twenty-eight. The problem was twofold: McQuinn was stuck in Cincinnati's minor league system while Frank McCormick routinely hit over .300 and led the NL in hits and RBIs, and then McQuinn lingered in the Yankees farm system while Lou Gehrig was a fixture at first base.

♣Barney McCosky starred in the outfield for the Tigers, A's, Reds, and Indians. In 1940, his 200 base hits led the AL. The peak seasons of McCosky's eleven-year career were spent in military service, yet he wound up with a lifetime batting average of .312. Still another excellent Irish player overlooked in Hall of Fame voting.

♣Tommy "Kelly" Holmes was the ultimate contact hitter, whiffing only 122 times in 4,992 at-bats. No wonder he batted .352 in 1945, a performance aided greatly by a 34-game hitting streak. From 1942 to 1952, Holmes was just as valuable as a sure-handed centerfielder for the Braves and the Dodgers. His lifetime average was .302, yet even more impressive was his reputation for being a class act.

♣Jim Hegan never hit much—.228 over seventeen seasons—yet he was the best defensive catcher of his generation. Also renowned as a handler of pitchers, Hegan caught three of Bob Feller's no-hitters, and four of his battery mates are in the Hall of Fame—Feller, Bob Lemon, Early Wynn, and Satchel Paige. Despite his week bat, Hegan was named to the AL's all-star squad five years running, starting in 1947.

♣From 1943 to 1949, Pat Seerey was an all-or-nothing hitter with the Indians and the White Sox. He always had home runs in mind and did clout 86 in 561 games—with a high of 26 of 1946. On June 7, 1948, Seerey earned a share of baseball immortality by hitting four home runs in a single game, albeit one that lasted eleven innings.

If Irish players no longer dominated the game as they once had, they would again.

Part IV

POSTWAR TO THE PRESENT

Chapter Twenty-Six

The Fabulous Fifties

Well Casey was winning,
Hank Aaron was beginning,
One Robbie going out, one coming in.
Kiner and Midget Cadell,
The Thumper and Mel Parnell,
And Ike was the only one winning down in Washington.

—Terry Cashman

MIRRORING AMERICA'S EXUBERANT growth after the war, this new decade was highlighted by a resurgence of Irish influence in the major leagues.

1950

Connie Mack and three of his sons, Connie Jr., Earle, and Ray, united to purchase 100 percent of the AL Philly franchise. The old man continued to manage the A's for one last season—finishing in last place with a dismal record of 52-102. Another Irishman, Jimmy Dykes, was already named as his successor. Mickey Cochrane was the general manager, with Earle Mack becoming the chief scout.

♣Unfortunately, the A's were unable to find or sign more than a few Irish players: Barney McClosky, a career .312-hitting outfielder who was past his prime; Les McCrabb, a pitcher who was never any good but was attempting to make a comeback after eight years; and Bob Hooper, a Canadian-born pitcher and the ace of the staff with a record of 15-10.

Meanwhile crosstown, the offense of the NL pennant-winning Philadelphia Phillies was powered by a pair of full-blooded Irishmen and two with Irish roots.

♣Del Ennis was the NL's Rookie of the Year in 1946, but had his career year in 1950: .311, 31 homers, and a league-leading 126 RBIs. If the beefy Ennis was slow afoot in right field, he compensated with strong-arm throws.

♣In his third full season with the Phillies, middle infielder Granny Hamner had great range at either shortstop or second base, and was admired by his peers for his throwing arm. No matter what position he played, Hamner was a fixture in the sixth slot in the batting order and was the team's most reliable clutch hitter. His hustle and aggressiveness made him the fans' favorite in blue-collar Philadelphia. He was also the first player ever selected to an all-star team at two different positions—shortstop in 1952, then second base the following season.

♣Richie Ashburn came by his Irish heritage on his mother's side. A speedy center fielder, Ashburn was Philly's leadoff hitter and his .303 batting average and league-leading total of fourteen triples made him an excellent table setter.

♣Willie "Puddin' Head" Jones started at third base for the Phillies from 1949 to 1959, providing sensational fielding and rock-steady hitting. A two-time all-star (1950, 1951), Jones hit his career peak in 1950 when he produced 25 homers, 88 RBIs, and a .267 batting average.

He was still another strong but silent leader on the team that was nicknamed the Whiz Kids.

The Yankees' drive to their second straight world championship was immensely aided by two late additions to the team who both happened to be Irish pitchers.

♣Edward Charles "Whitey" Ford was promoted from the Yankees' Triple-A team in Kansas City in late June and made his major league debut on July 1 in Fenway Park. He relieved fellow Irishman Tommy Byrne (15-9 for the year) in the second inning, and pitched in a mop-up role through the sixth while allowing seven hits, five runs, and six walks in a 13–4 loss. However, Ford recovered from his stage fright to win his first nine starts—losing only in relief late in the season—and finish with a sparkling record of 9-1.

Ford went on to log the entirety of his eighteen-year career with the Yankees, finishing with certified Hall of Fame credentials that included eight All-Star Games, one Cy Young Award (1961), plus being the American League pacesetter three times in wins and winning percentage. Ford also distinguished himself in the eleven World Series he played in, setting records in total wins (10), games pitched (22), innings pitched (144), strikeouts (94), and consecutive shutout innings ($33^2/3$).

During his glory years, Ford's repertoire included a sharp curve, a sneaky-fast fastball, and unerring control. And his longtime catcher Elston Howard dubbed him "Chairman of the Board" because Ford was always calm and in control.

At the same time, Ford wasn't above doctoring the baseball, especially in his declining years. "I needed something extra to help me survive," Ford said. "I didn't cheat when I won the twenty-five games in 1961. I don't want anybody to get any idea and take my Cy Young Award away. And I didn't cheat in 1963 when I won twenty-four games. Well, maybe a little."

Aided and abetted by the grounds crew at Yankee Stadium and Elston Howard, Ford had several ways to procure the necessary "something extra."

The grounds crew would create a wet area just to the right of the catcher's box. Howard would pretend to lose his balance when catching a pitch so as to land on his right hand. But since the ball was still in Howard's possession, it would be partially covered in mud when he tossed it back to Ford. Only unleashed with two strikes on the unsuspecting hitter and the bases empty, the resulting "mudball" was literally unhittable. Moreover, after the inevitable strikeout, the ball would be whipped around the infield and be surreptitiously cleaned by the infielders.

Until he was apprehended by an alert umpire, Ford used the diamond on his wedding ring to gouge rough spots in the ball. Howard also contributed to Ford's outlawed pitches by slicing the cover of the ball with a sharpened buckle on his shin guard.

But Ford claimed that he only threw a spitball once. "Mickey Mantle and I were in San Francisco for the 1961 All-Star Game," Ford said, "and the owner of the Giants, Horace Stoneham, was the host. So we asked Stoneham if we could play some golf at the Olympic Club the day before the game, and Stoneham said, 'Oh, sure.' So Mickey and I played golf, but we also spent about six hundred dollars each in the pro shop on shoes and alpaca sweaters, and we signed Horace's name to everything."

But later that night at a cocktail party, Mickey and Whitey felt guilty and decided to pay Stoneham back the money. They each kicked in three hundred dollars, but Stoneham wouldn't take the money and proposed a wager instead. If Ford pitched in the All-Star Game the next day and got Willie Mays out, then the debt would be forgiven. But if Mays got a hit, then Stoneham would be due the entire $1,200.

Ford was dubious because Mays always hit him, but agreed.

"Mickey and I stayed out late that night," Ford recalled. "We didn't pay much attention to All-Star Games in those days. And Mickey woke me up the next morning and he said, 'You ain't gonna believe it, but you're starting the game.' And I said, 'Oh, boy.'"

Ford began the game by retiring the first two hitters, then yielded a double to Roberto Clemente before Mays stepped into the batter's box. "And old Mickey and I were thinking it's $1,200 or nothing.

Willie hit two foul balls down the left field line that went about five hundred feet, so I had him two strikes and no balls. This was the perfect time to throw a spitter. The pitch almost started at Willie's hip, and it just broke down over the plate. Willie actually jumped back, thinking the ball was going to hit him. And the umpire said, 'Strike three.' And Willie's lying on the ground. And in Frisco, to go to the dugout, you went near home plate. And as I was coming in to the dugout, I looked down at Willie, and he looked up at me and he said, 'What's that crazy SOB in center field clapping for?'

"Mickey was running in from the outfield celebrating the fact that we'd just saved $1,200."

♣Besides Ford, another late-arriving Irish pitcher who was of immense help in the Yankees' success was Tom Ferrick. In his previous seven years in the AL, Ferrick had mostly toiled in relief for second division teams. He was obtained by the Yanks in a multiplayer deal with the lowly Browns on June 15 after Joe Page, New York's all-star fireman, came down with a career-ending sore arm.

Ferrick responded to his first pennant race with an 8-4 record, a 3.65 ERA, and eleven saves. The perfect topper in Ferrick's clutch performance came in the World Series when he won Game 3 in relief.

His reward?

Precisely one year after he joined the Yankees, Ferrick was traded to the pitiful Washington Senators.

1951

♣Joe Collins was installed as the Yankees' regular first baseman and responded by hitting a clutch .286 and providing a catch-all glove. He would play in more than 100 games and bash double-digit homers for the next four seasons.

♣Gil McDougald could play shortstop, third base, and second base with equal brilliance. With his unorthodox batting stance that had the head of the bat hanging lower than his hands, McDougald batted .306, smacked 14 homers, and was the AL's Rookie of the Year.

♣Bob Cain's clan came from County Derry, yet he was a decidedly lackluster pitcher—37-44, 4.50 ERA in five seasons. On August 19, 1951, however, he was on the mound for one of the most bizarre at-bats in baseball history.

Bill Veeck, the owner of the St. Louis Browns, was a P. T. Barnum type of guy whose unorthodox promotions attracted more hometown fans than the inept Brownies deserved. Late on Friday, August 17, Veeck cleared roster space for a new player and sent his signed contract to the league office knowing that the contract would not be scrutinized until Monday. The player in question was Eddie Gaedel, who stood 3'7" and weighed 65 pounds.

In the bottom of the second inning of the first game of a doubleheader with the Detroit Tigers, Gaedel was announced as a pinch hitter. Then he grabbed a tiny bat and literally skipped to the batter's box. Gaedel had been told in no uncertain terms not to swing at any pitch. He'd also been instructed to crouch at the plate, so that his vertical strike zone measured a mere one and a half inches.

Cain was the Tigers pitcher, and time was called while his catcher strode to the mound to offer this profound advice: "Keep the ball low."

Instead of crouching, Gaedel assumed a clumsy imitation of Joe DiMaggio's spread-eagle stance. But his bat never stirred as Cain made two legitimate attempts to throw strikes—both of which were high. Cain completed the base-on-balls by lobbing another pair of pitches that were at least a foot over Gaedel's head.

On his way to first base, Gaedel paused twice to bow to the cheering fans. Cain couldn't keep himself from laughing. Gaedel was immediately replaced with a pinch runner.

On Monday, the AL commissioner nullified the contract, saying that Veeck had made a farce of the game. Veeck countered by threatening to file an official demand to determine if the AL's reigning MVP, Phil Rizzuto, was a short player or a tall midget.

Gaedel passed away ten years later. The only individual to attend

the funeral who was affiliated with major league baseball in any way
was Bob Cain.

"I never even met the guy," said Cain, "but I felt obligated to go."

1952

Two tall Irishmen had notable double-sports careers, and fame of
other sorts, as well.

♣Gene Conley measured 6'8" and 225 pounds, and was clobbered
in his inauspicious debut on the mound for the Boston Braves on
April 4; his rookie season continued to be a dud—0-3 with an elevated
7.89 ERA. He skipped the 1953 baseball season to play with the
Celtics. For his NBA career, he grabbed 6.3 rebounds even though he
only averaged 16.5 minutes per game. Projected to forty-eight minutes, Conley would have averaged 18.3 rebounds per outing.

He was the first athlete to win championships in two of the four
major American sports—with the Milwaukee Braves in 1957 and the
Boston Celtics from 1959 to 1961. In so doing, Conley performed
a rare double dip—striking out Ted Williams in the 1959 All-Star
Game, and routinely guarding Wilt Chamberlain.

According to Red Auerbach, the Celtics' brilliant coach, baseball
was a "sissy's game." But he couldn't care less what Conley did over
the summer.

If he was a specialist on the hardwood, Conley became a dominant presence on the mound with the Braves, the Phillies, and the
Red Sox. Three times an all-star, he was the winning pitcher in the
1955 All-Star Game. After the 1959 baseball season, the Phillies
offered him $20,000 to forgo the basketball season, but Conley nixed
the deal. He ended his eleven-year career in the bigs with a record of
91-96 and an ERA of 3.82.

"When I look back, I don't know how I did it, I really don't,"
Conley said. "I think I was having so much fun that it just kept me
going. I can't remember a teammate that I didn't enjoy."

♣Another major league baseball player who also played in the NBA made his movie debut in 1952: Chuck Connors. Born Kevin Joseph Aloysius Connors, he was an altar boy from Brooklyn who went on to be a high school and college two-sport star—and to make it up to the big leagues, albeit briefly.

Connors hated his given name of Kevin and tried out a couple of nicknames: "Lefty" and "Stretch." But because he always shouted to his fielders as they were about to throw the ball to him at first base— "Chuck it to me, baby"—he became known as "Chuck."

He actually had a good season in the minors, hitting .293 with 17 homers one year, and the Dodgers gave him an advance invitation to their Vero Beach training camp for the spring of 1947. But Connors got a call to join the Boston Celtics in the inaugural season of the Basketball Association of America (the forerunner of the NBA).

"[They] offered me five thousand bucks," said Connors. "Holy Christ, that was a lot of dough in those days. Since I was making only three-fifty a month at Newport News, I went to Boston with alacrity."

Connors, of course, went on to TV cultural fame as the Rifleman, but Connors is also one of only twelve athletes in the history of American professional sports to have played for both MLB and the NBA.

He is also credited as the first professional basketball player to break a backboard, doing so before the first game at the new Boston Garden, delaying the start of the game for over an hour.

1953

♣Mickey McDermott was a twenty-four-year-old lanky southpaw who had his career year with the Red Sox—winning 18 games (four of them shutouts). Considering the proximity of the Green Monster in left field, McDermott's success was all the more remarkable.

But the young man had a wild streak, both on and off the mound. His lifetime total of 752 strikeouts was exceeded by his yielding 838 walks. Between games, McDermott was a heavy drinker and carouser.

During the 1953 season, he punched a Boston sportswriter, and also cursed owner Tom Yawkey's wife. No surprise that shortly after the season, McDermott was traded to the Washington Senators.

♣Standing only 5'9", Johnny O'Brien was a high-scoring pivot man on the basketball court at Seattle University. His twin brother, Eddie, was a key reserve. On January 21, 1952, Johnny tallied 43 points in Seattle's 84–81 upset of the Harlem Globetrotters.

But both Johnny and Eddie also excelled on the baseball diamond, the former primarily playing second base while the latter played shortstop.

They were both rookies with the 1953 Pittsburgh Pirates and, quite appropriately, each played in 89 games. Although they were both excellent fielders, neither was a particularly dangerous hitter. Nevertheless, the brothers O'Brien were the first twins to play in the major leagues, as well as the first siblings to play on the same team at the same time.

1954

The Philadelphia Athletics relocated to Kansas City. As part of the deal, the Phillies bought and moved their games to Connie Mack Stadium.

1955

♣Al Kaline's initial claim to greatness occurred in 1955, when at twenty years and ten months he hit .340 to become the youngest batting champion in history (one day younger than Ty Cobb was at his title in 1907). Kaline also blasted 27 homers, drove in 102 runs, and led the league with 200 hits.

Kaline was born with a deformed left foot caused by a bone disease known as osteomyelitis. When he was eight, a two-inch section of bone was surgically removed, leaving the foot permanently scarred and misshapen, and frequently painful. Another result was that three of his toes never touched the ground when he walked. But Kaline compensated by teaching himself to run with only the outside of his damaged foot touching the ground.

Even so, Kaline was a standout player at Southern High School in Baltimore. John McHale, the farm director for the Detroit Tigers, was encouraged by one of his regional scouts to take a look at Kaline. McHale was so impressed that he signed Kaline for a $15,000 bonus and a guaranteed salary of $6,000 for two years.

Without the benefit of seasoning in the minor leagues, the eighteen-year-old Kaline, standing 5'10", was a scrawny 155 pounds. "I was so skinny," said Kaline, "they had to get a uniform made up for me, but that first night or two I had to wear a batboy's uniform."

Kaline is still celebrated as arguably baseball's finest all-around player in that he could hit for average (.297 lifetime, with nine seasons over .300, and 3,007 hits) and power (399 HRs). Moreover, he hit .379 with two dingers as the Tigers won the 1968 World Series. An eighteen-time all-star, Kaline could also run the bases (137 steals, 1,622 runs) and was an exceptional fielder (ten Gold Gloves).

Kaline's decorum, honesty, and modesty were legendary.

In 1970, he had what he considered to be an unsuccessful season—.278, 16 homers, 71 RBIs—and turned down a new contract for $100,000.

"I don't deserve that much money," he told Detroit's front office. Indeed the most he ever earned was $103,000, and that didn't happen until 1973 and 1974, his last two years in uniform.

In 1980, Kaline became only the tenth player ever to be elected to the Hall of Fame in his initial year of eligibility. While never a superstar along the lines of Babe Ruth, Joe DiMaggio, Willie Mays, and Stan Musial, Al Kaline is still honored in the Motor City as "Mr. Tiger."

1956

♣Bob Oldis had bulging eyes, a crooked nose, and a hole in his bat, but he was a terrific receiver whenever he donned the "tools of ignorance." Which wasn't often. From 1953 to 1955 he appeared in a total of only 24 games as the Washington Senators' third-string catcher. Then, after hitting a collective .260, Oldis was waived and wound up playing for Denver in the American Association.

He was always a cutup and during one game, he managed to stroke a single, but then wandered so far from the base as to be caught in a rundown.

"I had to do something quick," said Oldis, "so I unstrapped first base and put it behind my back. Then I ran up to the umpire and pointed out that there was no base, so how could I be tagged out? The miserable rat threw me out. Didn't even consult the rule book."

Oldis did make a return visit to the bigs in 1960, finishing his seven years there hitting .237 and only one homer in 135 games.

1957

♣A large part of Richie Ashburn's success was due to his ability to foul off a pitcher's best offerings, which is precisely why he drew 1,198 lifetime walks while striking out only once every 16.8 at-bats. Twice he led the NL in hitting.

On August 17, Ashburn's ability to spoil good pitches negatively impacted (literally) one of the Phillies' hometown fans. During one at-bat the lefty-swinging Ashburn lined a foul ball into the lower stands situated between home plate and third base. Unfortunately, the ball struck Mrs. Alice Roth with such force that her nose was broken and a stretcher had to be summoned to carry her to an ambulance.

Adding injury to injury, during the same at-bat, Ashburn flicked another foul ball that hit Roth in the leg even as she was being lifted from her seat to the stretcher.

Coincidentally, Roth's husband, Earl, was the sports editor of the *Philadelphia Bulletin*.

♣Led by a gathering of Irishmen, the Milwaukee Braves beat the Yankees in a seven-game World Series. Milwaukee's manager was Fred Haney, and his coaching staff included Connie Ryan, Bob Keely, and Johnny Riddle.

Among the players were Gene Conley, Don McMahon, Johnny Logan, Dave Jolly, and John DeMerit.

1958

♣In losing his major league debut (and only appearance of the season) with Cincinnati, Jim O'Toole showed the promise that would eventually make him the mainstay of the Reds' pitching corps. In seven innings, O'Toole was touched for only four hits and one run, but he was the losing pitcher.

Three years later, O'Toole went 19-9 as Cincinnati won the NL pennant. In the process he was third in wins, second in ERA (3.10) and win percentage (.679), fourth in whiffs (178), and fifth in innings pitched (25 $^2/_3$) and opponents batting average (.240).

♣Billy O'Dell's southpaw slants kept the Orioles respectable, and he was an all-star in 1958 and 1959.

1959

♣From 1959 to 1973, Joe Cronin served as the American League's president, and was an early (too early) proponent of the designated hitter.

♣As a catcher, Sherman Lollar's excellence was a given—he led the AL's receivers in fielding percentage five times and was a six-time all-star. But he was a grossly underrated hitter.

His career high in home runs was a hefty 22 (1959); in batting average, .293 (1956); and in RBIs, 84 (1959). All exceptional numbers for a defense-oriented catcher.

In 1959, Lollar was the backbone of the pennant-winning Chicago White Sox.

Overall, Lollar was the epitome of a quietly heroic Irishman.

♣Joe Cunningham was always a steady-fielding first baseman and a capable batsman, but his 1959 season was a huge surprise to everybody, including him. A career .297 hitter, he posted a .345 average—27 points higher than his previous best. No wonder he was a onetime all-star.

♣Bobby Bragan had a tour of duty as a backup catcher and utility infielder in the 1940s with the Phillies and the Dodgers. He was with Brooklyn when Jackie Robinson broke the color line in 1947. Being a solid son of the South (born in Birmingham, Alabama), Bragan was initially opposed to Robinson's presence on the team, going so far as to sign a petition advocating Robinson's being traded elsewhere, anywhere. But Bragan soon changed his mind.

"After just one road trip," Bragan said, "I saw the quality of Jackie the man and the player. And I was honored to be a teammate of his."

He went on to manage the Pirates (1956–57), Indians (1958), and Milwaukee-Atlanta (1963–66). By then, Bragan was renowned for his fairness, color blindness, and fierce disagreements with umpires.

In 1959, he was managing the Dodgers' top minor league team, the Spokane Indians in the Pacific Coast League. Among Bragan's players was a weak-hitting yet fleet-footed shortstop named Maury Wills, whose future seemed dim. Bragan had the brainstorm of converting the right-handed Wills into a switch-hitter to take full advantage of his warp speed. Then Bragan nagged the Dodgers' front office until they finally summoned Wills to Los Angeles in the tail end of the 1959 season. Wills, of course, went on to lead the Dodgers to glory and to set numerous records in the fine art of stealing bases.

An additional note: On August 16, 2005, Bragan came out of retirement to manage the Fort Worth Cats in the independent Central League. He was eighty-seven years, nine months, and sixteen days old, making him the most elderly manager (by seven days over Connie Mack) in the history of professional baseball.

But the years had not diminished Bragan's fire. After vociferously arguing an umpire's call in that same game, he was ejected in the third inning.

Thereby making the part-Irish Bragan also the oldest manager in pro ball to get thumbed from a game.

Chapter Twenty-Seven

The Crazy Sixties

Brooks never had a candy bar named after him. In
Baltimore, people named their children after him.
—*Gordon Beard*

WHEN DENNY MCCLAIN suffered a foot injury in September
1967 and had to miss six starts, Detroit's best pitcher came up with
several explanations as to how it had occurred:

- He had kicked a locker after a bad outing.
- He had fallen asleep while watching TV and then wrenched his
  toes when he got up in the dark.
- He had accidentally kicked some garbage cans while being
  "terrorized" by squirrels.
- He had fallen into a manhole in the street while being chased by
  wild dogs.

The truth was not discovered until several years later: McClain
had welched on a losing bet he had made with a mob-backed bookie,
and a goon had subsequently stomped on his foot.

After missing critical starts, McClain returned to the mound in the Tigers' last game of the season and was hit hard in a losing effort. Detroit finished one game behind the pennant-winning Red Sox.

But even as the glory seasons of his pitching career were soon to arrive, McClain's nefarious dealings with underworld figures continued.

In 1968, McClain had an all-time magnificent year. He compiled a record of 31-6 and an ERA of 1.96, while pitching 28 complete games and 336 innings.

McClain won his 31st game against the Yankees on September 19, and there was an historic sidebar to the game. The Tigers had already clinched the pennant and were up 6–1 with one out and the bases empty in the top of the seventh. The hitter was Mickey Mantle, who was in the last season of his glorious career. At that point, Mantle had hit a total of 534 homers, which tied him with Jimmie Foxx for fourth place on the all-time list. While Mantle settled into the batter's box, McClain made an unmistakable motion to inquire exactly where the Mick would like the first pitch to be. Mantle indicated that letter-high down the middle would be just fine.

But Mantle didn't really believe that McClain would accommodate him, so he took a pair of as-ordered batting practice offerings for strikes. Finally convinced, Mantle swung mightily at the next pitch but fouled it off. The fourth gimme-pitch was blasted into the right-field stands. As Mantle rounded third he said, "Thanks, Denny," and McClain just grinned.

Joe Pepitone was next up, and he shouted out to the mound, "Me, too!" But McClain flipped him with a brushback fastball.

Understandably bothered by some soreness in his overworked pitching arm, McClain was only 1-2 in the subsequent World Series—but the Tigers prevailed over the Cardinals on the back of Mickey Lolich's three wins.

McClain's regular season achievements were rewarded with his being named both the AL's MVP and the Cy Young winner. He cashed in on his celebrity by giving organ recitals in Las Vegas, and also issuing two albums—*Denny McClain at the Organ*, and *Denny McClain in Las Vegas*. In addition, McClain played a snappy number on *The Ed Sullivan Show*, where he was accompanied on guitar by Bob Gibson.

Even as the Tigers' lineup suffered a team-wide slump in 1969 to finish nineteen games behind the Baltimore Orioles, McClain continued to dominate opposing hitters. For his encore, McClain went 24-9, hurled 329 innings and 9 shutouts, had a sparkling 2.80 ERA, and repeated as the AL's Cy Young recipient. His future seemed to be both secure and unlimited, and there was little doubt that McClain was destined for the Hall of Fame.

McClain's potential had been evident in his major league debut. He was only nineteen when on September 21, 1963, he was called up from the minors and pitched a complete-game win, allowing only seven hits and one earned run. To make the game even more memorable, McClain also belted a home run—the only one he ever hit.

Still, it took one full season for McClain to feel comfortable, coming of age in 1965 with a 16-6 record and a 2.61 ERA.

And that's when his fondness for Pepsi Cola turned him to the dark side.

It was no secret that McClain drank a case of Pepsi every day and, when he was pitching, drank a bottle in the dugout between innings. Naturally, a representative from the soft-drink company contacted McClain to see if he might be interested in an endorsement deal. Unfortunately, the Pepsi rep also had an affinity for gambling and he and McClain decided to join forces to "take action on bets." They subsequently tried to set up a bookmaking operation in which they would be hands-off, silent partners. But they never could get all the pieces in place.

When their plan finally became known to federal authorities in the spring of 1970, McClain was suspended by baseball commissioner Bowie Kuhn for the first three months of the season. McClain's arm was still lame when he returned to action and, in fact, after his second

Cy Young award McClain would never have another winning season. Worse still, the Tigers' organization suspended him for several days late in that same 1970 season when McClain doused two local sportswriters with a bucket of water. McClain suffered a third suspension that ended his season after he was discovered to be carrying an unlicensed gun.

The Tigers were disgusted with McClain and traded him to the Washington Senators, where he quickly ran afoul of his new manager, Ted Williams. McClain became the leader of a group of players unofficially called the Underminers' Club, whose purpose was to get Williams fired. By then, too many cortisone shots had permanently degraded McClain's arm and turned his hitherto blazing fastball into a meatball. He was 10-22 in 1971, going from the AL's leader in wins to the leader in losses.

The Senators released him after the season and McClain connected with Oakland and then Atlanta in 1972, but with no better results. After brief minor league stints in Des Moines and Shreveport, McClain retired at age twenty-nine. He did, however, make a comeback of sorts in 1974 with the London Majors of the Intercounty Baseball League in Ontario, Canada. He only pitched nine innings there, but batted .380 in fourteen games, variously playing shortstop, first base, and catcher.

Within a few years, McClain's weight had ballooned to 330 pounds and he was imprisoned on various charges that began with drug trafficking (cocaine) and included racketeering and embezzlement in an alliance with some of the nation's most notorious criminal elements. Then, in 1994, McClain and several partners purchased a small meatpacking firm in Michigan, which quickly declared bankruptcy. Two years later, McClain was convicted of having stolen $2.5 million from the employees' pension fund and spent the next six baseball seasons behind bars.

There were happier outcomes for several other Irish players in the 1960s.

♣Bill Freehan was McClain's battery mate and was considered to be the quiet leader of Detroit's world championship team in 1968. Over the course of his sixteen-year career, Freehan won five Gold Gloves and was named to eleven all-star teams—the most by any eligible player not in the Hall of Fame.

♣During that same time period, Dick McAuliffe was Detroit's shortstop, leadoff hitter, and sparkplug. He was a three-time all-star who always played as if his life were at stake on every play in every game.

♣Some say that Brooks Robinson was the best-fielding third baseman of all time. Besides some video highlights of his more incredible diving-sprawling-leaping feats of legerdemain at the hot corner, his sixteen consecutive Gold Glove awards constitute convincing proof.

Here's what Rex Barney said after Robinson's Orioles won the 1970 World Series: "He's not at his locker yet, but four guys are over there interviewing his glove."

Not even his appearance in fifteen straight All-Star Games could inflate Robinson's ego. Unlike several of his peers, he was proud to consider himself a role model. And his courtesy, decency, honesty, humility, and integrity made him an all-star both on and off the field.

"Fifty years from now," Robinson said, "I'll be just three inches of type in a record book."

♣"Sudden" Sam McDowell was a strong-armed southpaw with an explosive fastball. The workhorse of Cleveland's staff throughout the 1970s, he led the AL in strikeouts four times and in ERA once, and was chosen to compete in four midsummer classics.

Through it all, though, McDowell was troubled by a lack of control, an aching back, and over-the-top drinking. His sixteen-season career ended in 1975, whereupon his alcoholism became even more serious. After a failed business venture, McDowell was reduced to moving back in with his parents.

The character Sam Malone, a recovering alcoholic and former

Red Sox pitcher played by Ted Danson in the long-running TV series *Cheers*, was modeled on McDowell.

But McDowell's enrollment in a rehabilitation program turned his life around to the point where he was employed as an addiction counselor by several major league teams. At last report, he is the founder and CEO of a retirement resort in Florida for former players.

♣Mike Shannon was both a clutch hitter and a rifle-armed right fielder for the Cardinals from 1962 to 1970. He played in three World Series and hit key clutch homers in each. His career ended prematurely once he was diagnosed as having nephritis, a kidney disease. These days, Shannon is the radio voice of the Cardinals.

♣In 1960, Baltimore's Clint Courtney became the first catcher to use an oversized mitt whenever a knuckleball pitcher (in this case, Hoyt Wilhelm) entered the game. However, during his eleven-year career, Courtney gained more notoriety as being an aggressive throwback to the heyday of John McGraw.

Nicknamed "Scrap Iron," Courtney appeared in one game for the 1951 Yankees before being traded to the lowly St. Louis Browns and was forever resentful of the Bronx Bombers. Courtney got his revenge on the base paths, first in 1952 when he spiked Billy Martin while sliding into second base, and then in 1953 when he spiked Phil Rizzuto.

On both occasions, punches were thrown (but not, of course, by the Scooter) and heavy fines were imposed.

Overlooked by the tumults he initiated, Courtney was an excellent receiver who committed only 50 errors in 3,985 chances handled in 946 games. Courtney was also the first catcher to wear glasses.

♣Tim McCarver played in the bigs for twenty-one years, a long tenure for a catcher. Twice an all-star with the Cardinals, McCarver was the receiver of choice for a pair of incredibly talented but incredibly picky pitchers.

Bob Gibson and McCarver were both rookies in 1959 and soon developed a solid connection. Besides McCarver's obvious skills and remarkable pitch calling, Gibson's total acceptance of him was initiated by a seemingly trivial occurrence. The big right-hander was always sensitive about how he was treated by his white teammates and, when McCarver requested a swig from a bottle of soda that he was drinking, Gibson handed the bottle over and studied McCarver's reaction. Rather than wiping any residual black man's saliva from the bottle top, McCarver simply took a modest drink. That small deed convinced Gibson that McCarver would be a worthy and respectful battery mate.

They would team up to play significant roles in the Cardinals' winning two NL pennants and one World Series.

When McCarver moved to the Phillies, he hooked up with Steve Carleton, primarily because McCarver could handle the southpaw's money pitch—a sharply breaking slider that, more often than not, raised a puff of dust after it crossed the plate. Indeed, Carleton insisted on working exclusively with McCarver. The joke was that when McCarver and Carleton died, their graves would be sixty feet, six inches, apart.

In his last year as a player, McCarver appeared in six games in 1980, making him one of only twenty-nine players who had played in four decades. After McCarver retired, he began another successful career as a broadcaster.

♣During his initial eleven seasons (1956–66), Mike McCormick was a mediocre pitcher who periodically exhibited flashes of brilliance. On the basis of early-season successes, he had been named to a pair of All-Star Games but his combined record for those seasons ended up being only 28-28.

Then, in 1967, McCormick returned to the San Francisco Giants and had an astonishing turnabout. He went 22-10, with 5 shutouts and an ERA of 2.85, and was voted the NL's Cy Young Award winner. Plagued by a sore arm, however, McCormick never won more than twelve games thereafter.

McCormick's name is still in the record books for being the victim of Hank Aaron's 500th career homer, and also for clouting the 500th homer made by a pitcher in the history of the game.

♣Art Mahaffey was another Irish pitcher with wondrous stuff who was also beleaguered by arm trouble. An example of how good he was (and could have been) was a game played on April 23, 1961, the second half of a twin bill, when Mahaffey struck out at least one hitter in every inning, totaled seventeen in all, and led the Phillies to a 6–0 victory over the Cubs.

Unfortunately, Mahaffey's arm woes limited him to only two all-star appearances and a record of 59-64 over seven years. These days, Mahaffey is mainly remembered by veteran baseball watchers as having the absolutely best-ever pickoff move to first by any right-handed pitcher.

♣From 1963 to 1969, Jim Maloney was one of the most dominant pitchers in the game. His out-pitch was a fastball that routinely lit up the radar guns at 99 miles per hour.

During that stretch, Maloney was a brilliant 117-61 for the Cincinnati Reds, before their Red Machine phase. Among his wins were two no-hitters; he was denied credit for a third when the first hit he yielded was a game winner in the bottom of the tenth.

Although he was an all-star in 1965, Maloney was overshadowed by such contemporaries as Koufax, Drysdale, Marichal, Gibson, Gaylord Perry, and Ferguson Jenkins.

♣Norm Cash is of Scotch-Irish lineage and had a Hall of Fame season for the Detroit Tigers in 1961. That's when he led the AL by hitting .361 while also smashing 41 round-trippers, thereby earning his initial placement in what would be five All-Star Games. Unfortunately for Cash, he never again approached the same achievements.

Here's how he explained his extraordinary 1961 campaign: "I owe my success to expansion pitching, a short right-field fence, and my hollow bats."

Indeed, after retiring, Cash admitted that he'd drilled holes in his bats and filled the spaces with sawdust, glue, and cork. But his most famous bat was one he tried to use with two outs in the bottom of the ninth inning in a game played on July 15, 1973.

Nolan Ryan was pitching for the California Angels and was only one out away from still another no-hitter. Cash had whiffed in each of his previous three at-bats and approached the plate taking practice swings with the leg of a table. When the umpire refused to let him use the ersatz bat, Cash said, "Why not? I won't hit him anyway."

Cash then proceeded to end the game and complete the no-hitter with a pop-up.

♣Speaking of Ryan, now the Texas Rangers' president: MLB's first ever free-agent draft of high school, college, and sandlot players was conducted on June 8, 1965, and that's when the New York Mets selected Ryan in the tenth round. He worked in New York from 1966 to 1971, showing an explosive fastball and erratic control but, above all, a propensity to develop blisters on the fingers of his pitching hand. The accepted treatment was to soak his hand in pickle brine, but the results were never sufficiently effective for the Mets to feel they could depend on Ryan over the long haul. So in one of the most lopsided trades in history, he was dealt to the Angels in exchange for Jim Fregosi, a former all-star third baseman who was well past his prime.

Not only did the fireballing Ryan develop into baseball's all-time strikeout king, but he also threw a record seven no-hitters. Seven. With a lifetime total of 324 wins over an astounding 27 seasons, Ryan was a shoo-in for the Hall of Fame. However, he also lost 292 games (finishing ahead of only Cy Young himself, who lost 319), won twenty games only twice, and compiled a pedestrian winning percentage of .526. Accordingly, some critics brand Ryan a one-trick pony who was never a stopper.

Several other lesser-known Irishmen were named to all-star teams during the sixties:

♣Lindy McDaniel was a reliever for several teams throughout his twenty-one years in the big leagues. Relying mostly on his diving palm ball, he led the NL in saves three times.

♣Frank Bolling, a Gold Glove second baseman with the Braves.

♣Dick Donovan pitched for the Braves, Tigers, White Sox, Senators, and Indians, and was famous for his bottom-heavy sinker.

♣Johnny Edwards won two Gold Gloves as a catcher with Cincinnati until he was replaced by Johnny Bench.

♣Bill Henry was the Reds' closer, and also pitched for the Red Sox, the Giants, the Pirates, and the Astros, but without approaching the success he had had in Cincinnati.

♣Jim McGlothin ate innings and registered double-figure wins for the Angels, before strong seasons with the Reds.

♣Dave McNally was one of the stalwarts of the Orioles pitching staff and a four-time twenty-game winner. McNally is the only pitcher in major league history to hit a grand slam in a World Series game. His place in baseball labor history would come in the 1970s.

♣Claude Osteen twice won twenty games for the Dodgers after becoming the top lefty trying to fill Koufax's shoes.

♣Billy Moran played second base for the Angels and the Indians, and had surprising power for a slick fielder.

♣Phil Regan was known as "the Vulture" for his tendency to take the mound in a closer's role, give up the tying run, then get credit for the win when his team (Tigers, Dodgers, but mainly the Cubs) pushed across the winning run. His record for the 1966 Dodgers was 14-1, with a league-leading 21 saves.

♣Darold Knowles was a lefty with a nasty curve and a heavy sinker. A workhorse, Knowles became the first pitcher to work in every game of a seven-game World Series when the Oakland A's faced the Mets in 1968, tossing $6\frac{1}{3}$ shutout innings. Knowles was also renowned for his deceptive move to first. In fact, he still holds the lifetime record for picking off one runner every 24 innings he pitched.

Irishmen were also involved in significant off-field doings as well:

♣On February 18, 1960, Walter O'Malley purchased a Los Angeles property known as Chavez Ravine.

♣August 3, 1960, was the date of an historic trade when Detroit and Cleveland exchanged managers. The Tigers got the rather placid Joe Gordon while the Indians received the unquestionably fiery Jimmy Dykes.

♣Charlie Finley gave himself a Christmas present when he bought 52 percent of the Kansas City Athletics on December 20, 1960. Finley moved the franchise to Oakland eight years later.

♣On April 9, 1962, the return of major league baseball to Washington, D.C., was commemorated by John F. Kennedy throwing out the first ball.

♣The Red Sox were returning to their hotel after a game at Yankee Stadium on July 26, 1962, when Gene Conley's desperate need to relieve himself was frustrated while the bus was caught in heavy traffic. So manager Pinky Higgins gave Conley permission to disembark and find a bathroom. But Conley never returned. In fact, he stayed missing for nearly twenty-four hours.

Turned out that Conley was stricken with the sudden urge to fly to Israel and had taken a taxi to LaGuardia Airport. Conley reconnected with his team only after he was denied a plane ticket because he lacked a visa.

As seen, many Irish brothers played major league baseball; given time, fathers and sons had to follow.

♣When first baseman Mike Hegan of the Seattle Pilots was voted onto the all-star team in 1969, he and his dad became the first Irish father-and-son all-stars. Jim Hegan earned the honor four years running from 1949 to 1952, and Mike in 1969.

Mike Hegan also held the American League record for most consecutive errorless games as a first baseman (178), until it was broken by Kevin Youkilis in 2007.

The 1960s went out with a bang: the men on the moon, Joe Namath's Super Bowl prediction, and, of course, Casey's marvelous losers, now in the hands of Gil Hodges, finally winning it all.

♣Most famously on that Mets team was Irishman Tug McGraw,

who got his nickname for being an overly aggressive breastfeeder as an infant. He grew up to be an outstanding lefty reliever for the Mets and the Phils, and it was his rallying cry of "You Gotta Believe" that stirred the masses as the Mets copped the 1969 World Series.

He was always a free spirit: When asked how he planned to spend his salary, McGraw said, "Ninety percent on good times, women and Irish whiskey. The other ten percent I'll probably waste."

McGraw died of brain cancer on February 5, 2004, moving his son, country singer Tim McGraw, to write and record "Live Like You Were Dyin'" in his memory.

Chapter Twenty-Eight

Green and Gold

At home in Ireland, there's a habit of avoidance, an
ironical attitude towards the authority figure.

—Seamus Heaney

THE 1970S WERE a microcosm of all of the Irish influence in baseball rolled up into one: an Irishman was a key figure in the fall of the
reserve clause, an Irish owner shook things up (not all for the good),
Irish stalwarts dominated on the mound and at the plate, and a few
got overlooked for their accomplishments.

Several outstanding Irish players in the 1970s failed to make the
all-star cut:

♣Until his arm went bad, Dennis Leonard was a money pitcher
for the Kansas City Royals from 1974 to 1982. He had three 20-game
seasons (1977, 1978, 1980) and led the AL in innings pitched (1981)
and shutouts (1979).

It's hard to comprehend why Leonard was never an all-star.

♣Like so many pitchers of yore, Gary Nolan finished what he
began—247 complete games in 250 career starts from 1967 to 1977.
A kingpin of Cincinnati's rotation, Nolan led the NL in winning

percentage (15-5) and posted a 1.99 ERA in 1972. Arm and shoulder problems forced him to retire at age twenty-nine.

♣After being a dependable reliever for eighteen seasons with seven different teams, Don McMahon was forty-four when he finally retired in 1974. His cumulative stats include 153 saves, a record of 90-68, and a lifetime ERA of 2.96. The most amazing aspect of McMahon's career was that, as he got older, his fastball seemed to pick up speed.

♣Rick Dempsey caught in the bigs for twenty-four seasons. As his lifetime batting average of .233 attests, he earned his keep by being an agile defensive wiz and adroit handler of pitchers.

Dempsey was also valued for his performances in the "Rain Delay Theater." While a tarpaulin was spread over the infield and the rain was still falling, Dempsey would take off his spikes, assume a batless batting stance near home plate, then pantomime hitting an inside-the-park home run, topped off by his sliding into home on his belly.

♣Mike Caldwell went 22-9 and pitched to a 2.36 ERA for the 1978 Milwaukee Braves. This effort was good enough for him to be named the Comeback Player of the Year, as well as to finish second in the Cy Young balloting. Caldwell's encore in 1979 was to lead the NL in winning percentage—16-6 for .727. Yet he too was unjustly ignored when all-star selections were made.

♣Duffy Dyer is most likely the only major league player named after a radio show. His mother was listening to her favorite program when she went into labor: *Duffy's Tavern, Where the Elite Meet to Eat*. It seems that the tavern's proprietor—who never was actually heard—was in some kind of domestic trouble just as Mrs. Dyer was in the midst of her birthing. Her first words after her baby was born were, "How's Duffy?"

Dyer had a fourteen-year career as a catcher, most notably with the Amazin' Mets. He made up for his inadequate hitting with his solid defense.

For some unknown reason, a character named Ben (played by Rob Morrow) in the film *Into My Heart* refers to Duffy Dyer as a cultural icon.

But enough great and good Irish players did get their due in the decade:

♣Steve Garvey was the rock-jawed, velvet-gloved first baseman for the Los Angeles Dodgers who appeared in a total of ten All-Star Games and was an integral part of LA teams that won four pennants and one World Series. Upon signing with San Diego as a free agent in 1983, he then paced the Padres to a World Series appearance in 1984. And it was with San Diego that he continued (and concluded) his NL record of 1,207 consecutive games played. His lifetime stats included a .294 batting average, 2,599 hits, 272 homers, an MVP Award (1974), and four Gold Gloves.

Throughout his career, Garvey's spotless reputation earned him the sobriquet of Mr. Clean. However, it was later revealed that Garvey had actually been involved in several extramarital affairs. After his retirement from baseball in 1987, Garvey's past and present sexual escapades led to a divorce, plus innumerable simultaneous affairs, engagements, and lawsuits. His misadventures became the subject of jokes by late-night comedians, and his righteous reputation was irretrievably sullied.

Through it all, Garvey's interest in his Irish heritage seemed to sustain him. He's visited Ireland many times and has become an expert in Irish history.

♣Joe Coleman Jr. won 20-plus games twice and was selected for the 1972 All-Star Game. Back in 1948, his dad, Joe Coleman Sr., had his one all-star appearance during his ten-year career.

(A third-generation Coleman, with the lucky first name of Casey, is currently a promising pitcher for the Cubs. If Casey ever makes an all-star team, the Colemans will surpass Mike and Jim Hegan for Irish all-in-the-family all-star nods.)

♣Jack "the Ripper" Clark specialized in driving in runs, leading the NL three times in this category. The first of his four all-star appearances was in 1978.

In addition to RBIs, Clark's passion was for luxury cars. At one time, he owned or was paying for eighteen of them, including a $700,000 Ferrari. Eventually this extravagance forced Clark into a much-publicized bankruptcy that cost him his home.

♣Mike Flanagan played baseball and basketball at the University of Massachusetts. After trying to guard teammate Julius Erving one day in practice, he decided to concentrate on baseball. It was a wise decision.

In 1978, the crafty left-hander bedeviled AL hitters on his way to a 23-9 record with the Orioles. Toss in a lead-leading five shutouts, and Flanagan was a lock for the Cy Young Award. Yet he was an all-star only once, in 1978.

Family, friends, ex-teammates, and baseball fans of every persuasion were shocked when Flanagan committed suicide in 2011.

♣The other all-star Irishmen in the 1970s were Bill Campbell, Clay Carroll, Pat Dobson, Brian Downing, Matt Keough, Don Money, and Chris Short.

CONTRACTING TUBERCULOSIS WAS the best thing that ever happened to Charlie O. Finley. And Finley's purchase of a major league franchise was the worst thing that ever happened to several people.

Like so many of his generation, Charlie O.'s grandfather, Randolph Finley, was a *deori*—a Gaelic term for a wanderer or exile—one who did not choose to leave his homeland. He and his wife settled just north of Birmingham, Alabama, where he worked in the steel mills. Born on February 22, 1918, Charlie often boasted that he shared a birthday with George Washington and was convinced that he was also destined to be a great man.

The Depression cost Oscar Finley his job in Birmingham, but

he found similar employment in Gary, Indiana, through the efforts of his brother. When Charlie graduated from high school, he too wound up toiling in the hell-hot furnaces of the steel mills.

For the rest of his life, Finley never let anybody forget how he had risen up from such a back-busting, poverty-stricken childhood. Or as sportswriter Jim Murray once remarked, "Finley is a self-made man who worships his creator."

With the outbreak of World War II, Charlie tried to enlist in the Marines but was rejected because of an ulcer. Instead, he went to work in a defense plant and sold insurance on the side. After V-E Day, Finley concentrated on the insurance business and proved to be an award-winning salesman. However, in December 1946 he was diagnosed as having tuberculosis and was bedridden in a sanatorium for nearly a year.

He lost nearly seventy-five pounds but otherwise put his down-time to good use studying actuarial tables and figuring out profit margins. The outcome of his research was the development of a new idea—making affordable disability insurance available to groups of well-to-do physicians. With a few years, Finley was netting over $20 million annually. Finley moved his offices to Chicago and was thrilled to discover that the same building also housed the office of the American League. With his outwardly gregarious nature, Finley soon became friendly with Will Harridge, the AL's commissioner. From this fortuitous relationship came Finley's fervent desire to buy a baseball team.

However, when the chairman of the Baltimore Orioles was given the task of investigating Finley's qualifications, this was his brief report: "Under no circumstances should this person be allowed into our league."

But Finley's money spoke loudly enough to calm any official misgivings and, on December 19, 1960, he purchased a controlling share (52 percent) of the Kansas City Athletics for $1.975 million.

The franchise had relocated from Baltimore in 1955, when they had finished sixth in the standings, and since then the A's were even worse. Last-place finishes in 1956 and 1960 were only marginally improved when the team wound up in seventh place from 1957 to 1959, barely ahead of the pitiful Washington Senators.

Unfortunately, Kansas City's Municipal Stadium was in worse shape than the ball club. No surprise that the attendance was woeful, and persistent rumors abounded that Finley's first order of business would be to find a more promising and more populous metropolis for his new team. But in his introductory news conference, Finley swore, "I'm here to stay." To prove his intentions, he signed a ten-year lease on the ballpark with the only escape clause resulting from the team's failure to draw at least 850,000 paid admissions in any given season.

Finley did indeed invest over $500,000 in refurbishing the stadium and the parking lot, and he made himself and his players available for every publicity opportunity. But the team's on-field performance failed to improve. They were at the bottom looking up at the rest of the AL in 1961, 1964, 1965, and 1967. The A's were seventh in 1962 and 1966, sixth in 1963, and attendance rarely went above 500,000.

As a further demonstration of his good faith, Finley made a big show of burning the page on his contract with the ballpark that contained his escape clause. However, the page that Finley really put a match to was blank. When this deception was revealed, both the Kansas City city fathers and the other AL franchise owners were disgusted with Finley. His embarrassment was such that Finley signed another lease on Municipal Stadium that deleted the attendance clause.

But the show went on: in Kansas City, and later in Oakland, Finley hoped to make the turnstiles click by instituting a continuing series of "innovations."

- To supply game balls to the home plate umpire, a button would be pushed and a plastic rabbit would emerge from the ground holding a basket of new balls.

- The same umpire could depress another button to activate a device in the center of home plate that would remove dust and dirt with jets of air.
- A herd of sheep were let loose on a graded hill beyond the right-field fence. The attendant shepherd would ding-dong a bell whenever a home team player hit a homer. (The sheep officially became history when a home run ball struck a sheep on the head, killing it instantly.)
- Cow-milking contests were popular with the fans. As were fans' attempts to catch a greased pig.
- On September 8, 1965, Finley's promo stunt required the A's shortstop, Bert Campaneris, to play all of the nine positions, one in each inning. The stunt backfired when Campaneris, now catching, was bowled over by a runner trying to score, and was so banged up that he missed the next five games.
- Hot Pants Day attracted six thousand contestants.
- On September 9, 1965, Finley signed the fifty-nine-year-old Satchel Paige, ostensibly as a pitching coach. Finley's explicit rationale was to provide Paige with the time needed in the bigs to qualify him for a five-year pension. A rocking chair was set up in the bullpen, and a uniformed nurse shadowed Paige's every movement. On September 25, Paige was activated and pitched three scoreless innings against the Red Sox. Then, in a move that was both shameless and ruthless, Finley released Paige after the season, with the old-timer still several weeks short of making the pension cut. A subsequent stint as honorary coach with the Braves got Paige the in-uniform time he needed.

At the same time, several of Finley's sideshows were nixed by AL authorities. Like digging a tunnel from the A's bullpen to just under the pitching mound, where an elevator would present the new hurler in dramatic fashion. And using an orange ball to facilitate hitting, which Bowie Kuhn permitted for several exhibition games. Trouble was that pitchers found the ball too slippery, while the orange seams prevented hitters from picking up the spin of pitches. So Kuhn put an end to this particular experiment.

Also rebuffed were Finley's visionary proposals for interleague play and the designated hitter.

Finley disliked the white elephant that was the A's traditional emblem, so he bought a mule, named it Charlie O, and put it on perpetual display at the ballpark. Once, when the A's were playing in Chicago, Finley obtained a smaller, more easily concealed mule, smuggled it into the visiting team's clubhouse, and then persuaded one of his best players, Ken "Hawk" Harrelson, to help push-pull the mule out onto the field during a game. Harrelson was nursing what some said was a hangover and was therefore not in the lineup, so he agreed.

After much effort, the mule did clomp his way onto the field, forcing the game to be interrupted. Unfortunately, the mule also stomped on Harrelson's foot, incapacitating the A's outfielder for three more games.

Shortly thereafter, Harrelson was publicly quoted as calling Finley a "menace" to the game, and he refused to back down under his boss's intense pressure. In a foolish fit of temper, Finley's response was to simply cut Harrelson, allowing the Hawk to become baseball's first free agent.

The A's play-by-play radio announcer was the venerable Harry Caray, whose exclamation of "Holy cow!" emphasized every critical play. But Caray quit when Finley demanded that he change his trademark reaction to "Holy mule!"

Despite his promises and his showmanship, Finley made it clear that he was looking for a way out of Kansas City.

Through it all, the AL tried to arrange local buyers to purchase the A's, but Finley always demurred. His routine attempts to move the team—variously to Atlanta, Louisville, Dallas, Milwaukee, New Orleans, Seattle, and Oakland—were turned down by the AL's executive committee.

Finally the league relented in 1968, allowing Finley to move to Oakland and promising Kansas City an expansion team a year later. Once ensconced in Oakland, Finley took it upon himself to function as both the team's owner and general manager. He also spent considerable sums to enhance the team's scouting staff and its farm system.

With the signing and nurturing of such future stars as Vida Blue, Reggie Jackson, Joe Rudi, Sal Bando, Blue Moon Odom, and Rollie Fingers, the Oakland A's became the world champions in 1972, displacing the Big Red Machine.

Finley was named Man of the Year by the *Sporting News*, and Oakland succeeded themselves with World Series triumphs in 1973 and 1974. But Finley's frugality, inflated ego, and stubbornness raised a new series of problems for him.

As GM he routinely mortgaged the franchise's future by trading young players for worn-out vets, looking for a quick fix. During one five-year period, Finley traded away twenty-seven minor league players while getting back only three, thereby decimating the A's farm system.

The one incident that precipitated his eventual downfall occurred in Game 2 of the 1973 World Series versus the Mets. New York was leading by a run with the bases loaded and two out in the top of the twelfth inning. That's when a seemingly easy ground ball was hit directly to Mike Andrews, the A's second baseman, and just as easily bounced between his legs, allowing two runs to score. The next batter struck a slow chopper to Andrews, who fielded it cleanly but had to make an off-balance, cross-body throw that forced first baseman Gene Tenace to make a mighty stretch to receive the ball. The umpire ruled the runner safe, even though replays demonstrated that Tenace recovered to tag the base in time.

After the game, Finley was so incensed at the two errors charged to Andrews that he insisted on immediately putting the player on the disabled list. At first Andrews refused to sign a document claiming that he was indeed injured, but when Finley threatened to have him permanently barred from baseball, he relented. Finley then coerced the team doctor into making up an injury and sending the report to the league. Andrews's teammates were appalled, and wore black armbands in Game 3.

Hearings were held, witnesses questioned, and Finley was ordered to reinstate Andrews. But his players, and those around the league, never trusted or respected Finley again.

The brouhaha ended Andrews's career and, within a year, he sued Finley for $2.5 million for restraint of trade. The suit never came to court only because Finley settled with Andrews for an undisclosed but undoubtedly hefty payment.

Finley survived two heart operations without losing any élan. Of Finley's most recent surgery, Steve McCatty, one of the A's many disgruntled players, said this: "The operation took eight hours, seven-and-a-half just to find his heart."

Another heart attack felled Charlie O. Finley on February 19, 1996.

AN IRISH PITCHING star of the 1960s continued his success in the '70s, and made baseball history in several other ways.

♣Dave McNally has the unique distinction as the only pitcher in major league history to hit a grand slam in a World Series game (Game 3; 1970). Then, his fourth twenty-win season in a row came in 1971, and that was the year the O's had four such winners: McNally, Jim Palmer, Pat Dobson, and Mike Cuellar. In 1974, he gave up fellow Irishman Al Kaline's 3,000th hit.

Also in '74, McNally and Dodgers pitcher Andy Messersmith challenged the reserve clause—and won their free agency. Their stand, along with Catfish Hunter's bolting from Finley's A's, helped end the reserve clause era in baseball and launch the time of free agency.

An Irish labor issue of almost a hundred years before was finally resolved.

Chapter Twenty-Nine

The Hidden Potato Trick

Life is no "brief candle" for me. It is a sort of splendid
torch which I have got hold of for the moment, and I want
to make it burn as brightly as possible before handing it
on to future generations.

—*George Bernard Shaw*

THE 1980S SAW Irishmen thrive and barely survive success and defeat, and several sons of Ireland made a lasting mark on the game, often in unusual ways.

♣Dale Murphy's deserved reputation for being a clean-living model citizen was certainly not unusual for an Irishman in his chosen profession. If, for example, Connie Mack had lived in modern times he might also have sought to endorse wholesome consumer products like milk, ice cream, and cameras. However, in the wonderful world of Irish baseball players, Murphy was an anomaly in many other ways.

Like Mickey Cochrane, Murphy earned a pair of MVP trophies, but he was the only Irishman to win back-to-back MVPs (1982 and 1983).

Murphy was always celebrated for his charitable works and instincts, and before a 1983 game against the San Francisco Giants, he went into the stands to present a T-shirt and a baseball cap to a six-year-old girl who had lost both hands and a leg when she stepped on a live power line. The girl's attendant nurse hopefully asked Murphy if he'd hit a homer and dedicate it to the unfortunate victim.

"I didn't know what to say," Murphy recalled, "so I just sort of mumbled, 'Well, O.K.'"

He then proceeded to knock in all of the Braves' runs in a 3–2 victory with a pair of round-trippers.

Murphy's lifetime batting average of .265 is the lowest of any Irish nonpitcher in the Hall of Fame. At the opposite end of the spectrum, his 398 career home runs is the highest total of any Irishman honored in Cooperstown.

Yet the most unusual aspect of Murphy's vita is that this particular Irishman is also a Mormon.

♣Lee MacPhail was not nearly as obnoxious as his dad, Larry. He was a front-office executive for the Reds, the Dodgers, and the Yankees, achieving admirable levels of success at every stop. From 1974 to 1984, MacPhail was the president of the American League. It was he who reversed the umpire's game-time decision in the famous 1983 pine tar incident and allowed George Brett's home run to stand.

Born on October 25, 1917, as of this writing Lee MacPhail is the oldest living member of the Hall of Fame.

Several standout Irish players in the last twenty years of the twentieth century were frequently selected to All-Star Games:

♣Besides Sean Casey's skills and his lifetime .302 batting average, Casey had other attributes that were even more appealing. Playing first base, Casey would habitually initiate good-natured dialogue with any opposing runners in his sphere of influence. That's why he was dubbed "Mr. Mayor" and in 2007 was voted by his peers as the "friendliest player in baseball."

The testimony of veteran sportswriter Hal McCoy went even

further. "There's no debate and there never will be a debate. Sean Casey is the nicest guy in professional baseball. Ever."

♣Will "the Thrill" Clark was a Gold Glover at first base and a six-time all-star, yet one particular at-bat had a profound and lasting influence on the game.

Clark was due up with the bases loaded in Game 1 of the 1989 National League Championship Series. He had previously taken Cubs' pitcher Mark Prior deep, so while Clark was in the on-deck circle, Cubs catcher Joe Girardi went to the mound to discuss how Prior wanted to deal with this dangerous situation.

But Clark was able to read Prior's lips: "Fastball, high inside." When Prior's first offering was indeed a high, inside fastball, Clark promptly cleared the bases with a grand slam.

Ever since then, pitchers and catchers cover their mouths when convening to explore strategy on the mound.

♣The two main weapons in Bob Welch's arsenal were a blazing fastball and a drop-dead splitter. No surprise then that he hurled a no-hitter, made three All-Star Games, and was the NL's Cy Young winner in 1990 on the strength of his major league–leading 27 wins.

♣Bruce Hurst was a cagey left-hander who made the all-star team in 1987. But in some quarters he's more known for his participation in the 1986 World Series. Boston had a 3–2 lead in the series and had the Mets down 5–3 with two outs in the bottom of the tenth in Game 6.

The scoreboard at Shea Stadium had prepared its final display— "Congratulations Boston Red Sox, 1986 World Champions"—and Hurst had already been voted the series MVP. But then the ground ball scooted between first baseman Bill Buckner's legs, and the Mets won the game.

Hurst started Game 7 on three days' rest, and was lifted after six innings, with the score tied 3–3. The Mets went on to win the game and the championship.

Brokenhearted Red Sox fanatics pointed out that the letters in BRUCE HURST can be rearranged as B RUTH CURSE.

♣Other Irish All-Stars of this generation include Tim Burke, Brett Butler, Terry Kennedy, Mike Moore, Phil Nevin, Paul O'Neill, Jeff "the Terminator" Reardon, Shane Reynolds, and Gary Ward.

♣Mark Sweeney never made an all-star team, but was a deluxe pinch hitter. He collected 175 off-the-bench hits in his career, trailing only Lenny Harris on this particular all-time list. However, Sweeney does hold the record for most RBIs (102) in a pinch-hitting role.

♣Jaimie McAndrew was a replacement player when the contracted major league players went on strike during spring training of 1995. After the strike ended, McAndrew and the other temps were blacklisted. But McAndrew persevered in the minor leagues and, in 1996, became one of the first replacement players to make it back into the majors.

♣Joe McGrane led the NL in hit batsmen (10) in 1987 and ERA (2.18) in 1988.

♣An Irishman completed the circle of catchers who invented new gear.

Charlie O'Brien was another in a long line of no-hit, good-field catchers. The lasting legacy of his fifteen-year career began when he was hit in the mask by foul tips on two consecutive pitches. Later, while watching a hockey game, O'Brien came up with the idea of designing a goalie-style mask to replace the traditional bar-front protectors that catchers wore. Eventually, O'Brien's mask was approved by Major League Baseball in 1996.

♣After an undistinguished nine-year career in the big leagues (.256), Tim O'Malley became a perennial .300 hitter and all-star in Japan. Playing center for the Yakult Swallows, O'Malley was named MVP for both the regular season (.307, 87 RBIs, 31 homers) and the postseason Japan Series.

♣Andy McGaffigan was an effective pitcher—lifetime 38-33, 3.38 ERA—but in 126 at-bats, he managed only six hits for a woeful .048. Some baseball watchers say that, indeed, McGaffigan was the worst-hitting pitcher ever.

♣In September 1989, Francis T. "Fay" Vincent was named baseball commissioner. But his toughness and integrity soon proved distasteful to the game's magnates, especially after he suspended Yankees owner George Steinbrenner for various illegal activities.

The outraged owners booted Vincent in 1992 and replaced him with Bud Selig.

♣Dave Bresnahan was a backup catcher for the Double-A Williamsport Bills, and is remembered only for his take on a stunt Casey Stengel once pulled.

Before a meaningless game in September 1987, Bresnahan peeled a potato and trimmed it into the shape of a baseball. He initially concealed the potato in his jersey, but when the opponents had two out and a runner on third, Bresnahan moved the ball to the webbing of his mitt. Then, after catching a pitch, Bresnahan threw the potato far over the head of his third baseman in an apparent attempt to pick off the runner.

Naturally, the runner trotted toward home thinking that he'd easily score, only to be confronted with Bresnahan with the baseball in hand. The tag was applied, but the outraged umpire ruled the runner safe and thumbed Bresnahan from the game.

Immediately thereafter, Bresnahan was fined, and then released for affronting the dignity of the game. But he quickly became a national celebrity.

So much so that early in the 1988 season, Williamsport arranged a "Dave Bresnahan Day" that drew six thousand fans to witness the retiring of his number, 59. Said Bresnahan, "Lou Gehrig had to play in 2,130 consecutive games and hit .340 for his number to be retired. All I had to do was hit .140 and throw a potato."

The infamous potato was recovered, cleaned, preserved in denatured alcohol, and offered to the Hall of Fame—which declined.

Chapter Thirty

Century's End and Irish Resurgence

PERHAPS THE MOST blemished Irishman, of course, is Mark McGwire. At the time, his thrilling home run duel with Sammy Sosa in 1998 was hailed as being instrumental in reviving public interest in baseball after the 1994 strike. McGwire blasted 70 home runs to Sosa's 66, both of them breaking Roger Maris's record.

Both McGwire and Sosa denied the accusations of steroid usage or simply refused to comment on the situation. Until, that is, January 2011, when McGwire fessed up. Apparently, McGwire's confession was demanded by the Cardinals before he was hired as the team's hitting coach.

Despite McGwire's home run heroics (583 lifetime), and the Gold Glove he won at first base, the Hall of Fame electors have demonstrated their unwillingness to vote him into the hallowed ground at Cooperstown. This is a dilemma that will not be easily resolved.

Even so, McGwire was a colossal talent, clearly the best Irish slugger of modern times.

♣Unfortunately, two lesser Irish players admitted to using steroids: Dan Naulty and Jay Gibbons. The former confessed after retiring with a 5-5 record and five saves in four years. The latter was fined $15,000 and suspended for the first fifteen games of the 2008 season.

Allowed to participate in the 2008 spring training with the Orioles, Gibbons performed so poorly that he was cut before the team broke camp—even though Baltimore remained on the hook for the remaining $12 million in his contract.

Gibbons then sent emotional letters to all thirty major league teams admitting the error of his ways, and promising to donate the full amount of any forthcoming salary to charities. The only positive response came from the Long Island Ducks, an unaffiliated minor league outfit. After playing well there, Gibbons was signed to a Milwaukee Brewers' farm team, and eventually made his way back to the Dodgers in 2010, where he played well enough to be in consideration for a starting spot in 2011.

Unfortunately, Gibbons contracted eye problems while playing winter ball in Venezuela, and they improved only slightly when he began the 2011 season in Los Angeles. Once considered a high-average hitter with surprising power, Gibbons hit only .255 before the Dodgers sent him back to the minors.

The new century saw some Irish players reach major milestones. One of them was quite unusual.

♣Don Kelly was drafted by Detroit in 2001 as a shortstop. But by the time the 6'4", 215-pound Kelly got to Pittsburgh in 2007, he was penciled in as a backup at second, short, left field, and right. After coming over to the Tigers in 2009, Kelly stretched his capabilities by playing third, first, and center.

He was already a one-man utility squad.

But his repertoire expanded even further in 2011 when, on June 29, he pitched to one batter in a blowout loss to the Mets. His fastball never rose above 86 miles per hour, and he considered himself fortunate when Scott Hairston flied out to center on a hanging curve.

Kelly completed his tour of the diamond on July 2, 2011, when he got behind the plate after Detroit's starting catcher, Victor Martinez, was nicked on his shoulder and forearm by foul tips. Since the Tigers had an afternoon game scheduled for the next day and the game was already lost, manager Jim Leyland decided to spare the normal backup catcher and plugged Kelly into the game.

Kelly thus became the second big leaguer to make appearances in all nine defensive positions. But unlike the case of Bert Campaneris, who did this in the 1970s, Kelly's accomplishments were no mere publicity stunt.

Which position was the most difficult?

"Catcher," said Kelly. "The strangest thing is when you go to catch the ball and they hit it, and there's nothing there. You're expecting a hard fastball and then you're squeezing air. It was pretty crazy."

There were still more unusual happenings:

♣On April 9, 2006, Cory Sullivan, a young outfielder with the Astros, became the first National Leaguer in eighty years to hit two triples in the same inning.

♣Off the field and down the aisle, the background music that played while Ian Kennedy and his soon-to-be bride approached the preacher was "Take Me Out to the Ball Game."

♣John Lannan made his major league debut on July 26, 2007, pitching for the Washington Nationals against the Phillies. His fifth pitch hit Chase Utley, breaking the all-star second baseman's hand. Lannan's very next offering hit Ryan Howard. Lannan then became the first pitcher ever to be ejected in his initial major league appearance.

Since then, Lannan has evolved into a serviceable player whose most recent efforts hover about the .500 mark. This is quite an accomplishment considering that the Nats were 308-439 since Lannan's rookie season.

♣Brian O'Connor never played in the major leagues. The closest he came was in 1993, when he went 4-2 with a 4.03 ERA in a Double-A league. However, his credentials as an Irishman are impeccable—as are his achievements coaching at the University of Virginia. Over the last seven years, O'Connor's record there is 372-130-1. In 2009 he was named the NCAA's Coach of the Year.

♣Mike Stanton was a lefty reliever who appeared in 1,178 games, the most for any Irishman and second only to Jesse Orosco's 1,252.

♣Not to forget slugger Adam Dunn, who has averaged one homer every 13.96 at-bats. This places him behind only McGwire, Ruth, Bonds, and Thome—but ahead of Hall of Famers Kiner, Killebrew, Williams, Mantle, Foxx, and Schmidt.

However, Dunn is just as menacing with a glove as he is with a bat. In 2009, he was rated the worst-fielding outfielder in history, an evaluation he duplicated when he switched to first base.

In the late nineteenth century, and through a variety of ways and means, it was mostly Irish players and managers who had the leading roles in establishing baseball as America's national pastime.

- To begin with, their hatred of the English caused the vast majority of famine immigrants to reject cricket and embrace the early forms of baseball. The various running, throwing, and ball-and-bat games that were traditional in Ireland, plus their eagerness for physical tasks and confrontations, gave these new citizens a distinct on-the-field advantage over the less desperate residual upper-class dilettantes who also enjoyed the game.
- The new and still evolving game attracted significant media attention as well as paying customers wherever large numbers of displaced Irish settled—Boston, New York, Philadelphia, Cleveland, Chicago, and in many cities and towns in between. And the resulting influx of money made baseball and its players increasingly respectable.
- No surprise, then, that in the 1880s and 1890s, roughly two of every five professional baseball players were Irish—as were an

even larger percentage of the top-flight players. Specifically, Mike "King" Kelly almost single-handedly transformed baseball players into national heroes, while simultaneously turning certain plays and games into front-page news.

- By boldly and imaginatively exploiting every loophole in the rulebook, the Irish forced the bylaws and customs of the game to evolve closer and closer to the modern version.
- They also pioneered the first players' rights and unions.
- They came. They played. They conquered.

However, the style of play that seemed endemic to Irish baseballers and encouraged by such managers as John McGraw eventually created a backlash. So, if the Irish played a huge part in popularizing baseball, their high-flying spikes, nose-smashing tags, and verbal assaults nearly marginalized the sport. Indeed, it wasn't until the emergence of Babe Ruth's long-distance hitting enabled runs to score quickly and in bunches that the rough tactics necessitated by the predominance of one-run games began to be deemphasized.

The increased presence of other immigrant groups, plus homegrown talent in the pro leagues during the 1920s, '30s, and '40s, somewhat diffused the preponderance of Irishmen. But a significant population of Irish stars still shone brightly, from Kaline to Ford, Murphy to McGraw, and many more.

♣Here is some good news for those who enjoy the wearing of the green. In recent years, there's been a dramatic increase in the number of Irish players in the major leagues.

According to the latest U.S. census figures, 12 percent of American citizens identify themselves as being Irish. Compare this to another number: as of the all-star break in 2011, 18.8 percent of current major league players are of Irish descent, however distant.

♣Add to this stat six of thirty major and several minor league managers. John Farrell (whose family roots go back to County Longford) is with the Toronto Blue Jays; Jack McKeon (Antrim) leads the Marlins; Joe Maddon (Galway) runs the Rays; Mike Quade (Northern Ireland) heads the Chicago Cubs; Jim Tracy (Tipperary) is with the Colorado Rockies; and Terry Collins (Cork) directs the fortunes of the New York Mets.

Since managers tend to people their staffs with longtime associates, it's only natural that, in addition, twelve more Irishmen are among Major League Baseball's coaches, including such great Irish names as Roger McDowell, Steve McCatty, Mick Kelleher, and Bob McClure.

And there's an increasing probability that the next generation of Irish coaches, managers, and players will be even larger.

That's because Ireland's economy has recently been stricken with the kind of downturn that virtually every other nation has experienced. In 2006 the unemployment rate in Ireland was a mere 4 percent. By the summer of 2011, the number had increased to 14 percent. As a result, in 2009 and 2010, nearly 35,000 citizens of the Emerald Isle left their homes to seek steady work and a better life elsewhere. Some of these modern-day *deori* have settled in Australia, but most landed in either Boston or New York. A few may very well have journeyed to Irishtown, New Jersey, or to Emerald Isle, North Carolina.

There's no question that baseball as we know it would not be the same without the many contributions of this vibrant race of adventurous Irishmen.

To all of them—past, present, and future—baseball fans of every persuasion owe a debt of gratitude. The most appropriate way to express our thanks is in a language that is commonly called Gaelic, but the Irish call "Irish":

Go raibh míle maith agat.
A million thank-yous.

Epilogue: Eire Apparent: A Visit to the Irish-American Baseball Hall of Fame

Ireland is where strange tales begin and happy endings
are possible.

—*Charles Haughey*

A photograph of Connie Mack *(middle)* using his scorecard to position
his fielders, surrounded by some of the hundreds of signed baseballs
(Allison Benoit)

FOLEY'S IRISH-AMERICAN BASEBALL HALL OF FAME

Foley's Pub and Restaurant is squeezed between and beneath two huge office buildings on New York's Thirty-Third Street, in the shadow of the Empire State Building.

Through a low door, one enters a long, narrow aisle with a friendly mahogany bar on the right. Foley's motto is printed across the back of their official T-shirt: "An Irish Pub with a Baseball Attitude."

Appropriately enough, the length of the aisle seems to be about sixty feet, six inches.

♣Lining the walls of the corridor are stacks of autographed baseballs, each in its own plastic case. Literally hundreds of them, signed by such notables as Mickey Mantle and Gerald Ford. Some of the wall space is hung with autographed photos, including head shots of Brooks Robinson and Larry Bird.

♣Bronze plaques near the front entrance depict the likenesses of Connie Mack, John Flaherty, Walter O'Malley, Steve Garvey, Paul O'Neill, Vin Scully, and Mike "King" Kelly. Also on view are representations of Brian Cashman; umpire Jim Joyce; Kevin Costner, who starred in *Field of Dreams* and *Bull Durham*; Pete Flynn, chief groundskeeper for the Mets; and Ed Lucas, a blind sportswriter who has covered the Yankees and the Mets for more than forty years.

The approach to the cozy dining room also features an occasional nook containing various other sports memorabilia and oddities: corks from champagne bottles that the New York Yankees drank and/or spilled in their locker room after winning the 2000 World Series; an authentic ring donated by someone who played in the 1968 All-Star Game; an umpire's ring from the 2008 World Series; and individual boxing gloves signed in silver script by Roberto Duran, Larry Holmes, Joe Frazier, and Don King.

♣One alcove contains a variety of plastic statuettes and bobblehead dolls representing a wide range of current and past Irish ballplayers.

♣There's St. Patrick leaning on a baseball bat.

One of the many showcases of autographed baseballs that occupy most of the wall
(Allison Benoit)

Hanging from the ceiling is a green jersey signed by the County Cork All-Ireland Hurling Champions. There is a red-and-green soccer jersey autographed by another championship team, the Irish Seagulls. A few feet past the men's room is a seat from the demolished Memorial Stadium in Baltimore.

And on an early afternoon in the middle of June, Foley's was bustling with several gray-haired men in business suits, some middle-aged guys in brand-name sweats, a handful of women in showoff dresses, casually dressed media folk, even more casually dressed tourists, and curious walk-ins. All were on hand to celebrate the annual highlight of Foley's year—the fourth annual ceremonies to honor the latest inductees into the Irish-American Baseball Hall of Fame.

♣Shaun Clancy is the Irish-born proprietor, and still speaks with a slight, lilting brogue. As do Diedre and Kathie, who take orders, tend bar, and generally keep the place running smoothly.

Clancy's broad shoulders, clean-shaven skull, and earnest smile suggest a gym rat more than a businessman.

"When I was a kid in Ireland," he recalled, "my parents gave me a baseball glove for Christmas. It was a Don Mattingly model. Not only did I not know who Mattingly was, I had no idea how to use the glove."

By dint of a burgeoning appreciation of his adopted country's national pastime, and some diligent studying, Clancy is now comfortable in identifying himself as "an amateur baseball historian."

Through his efforts the "I-A HOF" has received the official blessing of that other HOF, in Cooperstown.

The Irish honorees for 2011 were Ed Walsh, the last pitcher to win 40 games in a season; Nolan Ryan; John McGraw; Terry Cashman, who wrote *Talkin' Baseball*; Chuck Lennon, the longtime director of the University of Notre Dame's alumni association; Gene Monahan, the soon-to-retire trainer for the Yankees; and his successor, Steve Donahue.

Terry Cashman is a tall, slow-moving, slightly rusted "ginger" man, who once penned the hit tune "Sunday Will Never Be the Same" for Sparky and Our Gang, and also wrote several songs that Jim Croce recorded. "I pitched in the Tigers organization for two years," he said. "I never got above B-ball and, besides, I really didn't like playing baseball for money."

Cashman can trace his Irish roots back to County Clare, which his paternal grandfather left in the 1880s. "I've been back there several times. It's such a beautiful country, and I can really relate to the history of Ireland. Especially the joyous musical heritage and the Irish unique sense of humor."

After being introduced as "The Balladeer of Baseball" by John Mooney, Foley's public relations director, Cashman told a humorous anecdote:

There was a bar in the Washington Heights section of upper Manhattan that Cashman used to frequent when he lived in the neighborhood. An old-timer named Peter Donovan used to sit in the back booth right next to the phone. With a perpetual beer in his hand, Donovan would answer the phone and then summon the recipient of the call.

"Two of the bar's regulars were named Bill Cody," Cashman said. "One of them was a tough guy, the head of the Iron Workers Union, and he was known as 'Uptown' because he lived nearby. The other Bill Cody was known as 'Downtown' because he lived near the Lower East Side. When a caller wanted to speak to Bill Cody, Donovan would ask, 'Uptown or Downtown?'

"But Downtown Bill Cody was a criminal, who once broke into the home of Hume Cronyn and Jessica Tandy and held them for ransom. He was caught, convicted, and sent to jail.

"The very day after Downtown was incarcerated, the phone in the bar rang, and the caller asked for Bill Cody. Donovan then said, 'Inside or Outside?'"

After a good laugh by all, Cashman got more serious. He choked up when he regretted that his parents weren't alive to witness the ceremony. He closed with this: "Being Irish also means having active tear ducts."

The Texas Rangers were in town to play the Yankees, but John Glenn, the Rangers' director of public relations, accepted Nolan Ryan's award and offered an apology. "Nolan never travels with the team," said Glenn. "He doesn't even go up to Cooperstown for the Hall of Fame inductions. I guess he feels he did enough traveling during his twenty-seven years in the major leagues. Also, since he was born in Texas, played so many seasons with the Astros and the Rangers, and is currently part owner and team president of the Rangers, Nolan considers himself more of a Texan than an Irishman."

Because of the upcoming Yankees-Rangers game, both Monahan and Donahue were on a tight deadline. If Monahan was busy privately rehashing fond memories with several of his old buddies before the official proceedings, his son, Tim, was happy to chat.

"My dad's father came over from northeast Galway in 1860," said Tim. "He was a broom maker who grew his own broomcorn to make the bristles. This is a plant that's really related to sorghum but looks like corn when it's in the field. The business is still a going concern, but we now make bristles for brushes and wreaths, and we also manufacture broom handles."

Tim's blue Irish eyes are always smiling, and his good nature is immediately evident.

"For both me and my dad," he said, "the most important part of our Irish heritage is the sheer joy of being alive. Instead of being hung up on this problem or that one, life should be fun."

Steve Donohue's father came from County Cork and his mother hails from County Wexford. He's a full-faced man with a gentle mien. "I grew up just north of the city in Mount Vernon and my father was a cop in New York. We were always proud to be connected with our Irish ancestry and I can remember going to meetings of the Emerald Society."

When asked what is there about his Irishness that Donohue is specifically proud of, he answers: "Our work ethic. And what could be better proof of this than the fact that two Irishmen like me and Gene worked so long for a tough German boss like Mr. Steinbrenner?"

TV personality Regis Philbin, Notre Dame class of 1953, introduced the Yankees' dual entries. "I can remember the first contact I had with Gene Monahan," the magnificently dressed and coiffed Philbin said. "It happened one afternoon when I was invited to take a few batting practice swings before a game at Yankee Stadium. Willie Randolph was a Yankees coach back then and even though he lobbed the ball the best I could do was hit a few harmless grounders. But then I fouled a ball off my shin and I collapsed and was writhing in pain. 'Help me!' I shouted. 'Somebody help me!' Somebody brought out a stretcher and I was carried into the trainer's room. Next to me on a training table was Paul O'Neill, who was suffering from a hangnail. I was moaning and groaning for all I was worth, but Gene worked on O'Neill for an hour and a half before he even looked at me. It was a humbling experience."

Donohue thanked everyone who was responsible for this "great honor" as well as all those present. Monahan also expressed his appreciation, noting that, despite living in New York for so many years, this was the first time he'd ever been in an "Irish saloon. But I'll definitely come back here on a day off."

A creased, elderly Jewish man named Moe Resner stood in place of any surviving relative of John McGraw, the great manager of the New York Giants for thirty years. Resner once owned a minor league Double-A franchise in Dallas, and served as a special assistant coach in the Montreal Expos farm system. His undisputed field of expertise, however, was the history of the New York Giants; his video, *End of an Era: Last New York Giants Game at the Polo Grounds, September 29, 1957*, is a classic.

"My video made it to the Hall of Fame," Resner said, "but I didn't."

His closest connection to McGraw was meeting his widow in 1957. "And the closest I ever got to being Irish was to marry an Irishwoman."

Chuck Lennon played baseball at Notre Dame, where he was a teammate of Carl Yastrzemski. After his graduation in 1961, Lennon served many years as an assistant coach of both the school's varsity baseball and basketball teams. Later, as director of the Notre Dame alumni association, he was instrumental in forming alumni groups for such minorities as blacks, Hispanics, Asians, and Native Americans.

Only days before, Lennon had announced his retirement and had already been hailed by virtually every administrator of the college as the exemplification of the spirit of Notre Dame.

He recounted the privilege of being associated with "such a magnificent university," but soon enough, Lennon recollected how his grandfather was one of eleven brothers. And how, in 1890, the

Lennons beat the Whites in the World Series of Brothers' Baseball played in Joliet, Illinois.

"The box score of the championship game is in the Hall of Fame," Lennon said, "with only the players' first names given."

The only sour notes of the day involved a little griping about some big-name recent players who have turned down invitations to come to Foley's: Paul O'Neill, Mark McGwire, and Derek Jeter. The prevailing sentiment was expressed with that Irish duality of boundless cheer and chip on the shoulder.

The day ended on an inspirational note.

Jon Houston, a businessman who was on hand to address the assembled about his passion for baseball, said that his family hailed from Donegal, and that being Irish meant "always picking yourself up after being knocked down. I would like to think I've passed that same tenacity down to my son and daughter."

To conclude the official proceedings, Houston elicited contributions for baseball in Ireland, where the game has found new life and deepening roots.

"We need everything," he said: "balls, bats, anything, but above all, respect."

The names of the adult and youth teams playing in organized leagues in Ireland have a wonderful blend of the familiar and particular.

In the Irish adult leagues: Belfast Northstars, Cavan Comets, Dublin Blacksox, Dublin Hurricanes, Dublin Spartans, Greystones Mariners, and the Munster Warriors.

And in the youth league: Cavan Comets, Celtic Warriors, Clondalkin Cardinals, Druids Baseball Club, Galway Jays, Greystones Mariners, the Gruffalos, Kingdom Green Sox, Portstewart Eagles, Portrush Mustangs, West Clare Dolphins, and the best name of all: the Kerry Green Sox.

America's national pastime, to which the Irish have given so much, from curveballs to a combative style, from great hitters to magnificent managers, is now flourishing on the island from which more than fifty Irish Hall of Famers hailed.

Hopefully, they are playing the game for the pure joy of it, but perhaps, just perhaps, there's another Irish Hall of Famer taking his cuts on Irish sod right now.

Notes

PROLOGUE: THE IRISH GAME

1   *but never strike three*: Dennis Bingham and Thomas R. Heitz, Appendix, in John Thorn, Peter Palmer, and Michael Gershman, *Total Baseball*, 3rd ed. (New York: HarperPerennial, 1993), 2269–2323, passim; or John Thorn, Peter Palmer, Michael Gershman, and David Pietrusza, *Total Baseball*, 6th ed. (New York: Total Sports, 1999). All citations of rules and rule changes come from Bingham and Heitz. All statistics and uncited incidents come from *Total Baseball*, 6th ed., passim.

3   *punched the ump in the jaw*: Norman L. Macht, *Connie Mack and the Early Years of Baseball* (Lincoln: University of Nebraska Press, 2007), 142.

ONE: ARRIVAL

8   *were considered to be major league teams were Irish*: E. Woodrow Eckard, "Anti-Job Discrimination Circa 1880—Evidence from Major League Baseball," *Social Science History* 34, no. 4 (Winter 2010): 409.

8   *transported in the holds of ships*: *Digital History* website, www.digitalhistory. uh.edu/, accessed January 8, 2011.

9   *An Gorta Mór*: Donald L. Fleitz, *The Irish in Baseball* (Jefferson, NC: McFarland, 2009), 1.

9   *nation's potato production was ruined*: Ibid., 2.

9   *"Black 47"*: Ibid., 1.

10   *machinery of private enterprise*: Ibid., 2.

10   *dire conditions in the Emerald Isle*: Ibid.

10   *363-mile length of the Erie Canal*: Jerrold Casway, *Ed Delahanty in the Emerald Age of Baseball* (South Bend, IN: University of Notre Dame Press, 2004), 13.

10   *males aged fourteen to twenty-four*: Ibid., 8.

10   *environment rife with poverty, disease, unemployment, and crime*: Fleitz, *The Irish in Baseball*, 3.

11   *Irish men and women were already living in America*: Ronald H. Bayor and Timothy J. Meagher, *The New York Irish* (Baltimore: Johns Hopkins University Press, 1997), 19.

TWO: BLOCKED AT HOME PLATE

14   *"by the servants of the gods"*: John Thorn, *Baseball in the Garden of Eden: The Secret History of the Early Game* (New York: Simon & Schuster, 2011), 47.

14   *instead of attending church*: Ibid., 59.

14   *meetinghouse a violation of the law*: Ibid., 59.

15   *John McKibbin Jr. elected president*: Ibid., 90.

15   *"for saying s—t"*: Ibid., 70.

16   *"Tailteann Games"*: George B. Kirsch, Othello Harris, and Claire Elaine Noble, *Encyclopedia of Ethnicity and Sports in America* (Westport, CT: Greenwood, 2000), 239.

16   *"Irish Whales"*: Ibid., 237.

18   *profit of only $1.40*: Casway, *Ed Delahanty*, 7.

THREE: NINA

21   *pelted them with stones*: Benjamin G. Rader, *Baseball: A History of America's Game* (Urbana and Chicago: University of Illinois Press, 2004), 20.

21   *entire metropolitan area*: Ibid., 20.

23   *virulent anti-Catholic prejudice*: Leonard Koppett, *Koppett's Concise History of Baseball* (Philadelphia: Temple University Press, 1998), 4.

23   *"end crime in this country"*: Fleitz, *The Irish in Baseball*, 16.

23   *"get drunk and quarrel"*: Quoted in Thorn, *Baseball in the Garden of Eden*, 95.

23   *Jewish athletes at the turn of the century*: Alan S. Katcher, "I-A Athletic Club," in Kirsch, Harris, and Noble, *Encyclopedia of Ethnicity and Sports in America*, 238.

FOUR: THE FIRST IRISH STARS

24   *paying ringers on a per-game basis*: Ted Vincent, *The Rise and Fall of American Sport* (Lincoln: University of Nebraska Press, 1994), 158–59.

25   *"I became fully convinced"*: Wikipedia.

25   *for the* Brooklyn Eagle: Article by Chadwick on August 16, 1870, quoted in Wikipedia.

26   *"I'm sorry, but"*: As quoted in Fleitz, *The Irish in Baseball*, 33.

27   *a total of 1,500 paying customers*: Ibid., 8.

29   *abide by the "fairest testimony"*: Bingham and Heitz, Appendix, passim.

FIVE: MORE IRISH FIRSTS

32   *the news caused no reaction whatsoever*: Fleitz, *The Irish in Baseball*, 32.

34   *"I want you to understand"*: Thorn, *Baseball in the Garden of Eden*, 165.

34   *playing in the NL again*: Wikipedia.

35   *flamboyant lifestyle*: Fleitz, *The Irish in Baseball*, 21.

35   *Murray Silk Mill*: Marty Appel, *Slide, Kelly, Slide* (Lanham, MD: Scarecrow Press, 1999), 14.

35   *nearly cost him his job*: Ibid., 14.

36   *"hit me gloves, anyhow"*: Ibid., 98.

37   *game for good*: Fleitz, *The Irish in Baseball*, 33.

SIX: THEY WOULD BE GIANTS

43   *12 points in on-base percentage*: Eckard, "Anti–Job Discrimination Circa 1880," 410.

44   *right arm was fully healed*: John P. Rossi, "Glimpses of the Irish Contribution to Early Baseball," *Journal of Irish Studies* (Summer 1988), 611.

45   *four-by-seven feet*: Bingham and Heitz, Appendix, 2298.

46   *"My boys are not only"*: Ralph C. Wilcox, "The Shamrock and the Eagle," *Ethnicity and Sport in North American History and Culture* (Westport, CT: Greenwood Press, 1994), 74.

46   *bartender and had it framed*: Fleitz, *The Irish in Baseball*, 85.

46   *gatekeeper at the Polo Grounds*: Charles C. Alexander, *John McGraw* (Lincoln: University of Nebraska Press, 1988), 246.

47   *right cheek for a curve*: Fleitz, *The Irish in Baseball*, 18.

47   *483 strikeouts in 500 innings*: Appel, *Slide, Kelly, Slide*, 64.

48   *smoking, drinking, and gambling*: Ibid., 87–88.

49   *St. Louis Maroons*: Fleitz, *The Irish in Baseball*, 90.

50   *just as a pitch was being delivered*: Casway, *Ed Delahanty*, 127.

50   *circle the bases for a game-winning homer*: Thorn, Palmer, Gershman, and Pietrusza, *Total Baseball*, 1948.

50   *"proficiency in the use of a club"*: Casway, *Ed Delahanty*, 128–29.

SEVEN: MOLLY MAGUIRES

52   *Workingmen's Benevolent Association*: www.providence.edu/polisci/students/molly_maguires.

52   *guarded churches and church members*: "Ancient Order of Hibernians," Wikipedia.

53   *movement was rendered extinct*: providence.edu.

53   *the Knights to dissolve*: "The Knights of Labor," Wikipedia.

54   *rowdyism that plagued the sport*: Casway, *Ed Delahanty*, 29.

EIGHT: SUPERSTAR

57   *scored the go-ahead run*: Fleitz, *The Irish in Baseball*, 19.

57   *legs and tallied the winning run*: Appel, *Slide, Kelly, Slide*, 72.

58   *"a mile above my head"*: Fleitz, *The Irish in Baseball*, 19.

58   *cache at an umpire's feet*: Appel, *Slide, Kelly, Slide*, 197.

58   *stealing opponents' signs*: Ibid., 196.

59   *"too much temperance"*: Casway, *Ed Delahanty*, 98.

59   *"Sunday school or a baseball club?"*: Fleitz, *The Irish in Baseball*, 21.

59   *"I have to offer"*: Ibid., 22.

60 *"lessen the salary list of the club"*: Ibid., 27.
61 *life story presented by a baseball player*: Casway, *Ed Delahanty*, 114.
61 *named the team's captain*: Appel, *Slide, Kelly, Slide*, 104.
62 *snagged the ball in his bare hands*: Casway, *Ed Delahanty*, 122.
62 *Giants to win the NL pennant*: Appel, *Slide, Kelly, Slide*, 143.
62 *as it skipped at Kelly's side*: Casway, *Ed Delahanty*, 154.

NINE: BROTHERHOOD

65 *included an option clause*: Macht, *Connie Mack and the Early Years of Baseball*, 74.
65 *franchise owners were Irish*: Casway, *Ed Delahanty*, 56.
65 *never paid back the loan*: Ibid., 109.
65 *cover of the horsehide split*: Ibid., 300.
66 *only for the Phillies*: Ibid., 58.
66 *corned beef and cabbage*: Ibid., 33.
67 *"God breathed pure"*: Ibid., 84.
67 *president of the National League*: Fleitz, *The Irish in Baseball*, 66–67.
68 *"The poor, miserable"*: Ibid., 39–40.
70 *registered two strikes*: Macht, *Connie Mack and the Early Years of Baseball*, 56.
70 *attempting to score*: Ibid., 57.
70 *"I didn't tip his bat again"*: Ibid., 100.
70 *Anson took for strike three*: Ibid., 99.
71 *transformed into a victory*: Ibid., 65.
71 *"Goodbye Players' League"*: Fleitz, *The Irish in Baseball*, 42.

TEN: SPIKES UP

75 *plan in Cincinnati*: Casway, *Ed Delahanty*, 158.
75 *forfeited the game to St. Louis*: Ibid.
75 *were exterminated*: Fleitz, *The Irish in Baseball*, 101.
76 *sore arm ended his career*: Ibid., 57.
76 *position his fielders for each hitter*: Macht, *Connie Mack and the Early Years of Baseball*, 89.
77 *safe space for him on the bench*: Alexander, *John McGraw*, 24–25.
78 *Baltimore chop*: Fleitz, *The Irish in Baseball*, 84.
78 *inserting him in the lineup the next day*: Alexander, *John McGraw*, 30.
78 *assaulting McGraw*: Ibid., 34.
78 *tactics helped the Orioles to win*: Ibid., 36.
80 *"disorganizing baseball"*: Fleitz, *The Irish in Baseball*, 82–95, passim.
81 *"He'd wring his hands"*: Lawrence S. Ritter, *The Glory of Their Times* (New York: William Morrow, 1984), 53.

ELEVEN: LAST SLIDE

83 *iron-fisted rule over Ireland*: Casway, *Ed Delahanty*, 77.
84 *front entrance of his ballpark*: *Sporting News*, January 25, 1890.

84   *"Captain Anson"*: *Sporting News*, January 18, 1890.

84   *looked for Irish scapegoats*: Fleitz, *The Irish in Baseball*, 60.

84   *back-page headlines*: Casway, *Ed Delahanty*, 39–40.

85   *"a red-headed Irishman"*: Bill Felber, *A Game of Brawl* (Lincoln: University of Nebraska Press, 2007), 9.

85   *"malicious intent"*: Fleitz, *The Irish in Baseball*, 100.

86   *170 other buildings in the neighborhood*: Ibid., 100.

87   *infielders closer to home plate*: Ibid., 47.

88   *being a "gentleman"*: Felber, *A Game of Brawl*, 36.

89   *amounted to $160*: Ibid., 36.

89   *"a Tommy McCarthy"*: Ibid., 37.

90   *"Well, boyos"*: Appel, *Slide, Kelly, Slide*, 184–86.

TWELVE: NICE GUYS FINISH FIRST

92   *"lawn tennis business is killing baseball"*: Fleitz, *The Irish in Baseball*, 106.

93   *bickered during games*: Ibid., 104.

94   *railroad station and onto a train*: Felber, *A Game of Brawl*, 13.

94   *training tables in green*: Casway, *Ed Delahanty*, 112.

94   *captained by Harry Donaghy*: Ibid., 103.

95   *Hanlon's pitching staff in 1897*: Felber, *A Game of Brawl*, 23.

97   *newfangled product, chewing gum*: Casway, *Ed Delahanty*, 115–16.

98   *always played hard*: Felber, *A Game of Brawl*, 51.

99   *eventually forced Freedman to yield*: Rader, *Baseball*, 82–84.

99   *done for Brouthers before him*: Ibid., 85.

100   *several scribes in Baltimore*: Felber, *A Game of Brawl*, 244–45.

THIRTEEN: KILL THE UMP

101   *"Fans who despise umpires"*: Macht, *Connie Mack and the Early Years of Baseball*, 450.

101   *"All is fair in war and baseball"*: Casway, *Ed Delahanty*, 124.

102   *"Somebody dropped"*: Fleitz, *The Irish in Baseball*, 117.

103   *"I'm the best"*: Ibid., 117–18.

104   *"He was perfect"*: Ibid., 111–12.

104   *two-man umpiring crew in history*: Ibid., 113.

104   *forfeited two games in one week*: Felber, *A Game of Brawl*, 109–10.

105   *knockout punch of his own*: Ibid., 161.

105   *indication that he'd been nailed*: Fleitz, *The Irish in Baseball*, 120.

106   *"He is one of the best"*: Ibid., 118.

106   *sheriff's bloodhounds*: Felber, *A Game of Brawl*, 39.

FOURTEEN: MORE IRISH RECORD SETTING

108   *attack the players and the umpire*: Fleitz, *The Irish in Baseball*, 75.

108   *forewarned which spot to avoid*: Felber, *A Game of Brawl*, 14.

108 *Doyle scored the tying run*: Ibid., 96.

109 *lost this round to Keeler*: Alexander, *John McGraw*, 54.

109 *heaved in the same direction*: Felber, *A Game of Brawl*, xiii.

110 *Tenney was knocked cold*: Ibid., 156.

110 *O'Day, and the winning run scored*: Ibid., 162.

110 *easily advance to third*: Ibid., 111.

111 *Cincinnati's shortstop, Tommy Corcoran*: Casway, *Ed Delahanty*, 190–92.

111 *loggerheads throughout the season*: Fleitz, *The Irish in Baseball*, 63–64.

112 *temporary substitution was legal*: Felber, *A Game of Brawl*, 135.

112 *the Wandering Micks*: Rader, *Baseball*, 80.

113 *all-the-time hustle was nothing unusual*: Alexander, *John McGraw*, 59.

FIFTEEN: THE DELAHANTY BROTHERS

119 *"They're the product"*: quoted in Casway, *Ed Delahanty*, 18.

120 *Toronto in the Eastern League*: Ibid., 94–95.

120 *"The league has gone to hell"*: Felber, *A Game of Brawl*, 145.

120 *good-hit, no-field infielder*: Casway, *Ed Delahanty*, 233.

120 *with his brother Joe*: Ibid., 289.

121 *under threat of being arrested*: Ibid., 243–45.

121 *station in Fort Erie, Ontario*: Ibid., 266–70.

123 *to bear out such a theory*: *Boston Journal*, July 10, 1903, courtesy of America's Historical Newspapers website.

123 *working as a lithographer*: Casway, *Ed Delahanty*, 289.

124 *batting average was a paltry .226*: Ibid., 291.

124 *after a popular cartoon character*: Ibid., 149.

124 *"there is no one to take my place"*: Ibid., 291.

SIXTEEN: A NEW LEAGUE

127 *Stuart's Dyspepsia Tablets*: Casway, *Ed Delahanty*, 177.

127 *some form of higher education*: Steven A. Reiss, "Race and Ethnicity in American Baseball: 1900–1919," *Journal of Ethnic Studies* (Winter 1977), 47.

128 *"broken his jaw"*: Fleitz, *The Irish in Baseball*, 92.

128 *Tommy Lynch during a game*: Ibid., 73.

128 *action for several weeks*: Alexander, *John McGraw*, 71.

128 *Holyoke, Massachusetts*: Fleitz, *The Irish in Baseball*, 73.

128 *latest example of players' solidarity*: Casway, *Ed Delahanty*, 184–85.

129 *resolved by binding arbitration*: "Ban Johnson," Wikipedia.

SEVENTEEN: MR. MACK

133 *"The locker room"*: Macht, *Connie Mack and the Early Years of Baseball*, 52.

134 *spare mask so that game could resume*: Ibid., 125.

134 *dozen new balls before every game*: Ibid., 111.

134 *the only one of his career*: Ibid., 115.

135 *the ball dropped safely*: Ibid., 117.

136 *"I'd die before I took a drink"*: Ibid., 487.

139 *died two months later*: Ibid., 462–64.

139 *box score as "Sullivan"*: Dale B. Smith, "Eddie Collins: White Elephants and Black Sox," Philadelphia Athletics Historical Society.

140 *greatest infield in the history of baseball*: Bill James, *The New Bill James Historical Baseball Abstract* (New York: Simon & Schuster, 2003), 549–50.

141 *doom of the Federals*: Rader, *Baseball*, 119–20.

141 *McGraw never forgave Dunn*: Alexander, *John McGraw*, 179.

142 *enough to keep the club*: Macht, *Connie Mack and the Early Years of Baseball*, 4.

142 *rock back and forth on the bench*: Ibid., 397.

143 *"And to hell with you, too, Robert"*: James, *The New Bill James Historical Baseball Abstract*, 848.

144 *jingling the change in his pants pocket*: Macht, *Connie Mack and the Early Years of Baseball*, 449.

144 *"Toward the end"*: Bill James, *The Bill James Guide to Baseball Managers* (New York: Scribners, 1997), 29.

144 *"I'm not quitting because"*: Fleitz, *The Irish in Baseball*, 164.

EIGHTEEN: TAKE ME OUT TO THE BALL GAME

148 *asking to be taken to the "old ball game"*: "Take Me Out to the Ball Game," Wikipedia.

149 *finally purchased the franchise*: Fleitz, *The Irish in Baseball*, 169–70.

150 *"I'd rather win a pennant than an election"*: Ibid., 43.

151 *copied by other major league catchers*: Ibid., 142.

153 *"vaudeville surprise you ever enjoyed"*: Ibid., 143.

153 *dinner date with his wife*: Alexander, *John McGraw*, 130.

154 *Pulliam, supported O'Day*: Ibid., 133.

155 *apparently ended the game*: Ritter, *The Glory of Their Times*, 132–33.

155 *rolling toward the distant fence*: Ibid., 106–7.

155 *forfeited to the Cubs*: Ibid., 108.

156 *ended in a 1–1 tie*: Alexander, *John McGraw*, 134.

156 *both the game and the pennant*: Ritter, *The Glory of Their Times*, 108–9.

157 *"just the spit that went by"*: Quoted in Fleitz, *The Irish in Baseball*, 125–26.

157 *first on-field fatality in major league history*: Ibid., 162.

157 *recover from a bad fall*: Alexander, *John McGraw*, 299.

158 *buried on August 1*: "Harry Pulliam," Wikipedia.

159 *Opening Day in D.C.*: Fleitz, *The Irish in Baseball*, 110.

159 *seven hopeful base stealers*: "Jimmy Archer," Wikipedia.

160 *wild throw on a routine ground ball*: "John Corriden," Wikipedia.

NINETEEN: FAUSTIAN BARGAIN

161 *boneheaded plays at critical moments*: Alexander, *John McGraw*, 191.

163 *chronicled the doings of his heroes*: Ibid., 11–15.

163 *Bresnahan along with him*: Robert W. Creamer, *Stengel: His Life and Times* (New York: Simon & Schuster, 1984), 137.

163 *fifty additional runs per season*: Alexander, *John McGraw*, 7.

163 *$2,000 every year from him*: Ibid., 209.

163 *press box attendants at the Polo Grounds*: Fleitz, *The Irish in Baseball*, 140.

164 *"After he'd had a night out"*: "Bugs Raymond," Wikipedia.

164 *umpiring in semipro leagues*: Ritter, *The Glory of Their Times*, 96.

164 *"seven years off my own life"*: "Bugs Raymond," Wikipedia.

164 *"Sometimes Mr. McGraw"*: Ritter, *The Glory of Their Times*, 91–92.

164 *added $1,000 to his next contract*: Ibid., 91.

165 *Auburn Prison in upstate New York*: Leo Pinckney, "McGraw Left His Mark on Auburn," AuburnPub.com, May 3, 2003.

165 *the summons never came*: Alexander, *John McGraw*, 75–76.

166 *improve the Giants roster*: Ibid., 167–68.

166 *a dozen black youngsters*: Ibid., 204.

167 *bypassed his catchers and called every pitch*: Ibid., 322.

167 *and stoke up the cranks*: Ibid., 171.

167 *highest-remunerated vaudeville performer of the day*: Ibid., 160.

167 *local judge dismissed the charge*: Ibid., 105.

168 *to save McGraw from serving time*: Ibid., 224.

168 *"Mr. McGraw"*: "Charles Victor Faust," Wikipedia.

170 *exaggerated windup, the Giants broke their losing streak*: Ritter, *The Glory of Their Times*, 102–5.

170 *as the fans laughed and cheered*: Alexander, *John McGraw*, 156.

171 *perished of tuberculosis in 1915*: Ibid., 163.

171 *bloody pulp in a hotel lobby*: Fleitz, *The Irish in Baseball*, 144.

172 *employ three coaches*: Alexander, *John McGraw*, 233.

172 *"If he plays every day"*: Ibid., 213.

172 *O'Doul was dealt away*: Ibid., 288.

172 *McCovey Cove bears his name*: "Lefty O'Doul," Wikipedia.

173 *resulting from prostate cancer*: Alexander, *John McGraw*, 308.

TWENTY: SCANDAL AND WAR

174 *"in recognition of his bravery and skill"*: The Infinite Baseball Card Set: 71: "Billy O'Hara: Knowing How to Apply Skills," 2.

175 *harmony by repeating as World Series champs*: Fleitz, *The Irish in Baseball*, 172.

176 *"This business makes strange bed-fellows"*: Ibid., 115.

176 *O'Toole seemed like a bargain*: Daniel R. Levitt, *Ed Barrow: The Bulldog Who Built the Yankees' First Dynasty* (Lincoln: University of Nebraska Press, 2008), 81.

176 *most of the money over to the building fund*: "Charles Ebbets," Wikipedia.

178 *glass of beer over McGraw's head*: Alexander, *John McGraw*, 70–71.

179 *temptation to become a player-manager in the upstart league*: Carl Frederick

Wittke, *The Irish in America* (Baton Rouge: Louisiana State University Press, 1956), 270.

180 *"shared no-hitter"*: "Ernie Shore," Wikipedia.

180 *discussing the particulars of the deal*: Bill Felber, *Under Pallor, Under Shadow: The 1920 American League Pennant Race That Rattled and Rebuilt Baseball* (Lincoln: University of Nebraska Press, 2011), 30.

181 *"No ballplayers allowed"*: Felber, *Under Pallor*, 29.

181 *Collins made $14,500*: Fleitz, *The Irish in Baseball*, 132.

181 *played catch to warm up between innings*: Ibid., 133.

181 *certainly damage his own business*: Felber, *Under Pallor*, 41.

182 *managed his hometown Maple Leafs*: Infinite Baseball Card Set, 1–4.

TWENTY-ONE: THEY'RE ALL GOOD IRISH NAMES

184 *"Jennings and McGann"*: Jean Schwartz and William Jerome, 1911.

185 *Lizzie famously produced her own baseball card*: "Lizzie Murphy," Wikipedia.

186 *two triples, and a home run*: "Joe Dugan," Wikipedia.

186 *big leagues for another twenty-one seasons*: "Jimmy Dykes," Wikipedia.

186 *Girls Professional Baseball League*: "Marty McManus," Wikipedia.

186 *brawl with a Boston saloonkeeper*: Alexander, *John McGraw*, 186–87.

188 *that traveled 610 feet*: "Harry Heilmann," Wikipedia.

188 *"the worst player in the Hall of Fame"*: George Kelly," Wikipedia.

189 *his first name, Sean*: Felber, *Under Pallor*, 31.

189 *enabled Cleveland to score*: Ibid., 44.

189 *the winners' shares in the series*: "Charles Comiskey," Wikipedia.

189 *into a hard-hitting outfielder*: "Dickie Kerr," Wikipedia.

190 *minor injuries but Donovan was killed*: Creamer, *Stengel*, 133.

191 *no penalty was imposed on the others*: Alexander, *John McGraw*, 256–66.

191 *he would be served potatoes*: "Frank Hogan," Wikipedia.

191 *appearance his last in the majors*: "Garland Buckeye," Wikipedia.

192 *"bite of meat I've had in a month"*: "Bob Fothergill," Wikipedia.

192 *dirty blond hair and jutting jaw*: Mark Armour, *Joe Cronin: A Life in Baseball* (Lincoln: University of Nebraska Press, 2010), 14.

192 *"the luck of the Irish"*: Ibid., 30.

192 *"go upstairs and see Joe Engel"*: Ibid., 28.

193 *for her on this latest scouting trip*: Ibid., 30.

193 *Mildred and Cronin were wed in 1933*: Ibid., 64.

TWENTY-TWO: THE ALERT IRISHMAN

194 *"I'm going up with real Irish now"*: Alan H. Levy, *Joe McCarthy: Architect of the Yankee Dynasty* (Jefferson, NC: McFarland, 2005), 335.

195 *nickname was "Utility Joe"*: Ibid., 23.

195 *"Hibernian" intensity*: Ibid., 47.

195 *policeman in comedy skits*: Ibid., 22.

195 *protest since they won the game*: Ibid., 83.
195 *every time he stepped onto the field*: Ibid., 104.
196 *one-fingered salute in passing*: Ibid., 104.
196 *McCarthy was immediately fired*: Ibid., 144.
197 *the more Ruth grew to hate him*: Ibid., 154.
197 *"Joe could look at the dents"*: Ibid., 3.
197 *in a close play at the plate*: Ibid., 115.
197 *runner would be a few inches longer*: Ibid., 158.
197 *"Try not to find too much fault"*: Ibid., 219.
198 *stronger than they really were*: Ibid., 219.
198 *"there was never a better manager"*: Ibid., 2.
198 *by the score of 3–2*: Ibid., 272.
198 *And he was gone*: Ibid., 221.
199 *"Flatbush's Darkest Hour"*: Ibid., 277.
199 *hard-to-handle spitball*: Ibid.
199 *McCarthy and his new Irish boss*: Ibid., 302.
200 *wearing a uniform in public*: Armour, *Joe Cronin*, 192.
200 *Red Sox's general manager*: Levy, *Joe McCarthy*, 326.
201 *intrusive and ignorant questions*: Ibid., 124–25.
201 *and other temporary illnesses*: Ibid., 371.
201 *neither suggestion had lasting effects*: Ibid., 334.
202 *died at ninety in virtual anonymity*: Ibid., 380.

TWENTY-THREE: HOMER IN THE GLOAMIN'
203 *history to be credited with a win*: "John Quinn," Wikipedia.
204 *used in three games during the 1939 season*: "Larry MacPhail," Wikipedia.
204 *His protest got nowhere*: "Kitty Burke," Wikipedia.
205 *Billy Knickerbocker, who made the easy catch*: Armour, *Joe Cronin*, 82.
205 *pitch would suffice as retaliation*: "Mickey Cochrane," Wikipedia.
206 *willing to turn a called strike into a ball*: "Bill McGowan," Wikipedia.
207 *Dean did, with disastrous results*: "Gabby Hartnett," Wikipedia.
207 *use his own bat in the game, and carried it in a gun case*: "Earl Averill," Wikipedia.
207 *hit the ball into the left-center bleachers*: "Gabby Hartnett," Wikipedia.

TWENTY-FOUR: A REAL CASEY
209 *"I played for Casey"*: Creamer, *Stengel*, 195.
209 *epic swings of "Casey at the Bat"*: Ibid., 62.
209 *he abandoned dental school*: Ibid., 49.
210 *forgot to continue platooning Stengel*: Ritter, *The Glory of Their Times*, 212–13.
211 *humiliation on Stengel*: Ibid., 213–14.
212 *"he always did have birds in his garret"*: Creamer, *Stengel*, 129.
212 *willing to entertain a crowd*: Ibid., 131.
213 *"wear your pants that way too"*: Ibid., 131.
213 *"Wake up muscles"*: Ibid., 144.

213 *"I want one of my own"*: Ibid., 157.

214 *shins with the fungo bat*: Ibid., 177.

215 *third baseman would also freeze*: Ibid., 186.

215 *invested $43,000*: Ibid., 191.

215 *"Good pitching beats"*: "Casey Stengel Quotes," Wikipedia.

215 *Sportsman of the Year in Boston*: "Casey Stengel," Wikipedia.

216 *new manager until after the deed was done*: Creamer, *Stengel*, 199.

216 *"Please don't cut my throat"*: "Casey Stengel Quotes," Wikipedia.

216 *"I like the idea of bridges"*: Creamer, *Stengel*, 206.

216 *"getting paid for home runs someone else hits"*: "Casey Stengel Quotes," Wikipedia.

217 *Thomson, and Sal Yvars 1-2-3*: Creamer, *Stengel*, 15.

217 *Billy Martin switch uniforms*: "Casey Stengel," Wikipedia.

217 *glug some more champagne*: Creamer, *Stengel*, 239–40.

217 *"We'd have clubhouse meetings"*: Ibid., 235.

218 *no mention of Casey's slur was ever printed*: Ibid., 296.

218 *"the only one who can't run"*: Ibid., 282.

218 *"should lead the league"*: "Casey Stengel Quotes," Wikipedia.

219 *"mistake of being seventy again"*: Ibid.

219 *"You have to have"*: Ibid.

219 *"Sure I played"*: Ibid.

220 *"Now, that other fellow"*: Ibid.

220 *"I've been in this game"*: Ibid.

220 *"I just want to see"*: Creamer, *Stengel*, 305.

220 *"Can't anybody here play this game?"*: "Casey Stengel Quotes," Wikipedia.

220 *"I'm being embalmed"*: Ibid.

TWENTY-FIVE: WARTIME

223 *returning to play three more years*: "Hugh Mulcahy," Wikipedia.

224 *a record for a complete game*: "Charles Barrett," Wikipedia.

224 *"Without them, you're nothing"*: Fleitz, *The Irish in Baseball*, 122.

225 *shin guards and steel-toed shoes*: David L. Fleitz, "The Green and the Blue: Irish-American Umpires, 1880–1965," http://sabr.org/drupal/node/2869.

225 *"Richie"*: Fleitz, *The Irish in Baseball*, 122.

226 *"On we go"*: "A Brief History of Baseball and Softball in Ireland," baseballireland.com/history/htm.

227 *$1 million to be the league's president*: Armour, *Joe Cronin*, 162.

228 *traded to Pittsburgh after the 1948 season*: Neil Lanctot, *Campy: The Two Lives of Roy Campanella* (New York: Simon & Schuster, 2011).

228 *expanded it for black hitters*: Ibid., 189.

TWENTY-SIX: THE FABULOUS FIFTIES

233 *Earle Mack becoming the chief scout*: Macht, *Connie Mack and the Early Years of Baseball*, 568.

235 *"I needed something extra"*: "Whitey Ford," Wikipedia.

237 *"we'd just saved $1,200"*: Ibid.

239 *"but I felt obligated to go"*: "Bob Cain," Wikipedia.

239 *"When I look back"*: "Gene Conley," Wikipedia.

240 *he became known as "Chuck"*: "Chuck Connors," Wikipedia.

240 *"[They] offered me"*: Charley Rosen, *The First Tip-Off: The Incredible Story of the Birth of the NBA* (New York: McGraw-Hill, 2009), 46.

240 *game for over an hour*: Ibid., 37–38.

241 *traded to the Washington Senators*: Armour, *Joe Cronin*, 234.

242 *damaged foot touching the ground*: Jim Hawkins, *Al Kaline: The Biography of a Tigers Icon* (Chicago: Triumph Books, 2010), 21.

242 *guaranteed salary of $6,000 for two years*: Ibid., 31.

242 *"I was so skinny"*: Ibid., 39.

242 *until 1973 and 1974, his last two years in uniform*: Ibid., 215.

243 *"I had to do something"*: Sandy Grady, "A Great Guy for Laughs," *Baseball Digest*, February 1964, 64.

243 *sports editor of the* Philadelphia Bulletin: "Richie Ashburn," Wikipedia.

245 *color blindness, and fierce disagreements with umpires*: "Bobby Bragan," Wikipedia.

245 *oldest manager in pro ball to get thumbed from a game*: Ibid.

TWENTY-SEVEN: THE CRAZY SIXTIES

246 *"Brooks never had"*: "Brooks Robinson," Wikipedia.

249 *next six baseball seasons behind bars*: "Denny McClain," Wikipedia.

250 *"three inches of type in a record book"*: "Brooks Robinson," Wikipedia.

251 *retirement resort in Florida for former players*: "Sam McDowell," Wikipedia.

251 *heavy fines were imposed*: "Clint Courtney," Wikipedia.

252 *their graves would be sixty feet, six inches, apart*: "Tim McCarver," Wikipedia.

254 *complete the no-hitter with a pop-up*: "Norm Cash," Wikipedia.

256 *denied a plane ticket because he lacked a visa*: "Gene Conley," Wikipedia.

257 *"Live Like You Were Dyin'" in his memory*: "Tug McGraw," Wikipedia.

TWENTY-EIGHT: GREEN AND GOLD

259 *sliding into home on his belly*: "Rick Dempsey," Wikipedia.

260 *Duffy Dyer as a cultural icon*: "Duffy Dyer," Wikipedia.

260 *become an expert in Irish history*: "Steve Garvey," Wikipedia.

262 *poverty-stricken childhood*: G. Michael Green and Roger D. Launius, *Charlie Finley: The Outrageous Story of Baseball's Super Showman* (New York: Walker, 2010), 17–21.

262 *"Finley is a self-made man who worships his creator"*: ESPN Classic Quotes: Charlie Finley, 2.

262 *fervent desire to buy a baseball team*: Green and Launius, *Charlie Finley*, 32–34.

262 *Kansas City Athletics for $1.975 million*: Ibid., 34.

263 *paid admissions in any given season*: Ibid., 55.

263 *deleted the attendance clause*: Ibid., 56.

264 *dust and dirt with jets of air*: Ibid., 45–46.

264 *to catch a greased pig*: Ibid., 87.

264 *missed the next five games*: Ibid., 97.

264 *attracted six thousand contestants*: Ibid., 152.

264 *Paige the in-uniform time he needed*: Ibid., 93–94.

264 *new hurler in dramatic fashion*: Ibid., 48.

265 *put an end to this particular experiment*: Ibid., 182.

265 *A's outfielder for three more games*: Ibid., 89–92.

265 *to become baseball's first free agent*: Ibid., 108–9.

265 *trademark reaction to "Holy mule"*: Ibid., 141.

266 *decimating the A's farm system*: Ibid., 233.

267 *never trusted or respected Finley again*: Ibid., 1–7.

267 *undoubtedly hefty payment*: Ibid., 190.

TWENTY-NINE: THE HIDDEN POTATO TRICK

269 *3–2 victory with a pair of round-trippers*: "Dale Murphy," Wikipedia.

270 *"There's no debate"*: "Sean Casey," Wikipedia.

270 *Clark promptly cleared the bases with a grand slam*: "Will Clark," Wikipedia.

270 *B RUTH CURSE*: "Bruce Hurst," Wikipedia.

271 *O'Brien's mask was approved by Major League Baseball in 1996*: "Charlie O'Brien," Wikipedia.

272 *Hall of Fame—which declined*: Thorn, Palmer, Gersham, and Pietrusza, *Total Baseball*, 2338.

THIRTY: CENTURY'S END AND IRISH RESURGENCE

274 *Dodgers sent him back to the minors*: "Jay Gibbons," Wikipedia.

275 *"The strangest thing"*: Tyler Kepner, "Roaming the Field for Detroit: A Jack-of-All-Trades," *New York Times*, July 24, 2011.

275 *"Take Me Out to the Ball Game"*: "Ian Kennedy," Wikipedia.

275 *ejected in his initial major league appearance*: "John Lannan," Wikipedia.

277 *identify themselves as being Irish*: "Ethnic Populations of the United States," Wikipedia.

278 *seek steady work and a better life elsewhere*: Chris V. Nicholson, "In Tough Times, Irish Call Their Diaspora," *New York Times*, July 18, 2011.

Bibliography

Alexander, Charles C. *John McGraw*. Lincoln: University of Nebraska Press, 1988.

Appel, Marty. *Slide, Kelly, Slide*. Lanham, MD: Scarecrow Press, 1999.

Armour, Mark. *Joe Cronin: A Life in Baseball*. Lincoln: University of Nebraska Press, 2010.

Bayor, Ronald H., and Timothy J. Meagher. *The New York Irish*. Baltimore: Johns Hopkins University Press, 1997.

Bingham, Dennis, and Thomas R. Heitz. "Appendix." In John Thorn, Peter Palmer, and Michael Gershman, *Total Baseball*. 3rd ed. New York: Harper Perennial,1993.

Boston Journal, July 10, 1903. America's Historical Newspapers website.

"A Brief History of Baseball and Softball in Ireland." http://baseballireland.com/history/htm.

Casway, Jerrold. *Ed Delahanty in the Emerald Age of Baseball*. South Bend, IN: University of Notre Dame Press, 2004.

Creamer, Robert W. *Stengel: His Life and Times*. New York: Simon & Schuster, 1984.

Digital History. www.digitalhistory.uh.edu/. Accessed January 8, 2011.

Eckard, E. Woodrow. "Anti–Job Discrimination Circa 1880—Evidence from Major League Baseball." *Social Science History* 34, no. 4 (Winter 2010).

ESPN Classic Quotes: Charlie Finley.

Felber, Bill. *A Game of Brawl*. Lincoln: University of Nebraska Press, 2007.

———. *Under Pallor, Under Shadow: The 1920 American League Pennant Race That Rattled and Rebuilt Baseball*. Lincoln: University of Nebraska Press, 2011.

Fleitz, Donald L. "The Green and the Blue: Irish-American Umpires, 1880–1965." http://sabr.org/drupal/node/2869.

———. *The Irish in Baseball*. Jefferson, NC: McFarland, 2009.

Grady, Sandy. "A Great Guy for Laughs." *Baseball Digest*, February 1964.

Green, G. Michael, and Roger D. Launius. *Charlie Finley: The Outrageous Story of Baseball's Super Showman*. New York: Walker, 2010.

Hawkins, Jim. *Al Kaline: The Biography of a Tigers Icon*. Chicago: Triumph, 2010.

The Infinite Baseball Card Set: 71. "Billy O'Hara: Knowing How to Apply Skills." http://infinitecardset.blogspot.com/2011/03/71-billy-ohara-knowing-how-to-apply.html.

James, Bill. *The Bill James Guide to Baseball Managers*. New York: Scribners, 1997.

———. *The New Bill James Historical Baseball Abstract*. New York: Simon & Schuster, 2003.

Kepner, Tyler. "Roaming the Field for Detroit: A Jack-of-All-Trades." *New York Times*, July 24, 2011.

Kirsch, George B. "Othello Harris, Claire Elaine Noble." *Encyclopedia of Ethnicity and Sports in America*. Westport, CT: Greenwood, 2000.

Koppett, Leonard. *Koppett's Concise History of Baseball*. Philadelphia: Temple University Press, 1998.

Lanctot, Neil. *Campy: The Two Lives of Roy Campanella*. New York: Simon & Schuster, 2011.

Levitt, Daniel R. *Ed Barrow: The Bulldog Who Built the Yankees' First Dynasty*. Lincoln: University of Nebraska Press, 2008.

Levy, Alan H. *Joe McCarthy: Architect of the Yankee Dynasty*. Jefferson, NC: McFarland, 2005.

Macht, Norman L. *Connie Mack and the Early Years of Baseball*. Lincoln: University of Nebraska Press, 2007.

Nicholson, Chris V. "In Tough Times, Irish Call Their Diaspora." *New York Times*, July 18, 2011.

Pinckney, Leo. "McGraw Left His Mark on Auburn." http://auburnpub.com/sports/article_e47873cd-6114-51d6-844e-a8f8459fbb82.html?mode=story. May 4, 2003.

Rader, Benjamin G. *Baseball: A History of America's Game*. Urbana: University of Illinois Press, 2004.

Reiss, Steven A. "Race and Ethnicity in American Baseball: 1900–1919." *Journal of Ethnic Studies* 4 (Winter 1977).

Ritter, Lawrence S. *The Glory of Their Times*. New York: William Morrow, 1984.

Rosen, Charley. *The First Tip-Off: The Incredible Story of the Birth of the NBA*. New York: McGraw-Hill, 2009.

Rossi, John P. "Glimpses of the Irish Contribution to Early Baseball." *Journal of Irish Studies* (Summer 1988).

Smith, Dale B. "Eddie Collins: White Elephants and Black Sox." Philadelphia Athletics Historical Society.

Sporting News. January 25, 1890.

Thorn, John. *Baseball in the Garden of Eden: The Secret History of the Early Game*. New York: Simon & Schuster, 2011.

Thorn, John, Peter Palmer, and Michael Gershman. *Total Baseball*. 3rd ed. New York: Harper Perennial, 1993.

Thorn, John, Peter Palmer, Michael Gershman, and David Pietrusza. *Total Baseball*. 6th ed. New York: Total Sports, 1999.

Vincent, Ted. *The Rise and Fall of American Sport*. Lincoln: University of Nebraska Press, 1994.

Wikipedia. http://en.wikipedia.org/wiki/Main_Page.

Wilcox, Ralph C. "The Shamrock and the Eagle." In *Ethnicity and Sport in North American History and Culture*. Westport, CT: Greenwood Press, 1994.

Wittke, Carl Frederick. *The Irish in America*. Baton Rouge: Louisiana State University Press, 1956.

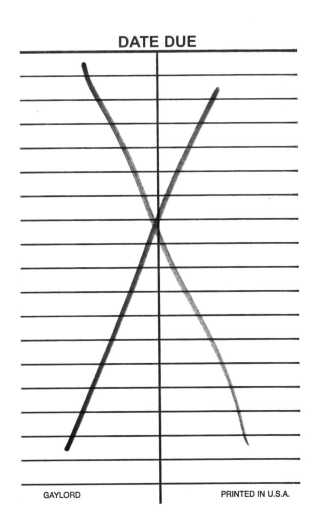

DATE DUE